# Art Rebellion

ALSO AVAILABLE FROM BLOOMSBURY

*Eco-Aesthetics: Art, Literature and Architecture in a Period of Climate Change*, Malcolm Miles
*Art, Politics and the Pamphleteer*, ed. Jane Tormey and Gillian Whiteley
*Working Aesthetics: Labour, Art and Capitalism*, Danielle Child
*Aesthetic Marx*, ed. Samir Gandesha and Johan F. Hartle

# Art Rebellion

## The Aesthetics of Social Transformation

**Malcolm Miles**

BLOOMSBURY ACADEMIC
LONDON · NEW YORK · OXFORD · NEW DELHI · SYDNEY

BLOOMSBURY ACADEMIC
Bloomsbury Publishing Plc
50 Bedford Square, London, WC1B 3DP, UK
1385 Broadway, New York, NY 10018, USA
29 Earlsfort Terrace, Dublin 2, Ireland

BLOOMSBURY, BLOOMSBURY ACADEMIC and the Diana logo
are trademarks of Bloomsbury Publishing Plc

First published in Great Britain 2023



Cover design by Ben Anslow
Cover image: London, United Kingdom. 3rd April 2021. Extinction Rebellion's Red
Rebel Brigade at the Kill The Bill protest outside Buckingham Palace.
(© Vuk Valcic / Alamy Stock Photo)



A catalogue record for this book is available from the British Library.

A catalog record for this book is available from the Library of Congress.

ISBN:    HB:     978-1-3502-3997-5
         PB:     978-1-3502-3998-2
         ePDF:   978-1-3502-3999-9
         eBook:  978-1-3502-4000-1

Typeset by Integra Software Services Pvt. Ltd.
Printed and bound in Great Britain

To find out more about our authors and books visit www.bloomsbury.com
and sign up for our newsletters.

# Contents

# List of illustrations

All photographs are the author's originals unless otherwise stated.

# Acknowledgements

I would like to thank the following for permission to use images which they supplied in this book: Eric Lesdema, Forensic Architecture, Freee Art Collective and Dr Valerie Holman. I am grateful to Dave Beech, Andy Hewitt and Mel Jordan of Freee Art Collective, Helen Evans and Heiko Hanson of HeHe, Gary Anderson of the Institute for the Art and Practice of Dissent at Home, Niamh Malone at Liverpool Hope University, art historian Valerie Holman, Jonathan Vickery of Warwick University, Murray Fraser of the Bartlett School, University College London and architects Kasia and Krzysztof Nawratek for conversations over several years which have contributed to the evolution of my thoughts on culture and society. And I am grateful to Liza Thompson and Lucy Russell at Bloomsbury Academic for their support and help through the process of writing and production of this book.

Malcolm Miles
Stroud, May 2022

# Introduction

In Bristol on 11 June 2020, a nineteenth-century statue of Edward Colston (1636–1721) was placed in storage by the City Council pending relocation to a museum. This followed a Black Lives Matter protest on 7 June when the statue was pulled from its plinth, sprayed with graffiti, dragged to the harbour-side and thrown into the river Avon. A year later, in June 2021, Colston's statue was exhibited at M-Shed, a nearby local history museum. It was placed horizontally and contextualised by placards used in the protest in 2020, with documentation on Colston's involvement in the slave trade. In January 2022, four people accused of criminal damage by pulling down the statue were found not guilty by a Jury. David Olusoga described the verdict as, 'a milestone in the journey that Bristol and Britain are on to come to terms with the totality of our history'.[1]

I discuss the toppling of the Colston statue in Chapter 6, in context of other cases of statues being removed during periods of historical change. I begin with this incident here because it is a recent example of the intersection of culture and politics, emphasising the inseparability of public representation from contestations of power. This applies to art within art spaces as well as in the street, and to art work (as a verb) done by artists' collectives working between political campaigning and aesthetics, and by campaign groups using visual and performative tactics. But the boundaries between aesthetics and politics are not merely blurred (as they always have been); an in-between terrain emerges where art and political campaigning meet, where values are acted out and contested, producing ephemeral yet illuminating glimpses of other ways in which a society might organise and sustain itself.

Throughout this book, I argue that aesthetic work can, sometimes, in some circumstances, stand as radically other to the dominant social order and power structures, which today means radically other to global capitalism. In this context, non-violent direct action is an inherently radical alterity, an incipient new society with distinct structures, cultures and values, within the old society.

In Chapters 6–9, I look selectively at how these two strands – artwork and campaigning – intersect, and how theoretical questions about revolution and aesthetics arise in that in-between terrain, which can be called political aesthetics. I remain cautious, and do not say that art changes the world, which would be simplistic; but I do suggest that art contributes to changing attitudes and perceptions, to the categories and lenses through which reality is apprehended, and to expansions of the imaginative horizon on which ideas of radically new kinds of world appear.

That is why I wrote this book. I hope it contributes to discussion. I do not attempt to be comprehensive in my coverage of historical and contemporary art and theory, nor to offer solutions to the problems raised; more to think again about the questions. My approach is careful, in my readings of existing theory – from twentieth-century continental philosophy – and, where it has been possible, in conversations with a small number of artists' collectives over some years. I am wary of assertion and pronouncement, equally of any formulaic or generalised application of an idea. For the most part, history is messy, and not all the ends add up. That is one reason for an element of caution, edging towards an understanding, and I hope bringing the reader into the material; another is, I suppose, my own temperament, as a critic not an advocate, as an academic not a campaigner, aware that each insight leads to further nuances of the problem, and to new questions. If my writing seems tentative, it is because doubt is the ground on which critical insight is built.

# Contents and organisation

To try to understand the terrain of political aesthetics, I go back to the first avant-garde in the mid-nineteenth century, tracing developments and arguments on aesthetics from that point, through modernism in the early twentieth century, and into recent and current controversies and practices. Between Chapters 1 and 2 on avant-gardes and later chapters on contemporary practices I reconsider theoretical problems in aesthetics, drawing on critical theory (the work of the Frankfurt School) and aspects of French post-structuralism. This material was produced in what might be called dark times, from the rise of fascism (which haunts the Frankfurt School) to regroupings after the failure of the revolt of May 1968 in Paris to bring down the regime. I look back on this material not merely because I have been reading it for most of my academic life but because I think it remains relevant now: the questions have not gone away, indeed are more urgent in face of the climate emergency.

Herbert Marcuse says at the opening of his last book, *The Aesthetic Dimension* (1978), that a concern for aesthetics is justified when real political change seems unlikely; but – he might have added – the prospect is never given up: art-work retains and embodies hope. Having been an art student in London from 1967 to 1971, I cling to the optimism of that time; as a retired academic in England today I do not try to recreate it, only to reimagine a world in which the values of life and hope are, or might be, enacted. I think that happens in non-violent direct action and, in another way, in art-work. As said above, I have no answers. I hope readers will have new ways of thinking about the questions.

The book is organised in three parts: part one (Chapters 1 and 2) reconsiders the European avant-gardes of the nineteenth and twentieth centuries. Part two (Chapters 3, 4 and 5) is where I reconnect to critical theory in the writing of Marcuse, Walter Benjamin and Theodor Adorno, juxtaposed to more recent thinkers on culture and politics including Julia Kristeva, Judith Butler and Isabell Lorey. Part three (Chapters 6, 7, 8 and 9) reviews specific cultural practices from the 1990s to the present.

In more detail: in Chapter 1, I discuss the first avant-garde, from the Realism of Gustave Courbet's depiction of ordinary lives after the 1848 Revolution in France, to the utopian vision of Georges Seurat in Paris in the 1880s. This is a politicised avant-garde, in an era in which radical social change is assumed to be produced by organised mass revolt. This avant-garde's pictures are now museum pieces framed in the aura of art's institutions, which does not detract from their interpretation as politically charged images. Yet there were, even before that, performative elements as well, as in the processions organised by Jacques-Louis

David in the Jacobin period of the French Revolution: means to enact revolutionary values in a new time marked by proclamation of Year One in 1793.[2] I return to the idea of embodied critique in Chapter 9.

In Chapter 2, I move to the modernist avant-garde of the early twentieth century, in which a series of artistic revolts – or mainstream of departures – continually renews art language in what might be called a revolutionary evolution. In the resulting aesthetic dimension, reality is refracted. Alternative realities emerge in art, if not in society, while what is called reality is seen as one polarity on an axis between what is and what might be. I argue that this remains vital to new ways of seeing and new categories of perception.

This leads me, in Chapter 3, to Marcuse's idea of an aesthetic dimension in which the reality of received ideas and perceptions is ruptured. Although Marcuse accepts that art affirms the existing order as compensatory escape, he argues that modernism's distancing of reality in a radical otherness enables its criticality, and that a new sensibility arises in protest culture in the 1960s. He argues, too, that in conditions of terror the last resort of freedom is not as might be expected in political writing but in a literature of intimacy whereby love poems carry a latent promise of happiness. I juxtapose this idea to Julia Kristeva's claim that the legacy of the May 1968 is a revolution in personal life – feminism insists that the personal is political – and her argument for a revolution *within* verbal and poetic language.

In Chapter 4, I turn to Benjamin's critique of history as a narrative from the perspective of power; against this, Benjamin calls for a history from the position of the oppressed. In his last text, written in 1940 in flight from Fascism, he fuses Marxism and Jewish Messianism in a redemptive history in which a leap can be envisaged: the rupture of continuity as opening of the new. I juxtapose Benjamin's critique of power and narrative in 1940 to Isabell Lorey's writing on present-day precarity, not to draw any direct parallel but to suggest that common issues of coercive narrative and imperative norm are encountered, and opposed.

In Chapter 5, I take Adorno's remarks on the impossibility of poetry after Auschwitz as a point of departure, asking whether it is possible to articulate responses to extreme history without rendering those histories acceptable through an aesthetic objectification. This prefigures controversies over the memorialisation of the slave trade, and the viability of the form of the public monument which I discuss in Chapter 6; but here I look to specific efforts to memorialise the Holocaust, for instance in buried monuments (denoting what was until recently a buried history in Germany), and in major memorials in Berlin and Vienna. The difficulty is that memories of annihilation are non-viable except from outside, taking meaning to, or over, an edge of communicability.

In Chapter 6, I address the issue of public monuments, beginning with controversies over the removal of Colston's statue in Bristol. I put this in context of earlier removals of monuments to defunct regimes. I argue that, since monuments represent the power-over of the regimes which produce them in a semblance of permanence, when a regime falls it is logical that its monuments are removed. An example was the removal or destruction of statues of Lenin and Stalin after the end of the East bloc in 1989 and collapse of the Soviet Union in 1991.

In Chapter 7, I consider an exhibition of the material culture of protest, *Disobedient Objects*, at the Victoria & Albert Museum, London in 2014. Exhibits included objects dating back to the Suffragettes in the 1900s, and documentation of barricades in the Paris Commune of 1871; and recent anti-capitalist and climate-change campaigns. The counter-cultures of protest enter an established cultural institution here, emphasising their materiality while signalling a reform within art's institutions. These objects demonstrate, too, the viability of art-work in political action. Looking to recent practices in visual culture, I cite the exhibition *Cloud Studies* (2020) by the research group Forensic Architecture; Eric Lesdema's collection of photographs, *Fortunes of War* (published as a book in 2021); and Freee Art Collective's use of a kiosk as a hub of public contestation in 2019–20.

Chapter 8 begins with another work by Freee Art Collective, *Revolution Is Sublime* (2009), a posed photograph for large-scale reproduction. The title echoes art's criticality as discussed in Chapter 3. If revolution is sublime – in an aesthetic terrain of licensed danger – then this implies that change occurs not in the conventional sense of organised mass revolt but more in other, distanced ways, as in changes of perception and value. Taking up that issue, I cite Friedrich Schiller's letters on aesthetic education, written in face of the Terror in Paris in 1793, setting out a function for culture as alternative reality; and Edmund Burke's more conservative reactions. I also look to practices which contribute directly to change, if in a localised way, citing *Bank Job*, a project, film and book by Hilary Powell and Daniel Edelstyn (2019) in which a rebel bank in East London produces its own money, a gold-painted van is exploded, and more than £1 million of local people's debt is cancelled.

In Chapter 9, I return to the argument that beauty acts as a radical alternative to the world produced by late capitalism, arguing that aesthetic realities interrupt the narratives by which that regime is coercively maintained. Focusing on the performative, I review projects by Liberate Tate aiming to stop oil sponsorship of art; the Women in Black who protest against men's wars and violence; Red Rebel Brigade, aligned to Extinction Rebellion, using street theatre for dramatic non-violent intervention; and, finally, the journey from Turkey through Europe to Britain in 2021 of Little Amal, a large puppet representing the thousands of refugees from conflict zones who face a dubious welcome here today. I hope that such cases of art-work contribute to a shift in public attitudes, and the way a new kind of public sphere of imagination emerges in contestations of values.

Non-violent direct action counters the violence of capital; and, in parallel, art-work collapses the boundaries of art and politics, and of art-forms, fusing static image and performative presence. I do not ask whether this remains art, but look at how wit, beauty and sublimity are means towards what Marcuse called the new sensibility which inherently produces a new society. I am, as said above, an academic (now retired, so just an old age pensioner) not a participant in direct action. But memories of anti-nuclear protests in the late 1960s and 1970s in which I did participate shape my insight that participation in such action is in its own way transformative. That was when I first read Marcuse, and began to think about art and politics. The threat then was nuclear war, returning in the war in Ukraine as I write.

There is also the climate emergency which threatens life on Earth in its totality. Floods, fires and other effects of extreme weather are, beside wars and forced migrations, the price of business-as-usual under global capitalism. When representational politics fails, the politics of non-violent direct action is the new society in incipient form, not signposting a future yet to dawn, but here and now.

T. S. Eliot said in *The Wasteland* (1922) that he shored up the poem's words against his ruin. I write academic prose, not poetry, look at art and critical theory, not the vegetation cults in which Eliot sought quaint comfort, and am – or might be (tentative again!) – less pessimistic. My optimism may be a product of spending time outdoors, walking in the woods near my house in the West of England; or evidence of clinging to the hope gained in my formative experiences in the 1960s. Yet… I wonder, is my hope really a cover for a despair so deep I cannot admit it? I simply do not know.

# PART ONE

# Avant-gardes

# Chapter 1
# Signed in red: The first avant-garde

Gustave Courbet's painting *The Stonebreakers* (1849, Dresden, Gemaldegalerie, destroyed) was signed in red. This may seem an obvious gesture towards Socialism – red as the colour of the workers' flag – but the circumstances in which the gesture was made are complex. On one hand, a year after the 1848 Revolution, the subject-matter expresses a commitment to the dignity of labour; on the other hand, the period was politically fraught. Louis Napoleon initially became President of France but increased his hold on power, staging a coup in 1851 to become Emperor Napoleon III. Censorship was tightened, and the regime was identified with commercialism, financial speculation and corruption. One outcome was the demolition of the inner-city working-class quarters of Paris to make way for new boulevards lined with apartments for the bourgeoisie; but the boulevards were designed, too, as routes by which troops might rapidly enter the city to quell any future insurrection.

In these conditions of capitalist modernisation, *The Stonebreakers* indicates Courbet's turn to a new realism, not only against the conventions of academic art but also in an allegiance to the Left coded by a shift in the language of painting. That is my point of departure in this chapter, taking Realism as indicative of a politicised avant-garde beginning in 1848 (while also drawing on French critical writing from the 1820s onwards). I examine the claims and contradictions of this avant-garde as a means to social change. But I am not concerned with efficacy in a mechanical sense, more with testing the arguments involved, and whether the means used enact or contradict the values of an envisaged future social formation. After considering Courbet's contribution to the avant-garde, and looking briefly back to art in the Jacobin period of the French Revolution, I end by reconsidering two paintings by Georges Seurat from the 1880s, reading them as implicitly aligning the avant-garde to utopianism, inventing a new artistic language for a new age. But I begin more generally, asking what constitutes an avant-garde.

# What was the avant-garde?

The term 'avant-garde' derives from Napoleonic military tactics: a small force going ahead of the army. The term is used culturally in the 1820s by utopian Socialist Henri de Saint-Simon in an imagined dialogue between an artist, a scientist and an industrialist. Saint-Simon looks towards a society in which politics becomes, 'the science of providing the people with as many material goods and as much moral satisfaction as possible'.[1] In this quest for social transformation, artists, scientists and industrialists contribute in different ways. The artist says,

> We… will be your vanguard. The power of the arts is in effect the most immediate and most rapid of all powers. We have all kinds of weapons. When we wish to spread new ideas among men [sic], we inscribe them on marble or canvas; we popularize them in poetry and song; we use, in turn, the lyre or the tabor, the ode or the ballad, the story or the novel; the drama is open to us, and through it, above all, we are able to exercise an electric and victorious influence.[2]

The role of scientists is to extend knowledge of, and human power over, the natural world; industrialists are what might now be called social entrepreneurs, 'the physical force of the social body' taking progressive ideas to the workforce. The latter maintains a hierarchy of masters who enlighten workers, and conventionally views Nature as resource; the model of change is evolutionary rather than revolutionary, too, and elsewhere Saint-Simon affirms the position of the monarchy:

> The philosophers of the eighteenth century decried monarchy by showing it to be inevitably allied with theology and feudalism; those of the nineteenth century will be essentially royalist, and will show that monarchy must have as its support and close advisers the most distinguished scientists and artists... [3]

This is thirty-two years after the execution of Louis XVI; and eleven after the restoration of the Bourbon monarchy, notionally as a constitutional monarchy on Bonaparte's abdication in 1814, and ten after the defeat at Waterloo. The reference to the monarchy – of Charles X – is thus topical rather than historical, settling for what transpired to be a dubious status quo. Five years later, in 1830, elections produced an antagonistic Chamber of Deputies which Charles tried to dismiss, amid strengthened press censorship. This produced the 1830 Revolution (the July Days), and installation of Louis-Philippe as a so-called citizen-king. This did not guarantee the presence of distinguished scientists and artists as royal advisors; but it did produce Eugène Delacroix's painting *Liberty Leading the People* (1830, Paris, Louvre).

Delacroix produced *Liberty* for public consumption, depicting people of mixed social classes, differentiated by dress, surging over a barricade with bodies strewn before it. Liberty is a female neo-classical figure, with bare shoulders and breasts, like a statue raising the flag of the Republic. This sets up an axis between feminine-classical and masculine-real which, for me, splits the image into two unintegrated parts. At the time, perhaps, the juxtaposition of visual languages reflected unresolved debates within art and representation: old and new pictorial languages. It was bought by the state but withdrawn from exhibition two years later, then brought out briefly in 1848 as the barricades were built again.

A further problem with *Liberty Leading the People* is the tension between documentation – as in the emergence of photography and journalism – and the more traditional role of the artist as narrator, which implies a privileged position, as if artists can foretell future social formations. Saint-Simon's followers through the next decades retained a reliance on their privileged status as mainly middle-class professionals. Jacques Rancière cites reports of Saint-Simonians showing, 'the philanthropic gaze of the visitor to the poor'.[4] But he also quotes a Saint-Simonian carpenter-poet who describes real conditions and, 'how to live the working-class condition philosophically'.[5] This entailed a split between the routine imposed by employers and skills learned amid fellow workers, the latter ignoring the dictates of the clock and reclaiming work as a creative practice. For Rancière, this means the capacity, 'to become different: not by becoming conscious, but by dizziness and loss of identity', when, 'only the words of the poet, the apostle, the young Saint-Simonian… can express reasons for revolt that are not those of egoism'.[6] The young Saint-Simonian, still, preserves a class difference from those whom his or her philosophy is deemed to educate. Put simply, when one person interprets the world for others, this assumes a privileged awareness which those others do not possess. I explain later why I think this undermines the avant-garde. Before that, I look back, following T. J. Clark in situating the origin of the European avant-garde in the 1790s, with Jacques-Louis David, a Jacobin and member of the Committee for General Security who voted for the execution of Louis XVI.

# Looking back

1793 is Year One in the Jacobin re-ordering of time. On 25 Vendémiaire (16 October) David organised a procession to the tomb of revolutionary martyr Jean-Paul Marat (assassinated the previous summer). David's portrait of Marat was carried (completed just in time), but equally important were the choreography, timing – the afternoon after Marie Antionette's execution – and negotiation of the route with the Museum Section (the citizens' group for the district concerned): 'all the arts contributed their magic to the exaltation of the faithful; the sans-culottes communed in memory of their martyrs'.[7] Clark reads the procession as indicating, 'the nature of David's presuppositions as an artist'.[8] He adds, 'What marks this moment of picture-making off from others (what makes it inaugural) is… that contingency rules'.[9] That is, all past assumptions are now void; there is nothing which a public 'could be taken to agree on anymore'.[10]

For Clark, contingency inaugurates a modernism which has not yet been named but which is characterised by a succession of movements which sweep away past art. Contingency is the defining aspect of modernism and the condition of its production, without either fixed mode of representation or a given social order. *The Death of Marat* is integral to the procession of 25 Vendémiaire, and its public display is integral to its meaning as a radically new, politicised art. Clark notes that David painted Marat's body quickly, as less important than other details of the scene such as the sheet of paper with Marat's writing.[11] In Year One, such details had an immediacy in public debate, emphasising the contingency of subject-matter.

Walter Benjamin writes, in 'Theses on the Idea of History' (1940), that history is, 'filled by the presence of the now', and that for Robespierre, 'ancient Rome was a past charged with the time of the now which he blasted out of the continuum of history'.[12] And Michael Lowy, reading Benjamin, argues that the Roman Republic provided Robespierre with a model for the Revolution, charged with what Benjamin calls now-time (*Jetztzeit*); but, he continues, 'the link is a fragile and fleeting one… a momentary constellation that has to be seized'.[13] That momentariness is, I think, what Clark means.

# Dignities of labour

Perhaps Courbet's red signature on *The Stonebreakers* also indicates a moment which has to be seized, the now-time of the Republic, coloured by tensions between Courbet's provincial background and his life in Paris, and between art and Socialism. These tensions increased under the Second Empire, from 1851, putting old craft skills against mass production, old provincial money against the profits to be made through speculation in Paris, soon to be remodelled as a bourgeois city. As Rancière notes, the introduction of inferior goods led craft-workers to seek the regulation of standards, placing, 'the avant-garde worker… and the utopian activist on the same side'.[14] Courbet's response in 1848 is to return to where he came from, in Franche-Comté, in North-East France, where he painted *The Stonebreakers*.

The two labourers are clearing rocks for road building, a common sight at the time; although forced labour on the roads was abolished in the 1789 Revolution, in 1849 casual labourers remained among the poorest members of the community. Their clothes are ragged; and the work soon ages them, seen in the juxtaposition of a young apprentice and an old man. The setting in the landscape of Franche-Comté asserts a refusal of the fashionable circles of Paris and a positive provincialism, as in several works which Courbet made there, elaborating, in effect, the artist's role in social change. That role is partisan in supporting socialism and the peasant class, although provincial farmers and smallholders – beneficiaries of land reforms – were not all Socialists, many being petit-bourgeois in outlook. Some became merchants in agricultural produce and tools, and many voted for the restoration of Empire in 1851. It is inaccurate, then, to see Courbet as simply standing for working-class aspirations, and his time in Paris was paid for by his family's profits from trade. Nonetheless, Courbet celebrates his peasant background. But he equally aspires to gain the professional recognition of the Artist, with its patronage and freedoms. Still, the point remains that he depicts people who were hitherto excluded from the polite language of art, using a language of recognisability. This insists on their dignity as ordinary people living everyday lives, the value underpinning Realism as an avant-garde; and, in a way, this represents a new society through a reordering of the categories through which the world is apprehended. Realism is revolutionary in its empathy, and in its ordinary, rough brushwork and realistic colour. The red signature adds to the effect.

In 1851, Courbet described himself as a Socialist, a democrat and a Republican,[15] while the regime harassed radicals, not least through censorship. Courbet says of the older labourer in *The Stonbreakers*, 'Let the poor devil decide to turn to the Reds, let him be caught with a stray copy of *Démocracie Franche-Comte* [a Left paper] in his pocket, and he will be envied, denounced, expelled, dismissed'.[16] That might apply to the artist, too, except that art is not daily life but its representation, hence its mediation through an aesthetic distancing as well as its politicisation for publics who can read the codes.

# Advancing with the avant-garde

Courbet's paintings in the late 1840s and the 1850s constitute an advance force for social change: *The Stonebreakers* is a Realist work depicting a real scene; six years later, *The Studio* (1855, Paris, Louvre) offers a social programme. Between are works depicting provincial life and landscape; and, incidental but establishing Courbet's Left credentials, a cover image for the radical paper *Le Salut Public* (edited by Charles Baudelaire) showing a man in a black hat standing on a barricade, rifle in one hand, banner in the other.[17] Drawn in 1848, this seems to parody Delacroix's *Liberty Leading the People*. Liberty becomes a man in a hat, a symbol of an aspiration to social status. For Clark, 'Delacroix pictured the worker and bourgeois side by side', while, 'Courbet simply combined them'.[18] He adds that engagement was dangerous in 1848: 'politics did not sell newspapers ... fantasy did'.[19]

This is a long way from Saint-Simon's dialogue of artist, scientist and industrialist advising a benign monarch, closer to the ideas of Pierre Joseph Proudhon, a utopian in a frock coat who went out in 1848 to interview people at the barricades, writing, 'I wept for the poor worker ... delivered up in advance to unemployment ... [and] for the bourgeoisie, whom I saw ruined, driven to bankruptcy, incited against the proletariat.'[20] Proudhon, like Courbet, seems held in a tension between his background and his politic:

> But, you will say, what can art do with such as we who are a wretchod, servile, ignoble, uncouth, ugly mob? It could do something most interesting, the most glorious thing of all. Its task is to improve us, help us and save us. In order to improve us it must first of all know us, and in order to know us, it must see us as we are and not in some fantastic, reflected image which is no longer us.[21]

Proudhon saw Courbet as the first to paint people, 'as our passions and our vices have made us'.[22] Clark reads Courbet's work in these years as moving, 'from painting to politics, from a judgement of colour to ... concerns which touch the State, which move anger and delight because they are the concerns of many'.[23] The evidence is in *The Burial at Ornans* (1849–50, Paris, Louvre), *After Dinner at Ornans* (1849, Lille, Musée des Beaux-Arts), *The Peasants of Flagey returning from the Fair* (1855, Besançon, Musée des Beaux-Arts) and *Young Ladies of the Village, Giving Alms to a Cowherd* (1851, New York, Metropolitan Museum), among other works. The subjects depicted range from labourers and agricultural workers to the 'fashionable young women from Ornans, parading their parasols and bonnets'[24] of *Young Ladies of the Village*. They are Courbet's sisters wearing their town dresses as they give out charity – a bourgeois pursuit – to a female cowherd. Courbet's father appears in *The Burial at Ornans* in a black hat, a respectable man who paid enough tax to vote, who owned two houses, and could support his son financially in his pursuit of art despite a bad harvest in 1846 and a glut in 1847. Such circumstances had major economic impact for others, some members of the community having their land and houses expropriated by speculators from Paris. Amid these tensions, Clark notes, unrest in 1851 was a 'last great act of resistance to the new order'.[25] Meanwhile, literature buried politics in pastoral subject-matter to evade censorship, as in Jules Champfleury's *Les Oies de Noel* (*The Christmas Geese*, 1852) which narrates usury and wrongful arrest within a provincial romance.

By 1851, Courbet was a political outcast. By the mid-1850s, reaction had become the new norm. In these conditions, his epic-scale painting *The Studio* is a potentially revolutionary statement, the indirectness of its use of imagery and specific subjects avoiding censorship while producing multiple interpretations within the pictorial language of Realism.

## The Studio

*The Artist's Studio: A Real Allegory of Seven Years of My Artistic and Moral Life*, to use its full title, shows Courbet seated at an easel bearing a landscape, a female model beside him, a child and a white cat on the floor nearby. Groups of figures fill each side: on his right (the viewer's left) are workers and peasants; on his left, intellectuals and patrons. The cavernous space suggests a workshop specially hired for a large work. The figures rely on past images, and the landscape (of Franch-Comté) is imported, none of this requiring the services of a nude model. Immediately, the scene needs explaining. The artist is its fulcrum, the literal as well as metaphorical centre between the two groups of figures, and centre of the pictorial world. In a politicised reading, the artist is the agent for change in a society categorised by distinctions between workers and intellectuals, expanded to include veterans of 1793, the poor, the aspirant middle class and the patrons of art.

At around six metres long, the painting is intended for public exhibition and debate. Leaving aside an explanation as depicting a masonic lodge – which Hèléne Toussaint justifies by taking the word *atelier* as a synonym for *loge* (masonic lodge), and through symbols such as a painting of a figure in a reddish hue from Diego Ribera's *Descent from the Cross*, sold in Paris in 1843, as the sun in masonic symbolism – and even less plausible allusion in the title to *L'Atelier*, a newspaper from the

1840s (a mouthpiece for the populist Right),[26] I follow Courbet's own description of the work as showing, 'the moral and physical history of my studio' extending to 'the people who serve my cause, sustain me in my ideal and support my activity; people who live on life, those who live on death; society at its best, its worst and its average… the whole world coming to me to be painted.'[27]

Most of the figures are identifiable from documentation. The veteran is Lazare Carnot, a member of the Convention and organiser of revolutionary armies, from a commemorative medallion. A hunter with a red scarf is Garibaldi, hero of the Italian Risorgimento, from an engraving. The labourer in a cloth hat (not the kind worn by French workers) is Alexander Herzen, a friend of Proudhon, founder of the Free Russian Press, exiled in London in 1853. On the other side are Courbet's patron Alfred Bruyas, Baudelaire (from a previous portrait), novelist Champfleury, and the Sabatiers, also Courbet's patrons.[28] The man with a beard and dogs (on the artist's right) looks like a game keeper; but critics briefed by Courbet called him *le braconnier*: dog trainer, poacher or libertine, all of which applied to Napoleon III, 'well known as a libertine and a dog-lover who… bagged the Republic for his own ends'.[29] Press cartoons represented the Emperor by a jackboot, echoed in the figure's thigh boots.

At one level, all this adds up to a picture of France after 1851, muddling through a period of suppressed but not extinguished hopes. At another, it suggests the utopian vision of Charles Fourrier: a society organised as phalansteries (assemblies of 600 carefully selected individuals of compatible temperaments), housed in purpose-built halls which will replace cities as the main form of modern human settlement. Fourier's theory revolves around the idea of affective passions: each Individual has a specific temperament, given to specific kinds of work, which is matched in a *complementary relation* producing an erotic (libidinal, life-affirming) society. Its name is Harmony.

A simpler model of complementarity appears in M. E. Chevreul's colour theory, evolved in his work at the dye works of the Gobelins tapestry in Paris. Chevreul's colour wheel places complementary colours in opposite positions, producing simultaneous contrasts (as in red-green or blue-orange), published in 1839. An English edition was published in 1855 as *The Principles of Harmony and Contrast of Colours, and Their Application to the Arts*.[30] I do not mean to establish any link between Chevreul and Courbet's art or Fourier's utopianism; only to say that complentarity is part of what is called, in general history, the background.[31] Having said that, Fourier's universal Harmony does provide a key to understanding the array of disparate figures in *The Studio*. For Linda Nochlin, *The Studio* is, 'a Fourierist … allegory', informed by the work of another painter, Dominique Papety – reviewed by Baudelaire in the 1846 Salon – whose *Rêve du bonheur* (1843, Compiegne, Musée Vivenel) is Fourierist in its content.[32] There is circumstantial evidence: François Sabatier, the male patron in *The Studio*, owned Papety's *The Last Evening of Slavery* (1848); and Courbet saw Papety's sketch for a Fourierist allegory when he stayed with the Sabatiers in 1854. This is compatible, too, with an analysis of the figure groups as a cross-section of French society, juxtaposing manual and intellectual workers.

Papety died of cholera in 1849, unaware that Courbet would borrow the intention of his allegory. As Nochlin summarises, *The Studio* is avant-garde in representing, 'a union of the socially and artistically progressive … a concrete emblem of what the making of art and the nature of society are to the Realist artist'.[33] It was rejected for the 1855 World Exhibition in Paris, for which Courbet painted it; he hired his own pavilion, as he previously hired a hall in Besançon to show the work from 1848 to 1851 to the publics depicted in it.

Clark asks if Courbet's subject-matter and public stance constitute, 'political art' when art is made in the studio and politics in tracts, manifestoes and action.[34] He suggests that there is a wordless politics which 'ends in a wordless gesture – a scythe on the shoulder, a burning rick, a barricade … the kind of politics the artist thrives on'.[35] This is the politics of barricades and an 'absolute refusal of bourgeois society' for Parisian bohemians whom Clark sees as 'a real social class, a real locus of dissent'.[36] It is not the production of art objects, more of art-work (verb). It reaches a peak in the Paris Commune of 1871, in which Courbet supervised the dismantling of the column bearing an effigy of Napoleon Bonaparte at Place Vendome.

# The Commune and after

During the Commune, barricades reappeared. Women bared their breasts (like Liberty) on them, assuming naively that government soldiers would not fire at people like their own girlfriends, wives and mothers. They did. Women also organised barricades, notably the Russian dissident Elisabeth Dmitrieff, who initiated the Women's Union for the Defence of Paris and Aid to the Wounded, on 11 April 1871. Dmitrieff knew of Karl Marx's theories, and had read Nicolai Chernyshevsky's utopian Socialist novel *What Is to Be Done?* (1862) in which the protagonist, Vera Pavlovna, turns the factory she owns into a phalanstery. Kristin Ross reads the Women's Union as a prototype of such a settlement, writing that the Women's Union envisioned the 'reorganisation of women's labour and the end of gender-based economic inequality... geared toward the immediate combat situation and the need to serve ambulances, to make sandbags for – and to serve on – barricades'.[37] Clearly, gender was as important a category as class, although perhaps less so for Courbet, the male centre of the world in *The Studio* sixteen years earlier.

The situation had changed in other ways, too, since the 1850s: the intellectual emerged as a distinct category of labour; the press expanded, with reviews of art exhibitions from overtly Right or Left positions; and Paris was remodelled by Baron Haussmann as a bourgeois city. It was also increasingly surrounded by aspirant, petit-bourgeois suburbs. All this indicates the process of modernisation inscribed by finance capital and speculation. Benjamin writes that Haussmann's work alienated the city's citizens so much that 'they no longer felt at home in it. They began to become conscious of the inhuman character of the great city.'[38] For a short while, the Commune took back the city, its sites and its feeling.

The defeat of the Commune was marked by executions, and construction of the Basilica of the Sacred Heart on the hill of Montmartre, a giant, ornate, white, Byzantine-style fist over the suppressed city.[39] Political messages in art were extremely coded, as in Eduard Manet's *Rue Mosnier with Flags* (1878, Los Angeles, Ghetty): in a street adorned with flags for the Fête Nationale on 30 June 1878 (designed to inscribe unity), a one-legged man walks away from the spectator, possibly an unemployed veteran; across the road a bourgeois couple wait beside a carriage. Next to the veteran is a ladder. John House reads the juxtaposition as 'a comment... on the evasion of politics and history, which the Fête imposed'.[40] For other artists and writers, aesthetic withdrawal was passive resistance to a regime veering between the Monarchist Right and the Republican Left – both claiming Jeanne d'Arc as emblem – and against bourgeois modernisation. That withdrawal produced the esoteric images of Symbolism, to me too easily interpreted as a-political when passive resistance remains resistant.

By the 1880s, the Republic had won, and a watershed appeared between a first, more overtly political avant-garde – from *The Stonebreakers* to the dismantling of the Vendome Column – to a second, aesthetic avant-garde spanning from the 1880s to modernism in the first half of the twentieth century. I discuss the modernist avant-garde in Chapter 2. Here, I end by reconsidering Seurat's two paintings, on opposite banks of the Seine, which I read (not alone, but against some recent interpretations) as utopian in content.

# Divisionism and anarchism

In the 1880s, Divisionism represents a new language for a new society, drawing on optical science. Small dots of colour deconstruct light, reconstructed optically by the spectator in a transposition from the eye to the cerebral cortex. Seurat's painting *Bathers, Asnières* (1883–4, London, National Gallery) is set on the bank of the Seine in the new suburb of Asnières. Members of the artisan class sit on the bank or bathe, as if on a Sunday afternoon. But this is *Saint Lundi* (Holy Monday), the day on which work is replaced by play and every day is a holiday, because mass production – the factory chimneys on the horizon, in Clichy – is able to solve the economic problem of scarcity. Goods are distributed according to need, made according to ability, as in the writing of Anarchist philosopher Peter Kropotkin.

Seurat's picture could be seen as merely a stylised image of everyday suburban life, but I suggest mine is not a fanciful reading. There is a genre of images of *Saint Lundi*, like Emile Friant's *Monday's Work* (1884, Nancy, Musée des Beaux-Arts), but most are satirical, playing on a mythicised idleness designed to appeal to bourgeois taste. John Leighton and Richard Thomson write that moral superiority is produced 'by having the spectator look down on these casual, furtive types' in Friant's picture.[41] For me, Seurat approaches *Saint Lundi* from the opposite position: as the future, modern and millenarian. And Asnières is an appropriate setting for the vision, a district of lower-bourgeois villas and cottages for the skilled working-class (or artisans). New bridges replaced those destroyed in fighting in 1871, and Asnières resumed a role as a site for boating trips from the city although these moved downstream to Argenteuil when industrial development affected

Asnières. In the 1880s, when Seurat painted it (from sketches, not outdoors), it was 'a prosperous suburban centre', its main employers being a railway works, a fine art print firm, Goupil, and the Louis Vuiton leather workshop.[42] In 1883, the Left succeeded in introducing a law to limit rail fares, making the city centre more accessible to commuters.

Seurat depicts emancipation from toil in this suburban site, a zone of multiple publics. It is a society of ease, a Land of Cockaigne in which the needs of all are met and each contributes by ability: again, Kropotkin's future vision. Although there is no documentary evidence for Seurat's allegiance to Anarchism, he did belong to an Anarchist milieu which also included the painter Paul Signac, another Divisionist. Then, in 1885, Seurat joined an Anarchist circle around the writer Robert Caze, which argued for jury-free exhibitions and a society in which the privileged positions which governed social organisation, the distribution of goods and ideas, and academic art, would be abolished. The artists in this milieu saw colour, freed from naturalistic depiction, as a medium of avant-garde ideas. Paul Smith says of Camille Pissarro (also an Anarchist), 'he thus came to identify colour on its own as a signifier of anarchist beliefs'.[43] Seurat knew of Chevreul's work and that of Hermann von Helmholtz, who extended colour theory from pigment to light. This is *modern* science, enabling a new way of seeing for a new age of human evolution. Although Impressionism offered pictures of fleeting sensations, Divisionism deconstructed light so as to reconstruct its subject-matter with a seeming permanence, an a-temporality previously found in the work of artists such as Pierro della Francesca (or, in modern France, Puvis de Chavannes).

An intermediary from 1885, when Seurat began preparation for the companion piece to *Bathers, Asnières*, was the writer Charles Henry whose cultural criticism appeared in the magazines *Revue Indépendent* and *Revue Blanche*, both symptomatic of the new cultural milieu. In Henry's aesthetic theory, the juxtaposition of complementary colours (as seen in light, transposed to pigment) is not oppositional but harmonious. José Argüelles reads this as 'a strange blend of mathematical idealism and rigorous scientific application' in a world of numbers which is 'the revelation of a mystic order'.[44] Hence images of harmony reveal the imaginary of a society *as* Harmony. Again, although Seurat left no document aligning himself to Henry's theory, he was part of a milieu, meeting at the Café le Panier fleuri in the mid-1880s, a nucleus of

Symbolism including Seurat, Signac, the writers Paul Adamand and Jules Laforgue, and Maurice Raymond, the latter arguing that archaic sculpture was not originally white (as in museum displays) but polychrome.[45]

Of course, circumstantial evidence is not conclusive. Smith takes Seurat's non-contribution to a fund for striking minewokers as disproving his Anarchist allegiance but this, too, seems circumstantial; and when he asserts, 'Seurat was a poseur', wearing 'a demotic and motley costume in the daytime' but a frock coat to dine with his mother in the evening,[46] I wonder if his motivation is merely an aversion to political content in art. To me, neither art historian nor empiricist, the circumstances of the work's production and the artist's milieu contribute to its understanding, and the alignment towards Anarchism fits with observation of what is in *Bathers, Asnières* and *Sunday Afternoon at the Grande Jatte* (1885, Chicago, Art Institute). I agree, too, with John House when he argues that the paintings should be read as a pair, as well as being politicised.[47] Indeed, the two are set on opposite banks of the same stretch of river. In the *Grande Jatte*, members of the bourgeois class take their ease just as the artisans do in *Bathers, Asnières*. A man in a black hat is being rowed across in the *Bathers*, making a topographical connection between the two banks and another kind of connection between social classes.

Walking the site in 2016, I deduced that Seurat had moved the chimneys, using them as a series of verticals which are key to the composition. A 1920s bridge obscures the view now but the central chimney was probably the gasworks at Saint-Ouen. This is a modern utopia, corresponding to what Clark says in a discussion of Pissarro:

> Anarchism … is a theory of the compatibility of freedom and order … dialectical moments of one another … Let us imagine a painter, then, who thought that pictures could be small epitomes of this repressed truth. In them order and freedom would be shown to be reconcilable – indeed, not entities or qualities at all without one another. Freedom would be shown to be a certain kind of orderliness, and order no more than a brittle armature … unless it be formed from the energies released by individual sensations.[48]

This is the Anarchism understood by Seurat and Signac. Its presence in Seurat's paintings is indicated by the picture's organisation: chimney (mass production, end of scarcity) moved to the centre of the horizon (imagined future) while members of all social classes reside in ease on the banks of the Seine. I cannot see why else Seurat would have composed the work as he did; and place more emphasis, perhaps, on trying to understand why and how the image is composed, by looking at it aware of circumstances and co-incidental matters, than on documentation or evidence from archives. That may be my limitation; or my insight.

# The intellectual

In the 1840s, artists and writers remained under the mystique of Romanticism. Courbet paints self-portraits against dark backgrounds; Baudelaire wears clothes which lend him the seeming legacy of an aristocratic past. By the 1880s, in a modernised Paris of boulevards – soon to see the Eiffel Tower as commemoration of tho centenary of the Revolution, and, in 1900, the first Metro line, opened during the World Fair – there were around 40,000 professional artists and 7,000 writers in the city.[49] The numbers fluctuate but show what would now be termed the cultural sector as larger than law or medicine. There were several reasons for this: writers benefitted from new technologies of printing, a rise in literacy and the growth of newspapers and small magazines; reforms in higher education aided the professions; and despite its uneven benefits, modernisation produced a wider market for cultural production. The high number of artists represents a saturation point, with a drop in sales after the 1882 stock market crash – although the same event led Paul Gauguin to become a full-time artist rather than a Sunday painter – but the rise of artist-organised exhibitions and popularity of artist's prints enabled more artists to make a living. Another factor is that metropolitan cities such as Paris, Barcelona, Berlin and Vienna attracted artists and writers by offering a critical mass of like minded professionals, dealers, critics and cafés in which to meet. I return to this in Chapter 2; here, I argue that the society of Paris in the 1880s moved generally from older forms of privilege to a new elitism of merit, across the arts, sciences and other professions (in an oblique way, what Saint-Simon hoped might occur).

Within this broad culture, political allegiances spanned social Darwinism and Marxism; both were Republican, but the former looked to survival of the strongest while the latter looked to a collectivity by which the under-privileged could reform the social order. Through the 1890s, and heightened by the Dreyfus scandal – the false accusation and imprisonment of Alfred Dreyfus, a Jewish army officer, in 1895 – Left intellectuals moved from critique to imagining new social structures. Lucien Herr, for instance, a librarian in higher education, undertook clandestine activism, and, Christophe Charle summarises, foresaw 'a new ideal of the critical *intellectuel* who hastens progress and prepares the necessary revolutions'.[50] He quotes Herr:

> All modern political life is premised on a negation of heredity … Heightening the independence of each new generation is the condition for progress. Since the average human being becomes rigid in his [sic] ideas and interests after reaching maturity, the condition for progress is initiative on the part of younger generations, who demand that social reality be better adapted to new desires, their will and ideas … Insurrection … is a duty not only in exceptional, grave cases, but always.[51]

Herbert Marcuse made similar observations in Paris in 1968 (Chapter 3). For artists and writers in Paris in the 1880s and 1890s, despite aesthetic withdrawal, the line between art and politics was indistinct. That is, progressive social visions included artists and writers as imaginative producers, and took imagination as the envisioning of a new society. While aestheticism tended, in one way, to self-marginalisation or a new elitism, in another way, it was an active refusal of the society of speculation, consumption and corruption (in which artist and writers unhappily relied on the market for a living). For Stéphane Mallarmé, the poet's attitude in such a time, 'on strike against society, is to sweep aside all the debased means offered to him'.[52] And that can be read as a possible point of departure into the aesthetics of modernism.

## Loose ends

History does not divide neatly into periods. Nor do the tendencies which are now taken to constitute modernism have defined memberships or programmes. There are exceptions – the Futurists and Surrealists had manifestoes – but, more often, from Impressionism in the 1870s to

Abstract Expressionism in the 1950s, the -isms are informal associations, defined by critics and used retrospectively as terms of convenience. Some – Symbolism, Divisionism and Fauvism – are sometimes grouped together simply as Post-Impressionism while, Alan Bowness explains, 'the word post-Impressionism would not have been recognized by any of the major artists to whom it is now generally applied'.[53] Perhaps the term avant-garde is no less generalising, and likely to disintegrate on closer investigation. Nonetheless, I use it here and in the next chapter, differentiating the overt socio-political alignment of Realism from the aesthetic turn of what I take as a second avant-garde in modernism. Looking back, for instance to Saint-Simon, I identify a flaw in an assumption of a privileged ability to interpret reality for others (presumed unable to interpret their worlds for themselves), and see this in another but related form in modernism's distancing of reality in an aesthetic turn which is also, if paradoxically, its criticality. As I say in Chapter 2, I read elements of continuity in the evolution of modernism from the 1880s onwards, as in a move towards abstraction; but this does not mean that there is an even process of development, nor common agreement as to aims and means on the parts of the diverse artists, writers and critics involved. Art history is no more prone to neat definitions than general history.

Having said all that, there are watersheds which – again in retrospect – seem to accelerate the processes of change. One of these, I think, was the Paris Commune. Courbet oversaw the dismantling of the Vendome Column in 1871; and was subsequently arrested, briefly imprisoned, then sent the bill for the Column's re-erection. He died impoverished in exile in Switzerland in 1874, the year of the first Impressionist exhibition in Paris. As noted above, political content in art was coded after that, while the dominant political contestation was between a reactionary Royalist Right and a progressive Republican Left.

The Republic prevailed, and announced a competition for the design of a new monument in Place de la République for the ninetieth anniversary of the 1789 Revolution. The winning entry by Charles and Léopold Morice identifies the Republic as Marianne – symbol of the Republic in 1789, identified by her Phrygian cap – holding an olive branch in one hand and a tablet on which the Rights of Man are inscribed in the other. Another entry by ex-Communard Jules Dalou, recently returned from exile in London, in which Marianne rides a chariot, received strong public support, and was erected in Place de la Nation. But, despite any differences, both monuments use a neo-classical language, as if to re-run the tensions in Delacroix's *Liberty Leading the People*. Meanwhile, Paris had been modernised before the Commune, a bourgeois city in which the workers were peripheralised. As David Harvey writes,

> Capitalist urbanisation occurs within the confines of the community of money, is framed by the concrete abstractions of space and time, and internalizes all the vigour and turbulence of the circulation of capital under the ambiguous and often shaky surveillance of the state. A city is... nourished out of the metabolism of capitalist production for exchange on the world market and supported out of a highly sophisticated system of production and distribution... populated by individuals who reproduce themselves using money incomes earned off the circulation of capital (wages and profits) or its derivative revenues (rents, taxes, interest, merchant's profits, payments for services).[54]

The world which Harvey describes produced the department store in which goods from all around the world (colonised by the European powers) were displayed in a continuous array of luxuries, in surroundings resembling domestic interiors where middle-class women could safely exit domestic containment. That world of capital also produced the markets for art and literature, on which artists and writers depended increasingly from the Romantic era onwards. New print technologies enabled low-cost mass production of popular fiction; new art dealers emerged, establishing a trans-Atlantic trade, especially in landscapes. In the 1860s, Courbet joined Jean-François Millet, Charles Daubigny and Théodore Rousseau in the rural retreat of Barbizon, the resulting pictures being popular among these buyers, regardless of any political allegiances. Orlando Figes writes,

> The Barbizon painters were quick to take advantage of the new art market serviced by commercial dealers and auction houses in Paris, London, Amsterdam and even Boston, where they sold a lot of pictures... the Barbizon painters were sharp-eyed businessmen. Their main buyers were wealthy men from mainly middle-class

backgrounds… who identified with them because they too were outside the academic art establishment dominated by the aristocracy.[55]

As Figes also notes, landscapes were small enough to fit into living and dining rooms. Impressionism, too, cashes in on this market, with scenes depicting boating outings on the Seine as well as views of the new city, often from hotel or apartment balconies. There is clearly a tension between the idea of artistic autonomy – reflecting the bohemian lifestyle of artists and writers, beginning in the Latin Quarter of Paris in the 1830s – and the demands of dealers and buyers for continuity of production.

That tension runs through modernism, as it did through the mid-nineteenth century. But the way in which the tension is treated changes, again I suggest after the defeat of the Commune. In his novel *A Rebours* (1884), Joris Karl Huysmans conveys an outright disdain for the mediocrity of modern life, in a city dominated by speculators. In these conditions, aesthetic life offers highly coloured unrealities as well as the status of high culture. The novel's protagonist, the aristocratic Des Esseintes, invents increasingly extraordinary scenarios from an organ in which sounds are replaced by the flavours of unusual liqueurs to a villa filled with exotic flowers (which wilt) and a bejewelled tortoise (which dies). This exemplifies Decadence, a strand within Symbolism, in a matching style; Denis Dennisoff comments, 'with the prose sometimes going on for pages in its lists of collections of things such as esoteric books and freakish plants'.[56] The question is whether this is escapism, or passive resistance.

My reading, which underpins my reading of modernism in the next chapter, is that it is resistant to the dominant society. After the Commune's defeat, oppositionality gives way to covert, coded and oblique critiques of social and political norms. As Jacques Rancière writes, 'The arts only ever lend to projects of domination or emancipation… what they have in common with them: bodily positions and movements, functions of speech, the parcelling out of the visible and the invisible.'[57] The contested ground becomes visual and verbal language, and the ways in which reality is apprehended, categorised and lent value.

# Chapter 2

# Blue voids: The modernist avant-garde and the permanence of art

In Chapter 1, I reconsidered the first politicised avant-garde. In this chapter, I move to the modernist avant-garde and the ambivalence of its political allegiances. The background was a growth in urban centres of population accompanied by technological advances affecting daily life (such as electric light, metro systems and trams, cinema and newsreels bringing faraway events into immediate awareness). Metropolitan cities including Paris, Berlin, Munich, Vienna and Barcelona became hubs of artistic activity as artists, writers and critics were drawn to the polyglot diversity and critical mass of cultural activities and opportunities they offered. Before the outbreak of war in 1914, railways enabled members of emerging art-worlds to move more or less freely across Europe; and the avant-garde groups who comprised those art-worlds were themselves drawn from different nationalities and backgrounds. Most groups had no formal membership. And while there was a general alignment to an internationalism linked, in turn, to the political Left, there were notable exceptions. The Italian Futurists, strongly, welcomed the prospect of war – amid growing tensions between the European powers – as a purifying device for humankind. Cross-border exchanges ended in 1914, along with an incipient optimism that the twentieth century would be a new age not only of technology but also of harmony and human vitality. Even though some contacts were re-established after 1918, the politics of the modernist avant-garde were always subsumed in a shift of visual languages constituting an aesthetic reality: the autonomous, universal language of Form which stood outside the conflicts and changes of ordinary or political life.

In this chapter, I address two overlapping issues: what made the modernist avant-garde an avant-garde, given its political ambivalences, and what constituted the claim to autonomy of an aesthetic dimension. The issues overlap in that a move to new visual and literary languages may be read (then or now) as distancing art from a mass public, that public being potentially the constituency (in a literal sense) of liberal democracy. For art critic Clement Greenberg in the mid-century, it is precisely this distancing which constitutes an avant-garde. I suggest, counter to this, that the situation is more nuanced, involving coded political content, and the viability of withdrawal as passive resistance to the dominant, market-driven society. To address these issues, I focus on three moments in the development of the modernist avant-garde, located approximately at the beginning, middle and end of the modernist era. I admit that the terms avant-garde and modernist are generalisations, that history is not neatly divided into periods (as artists continue to work in the style which brought them public notice, even after it is overtaken by the next development), and that there are several avant-gardes in the twentieth century, with multiple histories. Such is the occupational hazard of writing at a distance, with limited space.

The first moment, drawn from Raymond Williams's commentary on the politics of the avant-garde, is a procession celebrating August Strindberg's birthday in Stockholm in 1912, as a point of departure for discussion of his work stretching back to the 1880s and 1890s. The second is broader: Cubism in Paris, from around 1909 onwards, looking at three distinct strands within the movement. The third is textual, and trans-Atalantic: Greenberg's 1939 essay on avant-garde and kitsch, which offers one argument as to what an avant-garde is, and is for. Many other incidents, works and texts could be interrogated, for instance, the Dadaists' fusion of art, poetry and music at the Café Voltaire in Zurich in 1916 as refusal of the bourgeois values which produced the war; or the on-off (and partly on-again) relation of the French Surrealists towards the Communist Party from the 1930s onwards, or between Existentialism and the Left in the 1950s. But, rather than attempting a representative survey of the modernist avant-garde, on whom there are several excellent books,[1] I focus on instances which illuminate the political ambivalences of modernism. These instances construct a spectrum from Williams's view that the avant-garde exhibits a 'violent rejection of tradition: the insistence on a clean break from the past',[2] to Greenberg's trajectory towards a purity of means, prescribing a permanence for art, as if outside temporality, with Cubism somewhere between the polarities.

# Strindberg's birthday procession

The torch-lit procession in Stockholm on 22 January 1912 marked Strindberg's sixty-third birthday. It was organised by the Stockholm Workers' Commune, a Communist organisation. Strindberg was Sweden's foremost intellectual, a playwright, poet, painter and polemicist, for whom the Commune called for a state pension. Williams notes, 'Red flags were carried and revolutionary anthems sung'.[3] But, although Strindberg was known for attacks on the religious, literary and military establishments, his politics were a mix of Right and Left. In his early work he supported radical causes; yet in his main works he is a, 'psychologically introspective writer'.[4] And when he engages with class conflict, he is pessimistic. Hence the strangeness of the procession (as it happened, for his last birthday). But this is not uncharacteristic of the inherent political ambivalence of the withdrawal of art and literature into aestheticism in the 1880s, when it seemed no longer viable to oppose bourgeois society, only to create a parallel, aesthetic society within it, in small groups of artists, writers and critics meeting in cafes and apartments, sharing ideas in small magazines, offering mutual support and becoming their own publics.

In this situation, art and literature took the artist's or writer's state of psyche as subject-matter. If this seems a retreat to solitude, I read it, equally, as a conscious refusal of the dominant society's materialism and market economics. The turn to immateriality thereby assumes a radical aspect, denying the values which shaped a society of speculation and consumerism – although artists and writers were increasingly dependent on the market for a living – just as artists in the 1960s took to Conceptualism as denying the art-market the objects of consumption on which dealers relied. In some cases in the 1890s, this extended to the esoteric – seances, spiritualism and appropriation of archaic cultures and Eastern religions – but this is the period, too, of psychanalysis and a realisation that human life exists in dreams as well as in waking actualities. For Dennis Denisoff, what is called Decadence is dissidence:

> Western culture... has habituated a view of birth and growth as positive, and decay as death and negative, when in fact they are all part of one indivisible, non-progressive package. In connection with this critique, decadence also challenged other false normativisations such as the fundamental importance of the middle-class family model, industrial progress and a common moral basis to beauty and the meaning of life. Aestheticism is similarly anti-conformist, supporting an aesthetic doctrine that suggests one's private utopia is at hand, if one would only learn to ignore the dominating bourgeoisie.[5]

Strindberg both illustrates and upsets this scenario. His plays are set in bourgeois or upper-class interiors, revealing the angst-ridden states of psyche of those who constitute polite society. He undermines that society (of which he is a member) by exposing its hidden tensions (and his own); and points to the brittle, fracturing aspect of the equilibrium which that society claims or seeks. Yet there is little or no glimpse of a private utopia, nor any retreat to an aesthetic idyll. Where there is such a hint (as in *Miss Julie*, discussed below) it is already denied, put less in an aesthetic dimension than in a realm of brutal impossibility.

Strindberg's version of everyday domestic life is akin to the extreme unease of, say, Edvard Munch's *The Scream* (1893, Oslo, National Gallery). And while he may not have seen that painting (of which Munch made several print versions), he was part of the dissident cultural milieu in Berlin in 1892, when Munch's exhibition was closed for its departure from sanctioned taste. But, if the new art and writing of the 1890s reveals hitherto prescribed traits of human emotion and desire, the depths thus plumbed are represented with a directness which, paradoxically, masks a distancing of reality through abstraction. Munch regarded madness as haunting modernity, yet he redirects attention from the conditions which might produce anxiety – social, economic, political – towards the individual, the human face and body as unique identity. Shearer West writes of Symbolism, its subjective qualities, 'were symptomatic of a range of escapist tendencies in contemporary culture... the product of a growing fascination with psychology, dreams and repressed desire'.[6]

All this positions the art and writing of the 1890s as a rejection of bourgeois materialism. For West, mindful of William Morris as well as aestheticism, Symbolism was 'a negative engagement with the actual circumstances of modern life', informed by an evident utopianism found either in 'the beauty of art', or social change.[7] But that is the dilemma: beauty or social reform? Strindberg offers no exit from the angst he exposes. The plays present social constriction, repression, sexual tension, nihilism and misogyny, not the new dawn which the Workers' Commune might have imagined. Indeed, he was drawn to the reactionary spectacle of social Darwinism, a misrepresentation of Darwin's theory of evolution not as survival by adaptation (as Darwin said) but as survival of the strongest, used to justify imperial power and white male supremacy.

## Strindberg's revolution?

When his plays were performed in Paris in the mid-1880s, Strindberg required that the lights were turned off during the play, limiting the audience's ability to watch each other and continue their conversations.[8] Darkness separated the stage from the life outside the theatre, and reflected a turn to seriousness in northern European cultural circles, epitomised by the text from Seneca displayed above the stage in the Leipzig Gewanthaus, '*Res Severa est Verum Gaudium*' (True Joy is a Serious Matter).[9] That, too, was a facet of modernism, and theatre critic Michael Billington takes Strindberg, together with the Norwegian playwright Henrik Ibsen, as founding figures of modern drama. But, he says, while Ibsen relays, 'the interaction of private and public... the dramatist as spokesperson', for Strindberg, 'absolute realism' evokes, 'love, hate, fury and desire' as personal emotions.[10] *Miss Julie* (1888) affirms this.

*Miss Julie* is a drama of class conflict. It is also a drama of gender relations, with two female leads. Julie, daughter of an aristocrat, and Christine, the cook, are rivals for the affection of Jean, the valet, Julie breaking the norm by which masters and servants live separate lives. In a preface, Strindberg writes of a struggle for survival, transposing this pseudo-Darwinian scenario to female roles on opposite sides of the class divide, acted out in the domestic spaces of the estate owned by Julie's father. To survive, Julie must act like a man.

The action spans Midsummer's Eve and the morning after, a time of almost endless daylight. At first, talking to Christine, Jean describes Julie as mad after she tries to partner him at a barn dance. Julie breaks off her engagement to a fiancé who has refused to jump over a riding crop she holds out as if training a dog, adding gender transgression to the class transgression of dancing with Jean. When Julie enters the kitchen, the mood changes and Jean agrees to dance with her as Christine remains mute in the background. Julie and Jean tell each other their dreams, go to Jean's room and have sex. They plan to elope but Julie insists on bringing her pet caged bird, saying she would rather kill it than leave it in the hands of strangers. Jean cuts off its head. But in the morning Christine tells the lovers she will instruct the stables not to release any horses, trapping them on the estate. Julie asks Jean what to do. He hands her his razor. She exits with it in her hand. Jean returns to Christine. The censor cut Julie's description of sex with Jean as bestial. Strindberg wanted his wife Siri von Essen to play Julie, and saw the play as establishing Naturalism as a realistic study of human behaviour. But the outcome is nihilistic: the escape from class boundaries and gender roles is, in Julie's final exit, death.

Naturalism was a major force in the arts in Scandinavia in the 1880s, appealing to a middle-class, Lutheran public. Strindberg aimed to found a Scandinavian Naturalist Theatre in Copenhagen, with *Miss Julie* as its first production but the play was banned during its dress rehearsal, performed later at the Students' Union. Its first performance in Stockholm was not until 1906 when, Williams notes, it, 'met furious denunciation. The new drama was low and vulgar … it threatened the standards of decent society.'[11] Perhaps that was the aim: to attack bourgeois society via its cultural institutions. And Strindberg realised his ambition in 1907, by founding the Intimate Theatre (*Intima Teater*) in Stockholm. This was the year in which he completed *Ghost Sonata*, in which the cast express their misfortunes in separate monologues. Its first performance occurred in the Intimate Theatre, in an auditorium of 150 seats, with modern lighting. Williams sees a move towards Expressionism in *Ghost Sonata* (1907) but argues that a 'fully public' drama would reverse 'the bourgeois evacuation of the sites of social power' of Strindberg's withdrawal into 'what was taken to be an inner consciousness or indeed an unconscious'.[12] The Intimate Theatre was boarded up after Strindberg's death in May 1912, later used as a trade union meeting hall. Perhaps members of the Workers' Commune went there.

Among Strindberg's other interests was contemporary art. In Paris 1894 and 1895 he attended Paul Gauguin's Thursday evening gatherings of artists and writers. Preparing a sale of pictures to finance his journey to Tahiti in June 1895, Gauguin asked Strindberg to write a preface for the catalogue. Strindberg said no, but his letter of refusal reveals mutually held values. Gauguin used it anyway:

> I should have willingly given you this souvenir to take away with you … where you are going in search of space and a setting in harmony with your own powerful stature … I saw on your walls this confusion of sunlit paintings that haunted me … I saw trees that no botanist would ever find … and people that you alone could have created … A sea looked as if it had flowed from a volcano, and a sky that no God could inhabit … you have created a new earth and a new sky, but I do not feel at ease in your creation. For me it is too ablaze with sunlight, I who prefer chiaroscuro. And your paradise is inhabited by an Eve who is not my ideal … Gauguin [is] the savage who hates the restrictions of civilisation … the child who takes his toys to pieces to make new ones, he rejects and defies, preferring to see sky as red instead of blue like the masses.[13]

Strindberg preferred tone and volume to flat colour but felt an empathy for Gauguin as someone rejecting the restrictions of European civilisation. Today, Gauguin is also seen as a misogynist and sexual predator, appropriating the exotic of a Polynesia already afflicted by sexually transmitted diseases and alcohol. Perhaps their affinity was in a shared gender-restricted horizon, looking to red sunsets, not female emancipation. But it also exhibits a lack of any coherent political position.

Strindberg was aligned to the Left in his early and late work, but not in the middle years. Williams notes that he 'declared that in a time of social eruption he would side with those who came weapon in hand from below'[14]; but that he also said his revolution was against himself.[15] Modernism is a play of opposites. As Williams observes, Expressionists raise this to 'a principle of form' and Surrealists, in the 1930s, leap beyond, 'contradictions such as action-dream, reason-madness, and sensation-representation'.[16] Boundaries are collapsed; yet there is no guarantee that the outcome is a better world. The revolution is a revolution in setting and language, the latter prevailing in Cubism in Paris from around 1909 onwards.

# Intersections, colliding coherences

Like modernism, Cubism is a term applied retrospectively. Groups within Cubism had divergent aims and publics, even within the Paris art-world (and there were Cubists in many other countries as well, from Portugal to the Baltic and the Balkans).[17] A common concern is to rebuild the means by which three-dimensional materiality is figured in the two-dimensional realm of the picture. In one way, this responds to the tendency to abstraction which began in the 1880s, moving from areas of flat colour within outlines of objects to the dis-assembly of things in intersecting planes. In another way, it is a reflection, not of realms of psyche, but of the material, interior spaces of the artist's studio. The still life objects which frequently appear – pots, bottles, musical instruments, pieces of newspaper or wood grain and wallpaper (like newspapers, already two-dimensional) – constitute a parallel reality in which the view of the world outside is framed by the window: enclosed space as *pictorial space*. And just as the objects re-constructed in art re-figure the daily life of the studio, so the space of the painting, collage or drawing is unique to art. Hence the claim to autonomy, not only freed from the norm of perception but also conjuring a separate realm of Form, with its own mechanisms and structures, its own immaterial permanence. This new way of seeing reflects a concern with the language of art, or dialectic of visuality, and with a continuity no longer rooted in the past and its traditions, but in a perpetualised present (if there is one).

All this occurs in, and carries the traces of, a world re-made, too, in new technologies, and in the speed not only of motorised or steam-powered transport and machines but also with which news reaches urban publics in newspapers and newsreels. The re-ordering of planes, light and surface is an equivalent, rather than representation in a conventional sense, of the vitality of modern, urban (especially metropolitan) cities, with crowds, changing displays in shop windows, reflections in the glass and shifting lights of trams. Everything intersects. Nothing is permanent except the rapid pace of change and overload of visual sensations. Subjects and objects dissolve in mutual immersion. For Paul Wood, the planes of Cubist painting 'have the appearance of shards or fragments that overlap each other in a shallow space that does not extend to… the horizon but just revolves around the overlapping planes themselves'.[18] Again, impressions collide, intersect and shift, permanently dis-continuous, in a realm of kaleidoscopic co-incidences.

The creation of an alternative realm of Form is art's equivalent to the suspension of the theatrical suspension of disbelief epitomised in the dramas of Bertolt Brecht. It suspends the picture frame's equivalence to a window frame, as said above, makes a space which exists only as itself, a basis for allusion but not illusion. The price of this, as well as the difference from Brecht's theatre of alienation, is art's distancing from what is called reality; but all worlds are real to those who inhabit them, even alone. As I elaborate later (and in Chapter 3), this distancing produces a critical space. But it is not necessarily politicised; abstraction looks in more than one direction.

# Factions, publics and outlooks

In Paris in the 1910s, there were at least three groups within the broad terrain of Cubism: Picasso and Georges Braque, working in cheap, live-in studios in Montmartre, exhibiting through dealers such as Ambrose Vollard and Paul Kahnweller catering for an emerging market of collectors of modern art; Albert Gleizes, Jean Metzinger, with associates around the writers' group (and press) l'Abbaye de Créteil,[19] meeting at the house of Marcel Duchamp and Raymond Duchamp-Villon in the suburb of Puteaux, formalising their position in the essay *Du Cubisme* in 1912; and Sonia and Robert Delaunay, designer and painter, showing in the annual salon exhibitions to be encountered by a broad public, and immersing themselves in everyday modern life.

Combining bohemianism with the cultivation of an emerging modern-art-market, Picasso, among others in Montmartre in the late 1900s and 1910s, retains a semblance of figuration: the pictures are either full of things, or depict people, or both. But I say a semblance because it may be that things are a point of departure, not the journey; the latter is a play of quasi-illusion in shading and collage, a punning on representation which is no longer representational, and a new geometry of line and plane which is almost Cartesian in its self-containment, except it is also a hint of space-time, adding the fourth dimension to the Cartesian world view. I think Tim Clark says something like this when he writes (using the term high Cubism to denote Picasso's work around 1911 to 1912),

> Nobody is going to say that reference to the things of the world has simply ceased in high Cubism. But it may not be the point any longer. It may not be what drives depiction toward the kind of orders it finally offers us. Might we do better to understand the world of high Cubism as one in which objecthood… or thing-ness… has been overtaken by the act of signification itself… a freer and freer play of the signifier, a set of devices discovering that simply the difference between them is enough to make a world?[20]

To be avant-garde is to pursue the logic of the new language on its own terms, wherever it leads.

Gleizes and Metzinger are avant-garde in this way, too, but formalise their position in the text *du Cubisme* (1912). They situate Cubism in a tradition from Realism to Eduard Manet and Paul Cézanne, as if in a trajectory which it logically extends. They also write, 'Let the artist deepen his [sic] mission more than broaden it. Let the forms which he discerns… be sufficiently remote from the imagination of the crowd to prevent the truth which they convey from assuming a general character.'[21] This is contrary to Courbet's intention in Realism, although they share the first avant-garde's assumption of the artist's privileged insight; and although Gleizes and Metzinger say that art *should* be for a wide audience, they insist it meets that audience on its own terms. David Cottington notes that while Metzinger showed at the salons his links were equally to Montmartre: 'Throughout [*du Cubisme*], the assertions of avant-gardism were couched in the elevated symbolist-inspired language', which limited, 'the engagement with the dynamic experience of modern life that characterized the work of the other salon cubists'.[22]

Among those others exhibiting at the salons, Robert Delaunay looked from his studio window to the Eiffel Tower – modern engineering commemorating the centenary of the 1789 Revolution – and the more recent Ferris wheel. He painted both, and the visiting Cardiff football team, in *L'Equipe de Cardiff FC* (1912, Paris, Musée d'Art Moderne). A biplane hovers, too, intersecting the wheel, in an image borrowed from a contemporary postcard. Delaunay was a hands-on painter, not given to intellectual justification: 'the world is not our representation recreated by reasoning... [it] is our *métier*'.[23] *Métier* means trade or profession, a *terme de metier* a technical term, which aligns him to a practical approach. And yet his work is the most abstracted among the Cubists in 1912, in a series of paintings in which the Tower becomes a motif and the surface dissolves into planes of colour, the refractions of light which insist that what is rendered here is not the view, but the medium of light itself. The most practical painter, then, is also the most advanced in non-representation (although, as Clark says above, Picasso does this, too).

Sonia Delaunay – whose work spans textile designs, posters, book covers, even a decorative pattern applied to a motor car – uses light, refracted into circular motions, in her collaboration with the poet Blaise Cendrars in the picture-poem *Prose du Transibérien et de la petite Jehanne de France* (1913). Jehanne is not Jehanne d'Arc but a Paris sex worker. The poem traces a series of journeys, ranging from Russia to Timbuctu, New York, and many European destinations, returning to Paris, the Eiffel Tower and the Ferris wheel, mixing free verse and rhyme, personal desires and cosmic scenes – a crescent moon, the sky lit up – and the music of drums, trumpets, clarinets and flutes. Virginia Spate glosses, 'memories of the endless journey ceaselessly generate new associations... juxtaposed in vivid contrasting images, unconnected by the usual transitions of narrative language'.[24] This is city life as simultaneity: conventionally, time prevented everything happening at once; now It enables that coalescence which is also a distribution, in time-space. Spate notes that *L'Equipe de Cardiff FC* fuses, 'different kinds of time – the moment of the game and the continuous movement of colours.'[25] She adds that both Sonia and Robert were inspired by the multi-coloured halos around streetlights recently installed on Boulevard Saint-Michel.[26]

# Divergences

The groups and individuals within Cubism shared a sense of modern life as new, but in different ways, drawn variously to the excitement of the metropolis and machines, the science of optics, the mathematics of the fourth dimension (space-time), or a trajectory of abstraction (seen by Wassily Kandinsky, working in Munich in 1912, as opening a new spiritual era).[27] While Picasso looked to the market, and the Delaunays to a broad public and fusion of art and craft in Sonia's designs, Gleizes and Metzinger stand out as the most intellectualised, their essay on Cubism prefiguring the turn to textuality as a revolutionary stance proposed, in the 1970s, by Julia Kristeva (Chapter 3).

# Avant-garde or kitsch?

Modernism's claim to autonomy rests on the primacy of visual language, advancing on the path to Form. John Roberts writes, citing Theodor Adorno's *Aesthetic Theory*, that if art leaves the new, 'it falls back into heteronomy and the academic … there can be no renewal of art without art resisting, reworking, dissolving what has become tradition'.[28] Such departures lead to a 'reflection on [art's] own conditions of possibility' as he puts it.[29] There are echoes of Strindberg's attacks on the literary establishment when Roberts continues,

> In order to delineate itself as modern, it is imperative that art define itself against those institutional arrangements, social circumstances and traditions in which it finds itself. Therefore there can be no critical future for art without this experience of disjunction with the traditions and institutions which have brought it into being. That is, the dynamic content of art continues to be implicated in the mediation of the critique of art as a … category.[30]

But there is a contradiction if modernism's development is constructed as a trajectory, not as a means to continuous critique. This is my objection to Greenberg's formula of a modernism which progressively realises its essence, shedding ornament and incident, narrative, autobiography and social comment. Painting is colour on surface. It has a limited public (almost does not need one, so much on its own terms), and by the 1970s produces monochromes: all-grey canvases, blue voids.

Greenberg idealises modernism by dividing art from popular culture, in his 1939 essay 'Avant-garde and kitsch'. He targets Socialist Realism, which reflected the daily lives of its publics in ways which could be easily understood, as kitsch. That is a limited reading of Socialist Realism, at least before a tightening of Stalinist cultural policy in 1936. But dates matter: Greenberg conveys an allegiance to purity as art's permanence, but his essay is historically specific, a reaction to the 1939 Hitler-Stalin pact whereby the Soviet Union undertook not to attack Nazi Germany. This undermined the Left for obvious reasons, trashing the oppositional dualism of Fascism-Communism instantiated two years previously, for instance, in the juxtaposition of Nazi and Soviet pavilions on the main avenue of the 1937 Paris International Exhibition.[31] *Guernica* was exhibited in the Spanish Republic's pavilion, evoking the perpetual horror of war, and sympathy for anti-Fascism. In France, the Popular Front united Socialists and Communists against Fascism. In 1939, Greenberg, a Left critic writing for Left journals such as *Partisan Review*, redefines modernism as incompatible with mass culture and the mass audience of Socialist Realism. He ignores public murals in Mexico, painted in the 1930s as mass education, and by 1962, has reached a more extreme position: 'there are only two kinds of art: the good and the bad'.[32] The implication is that he knows which is which, transposing the avant-garde's privileged insight from artist to critic.

Greenberg insists that the 'civilization' which produced T. S. Eliot's poems is incompatible with the mass culture of popular songs and magazine covers (citing *Saturday Evening Post*). Then, claiming that 'the first settlers of bohemia' were 'uninterested in politics',[33] a contestable assertion, he says, 'the true and most important function of the avant-garde was not to experiment, but to find a path along which it would be possible to *keep culture moving* in the midst of ideological confusion and violence'.[34] Keeping culture moving implies experiment; but it also reflects the pressure to keep style moving in fashion and the art market (whereby dealers introduce new artists and promote others, if they sell, to senior, more expensive, status).

Greenberg aligns aesthetics to 'spaces, surfaces, shapes, colours, etc., to the exclusion of whatever is not necessarily implicated in these factors'.[35] The function of advanced art is hermetically sealed, to which Greenberg sets up the Aunt Sally of kitsch. To prove this, Greenberg juxtaposes Picasso and Ilya Repin: the archetypal modernist and a nineteenth-century naturalist painter. Repin was not a Socialist Realist because, although his work was popular in the Soviet Union, he began his career in nineteenth-century Tsarist Russia, and later declined an invitation to return to the Soviet Union after moving to Finland, where he died in 1930. Greenberg's objection to his paintings is that they were liked by peasants, a view borrowed from another writer in *Partisan Review*, Dwight Macdonald, who writes on Soviet cinema. In passing, Macdonald asks why peasants prefer Repin's work to Picasso's 'whose abstract technique is at least as relevant to their own primitive folk art' and answers, 'they have been conditioned… to admire socialist realism'.[36] Greenberg does say, contra Macdonald, that the masses like kitsch for its easy content, not through conditioning, but largely follows Macdonald's ready-made line. Hence, he says, the peasant sees in Repin's battle scenes, 'values… far superior to the values he has been accustomed to find in icon art'.[37] But these are values based on perception, not on 'reflection upon the immediate impression left by the plastic values'.[38] In his final paragraph, recalling his Left roots, Greenberg says that anything of quality made in a capitalist society in decline is a threat to its existence; and that avant-garde art corrodes the society in which it is produced. He adds, 'we no longer look to socialism for a new culture… simply for the preservation of whatever living culture we have right now'.[39]

I find Greenberg's critique confused, not only in his mistaken alignment of Repin to Socialist Realism but also in his assumption that mass publics have no taste. It is the case that under capitalism mass culture is determined not by its publics but by the producers, who reproduce the consumerism on which their profits depend. As Adorno writes, 'the dream industry does not so much fabricate the dreams of the customers as introduce the dreams of the suppliers among the people'.[40] But Walter Benjamin reads film and photography as democratising culture, looking at experimental cinema and Expressionist theatre, not Hollywood, and assuming the audience's ability to understand how films are made. Citing Benjamin's essay (using a correctly translated title), 'The Work of Art in a Period of Technical Reproducibility', Esther Leslie comments,

> The copy can be manipulated. It is tactile. Exhibition, the ability to see and be seen, tactility, the ability to touch, are sensuous concepts that relate new art to the physical presence of the collective receiving body. Benjamin negates any idea of artistic autonomy in his version of art as embodiment of corporeal, material nature.[41]

This resonates with Marx's reference to 'sensuousness as practical, human-sensuous activity' in his *Theses on Feuerbach* (1845);[42] and with Clark's idea of an embodied politics (Chapter 1). It is also a more thoughtful critique than Greenberg's.

Greenberg's reputation as an influential critic grew, nonetheless, in the 1960s when he championed the colour-field painters in New York. But Agnes Heller questions his reductive approach (without naming Greenberg),

> Many contemporary artists speak with resentment of the theorists of high modernism… It is said that they have terrorized the artistic scene, excluded many deserving artists from recognition and included less-deserving ones., while being motivated by their ideological pre-judgements or even prejudices. There is some truth in these accusations…. Art theories could blame the corrupt taste of the culture-loving public, but their taste could not entirely be neglected.[43]

There are two issues: Greenberg's reductive art history makes a simplistic divide between high and low culture (while Cultural Studies sees social conditions sedimented in all culture and sub-culture, and in intermediate forms such as jazz and cinema); and, as said, his trajectory leads art into a dead end, a high point of non-reversibility which is also void of content (the agency of evocation which the modernisms of the 1880s to the 1930s retain in various ways). There *is* a case to be made against mass culture, as argued by English art critic Peter Fuller in the 1980s when he castigates the mega-visual culture of consumerism as degrading visuality (and in Adorno's remarks, above). But that is not Greenberg's position, and Fuller attacks colour-field painting, too.[44] But that politicised, economic case is not the one Greenberg makes.

# Frayed edges

Returning to my two issues: what made the modernist avant-garde an avant-garde, and its political ambivalence: the turn to states of psyche in the 1880s is transposed to the space of the studio, and the picture, giving rise to visual languages which express the multiple sensations and intersecting planes of metropolitan life, but which also separate art as intellectual work from that life, affirming the avant-garde's privileged position. That separation constructs the separation of aesthetics from politics. But the position has been challenged since the 1870s in a growth of public art museums – such as Tate, initially intended to improve the deserving working class by exposing it to middle-class taste and aristocratic values[45] – and in recent reforms whereby museums diversify their coverage as well as their publics (discussed in Chapter 7). Nonetheless, a split between art and politics remains, and the art market has converted radical innovation into a new mainstream in which all departures are subsumed, and colonised even the most immaterial, Conceptual practices, substituting name recognition for the art-object. But that is what capitalism does. If there is an exit it is in the work of artists and artists' groups who pursue politicised objectives while drawing on arts funding (and education) for a livelihood – biting the hand that feeds them, as policy – discussed in Chapters 7, 8 and 9. Here, before revisiting *Miss Julie*, I cite three voices echoing modernism's ambiguities. Wood sees modernism as caught 'between a technically radical art… and an art dedicated both to the criticism of existing social inequalities and the provision of models of social progress'.[46] Clark reads modernism as facing in two directions: 'its inward-turning and its outward-reaching, its purism and opportunism, its centripetal and centrifugal force'.[47] And Williams writes, 'radically innovating experimental artists and writers' produce 'a new kind of art for a new kind of social and perceptual world… which would revive and liberate humanity'.[48] That would be nice.

# Coda: *Miss Julie* again

In Liverpool in 2008, *Miss Julie* was adapted for walk-through performance in a social housing site, retitled *Miss Julie in Utopia*, with a Preface re-written from a feminist position, by the Institute for the Art and Practice of Dissent at Home. It was a free event for an audience of fifteen, with Cathy Butterworth as Julie, Gary Anderson as John (Jean) and Lena Simic as Tina (Christine):

> History revisited! The Internationale sung! This was Strindberg undone! A journey from 1888 via 1968 to 2008. Another world made possible. This was the revolution staged at home. This was Strindberg with a feminist make-over. This was about thinking class. This was about claiming history. This was about imagining Utopia.[49]

The new Preface, spoken by Butterworth from an upstairs window, begins,

> 120 years ago this summer in England, an authorized translation of the Communist Manifesto was published with a Preface by Engels. The opening goes, 'Workers of the world unite, you have nothing to lose but your chains.' 120 years ago this summer, in France, Eugène Pottier wrote words for the Internationale.... 120 years ago this summer in Sweden August Strindberg wrote *Miss Julie* – a new kind of naturalistic tragedy that deals with ... conflict between the classes.[50]

It comments on New Labour's turn to the Right after 1997, and retitles Liverpool's year as Capital of Culture in 2008 as Capitalism of Culture, when Liverpool becomes 'a toy shop for the developer'.[51] The Preface continues,

> The Institute believes that stating a political, ethical or philosophical position with rigour and integrity, is a productive practice for thinking through current issues. *Miss Julie in Utopia* is for us a thinking through of a political position through the filter of a play that suggests but does not deliver on a political promise.
> This play is deeply problematic. Strindberg was a left winger who had a demonstration of dock workers campaign for a pension for him on his 63rd birthday ... [He] was also an insufferable misogynist, a woman hater, subscribing to ideas about 'the weak dying out' making way for the 'stronger.' Our strategy to counter this was to rewrite, rewrite, rewrite.... *Miss Julie in Utopia* is a feminist intervention into a text that has for the past 120 years, in our theatres and our class rooms, been oppressing women.

> 120 years ago saw the seeds of revolution sown in the Communist Manifesto… it seems important not just to remember the seeds of revolution but to sow them again, for our time, our place.[52]

I quote this at length to show that modernist drama can be extricated from its contradictions, or from Strindberg's pessimism. The workers' procession in Stockholm responded to the undermining of bourgeois values through a theatre of domestic angst, and the Institute for the Art and Practice of Dissent at Home responds to Strindberg's misogyny and assumption of impenetrable class barriers by re-writing the play. *Miss Julie in Utopia* extends the unfinished task of a drama of personal life transgressing class and social norms, received by an audience aware of their own experiences. Such might have become the project of the Intimate Theatre. The performance of *Miss Julie in Utopia* was for an intimate audience, but not as an end-point in a trajectory, not a blue void but a red banner of revolt when the personal has become political.

# PART TWO

# Theories and critiques

# Chapter 3
# Society as a work of art?

The modernist avant-garde was politically ambivalent, and produced a series of departures from the mainstream which, in time, became a mainstream of departures. For Clement Greenberg, the purpose of an avant-garde was to keep art *moving*; yet there are aspects of modernism which look to an opposite possibility in autonomous and timeless laws of Form. Greenberg took art's formal qualities – such as colour on surface – to construct a trajectory towards purity; but a trajectory is a movement through time, which theoretically contradicts the potential *stasis* of a universal aesthetic. Perhaps, then, movement and stasis become polarities on an axis of potentially creative tension, on which the modernist work of art takes place.

Wassily Kandinsky wrote in 1911 of the inherent psychic qualities of colours, and how these are mediated by shape and juxtaposition within the whole composition of a painting; pulling away from naturalism, he concludes,

> We must find, therefore, a form of expression which… does not restrict the free working of colour in any way. The forms, movement, and colours which wo borrow from nature must produce no outward effect nor be associated with external objects. The more obvious is the separation from nature, the more likely is the inner meaning to be pure and unhampered.[1]

Although Kandinsky writes in terms of an advance (in art as a sign of a movement towards a realm of spirit, or psyche[2]), he sees this as a continuous negotiation of form within each art work. Rather than constituting a linear development, I suggest, this sets out a polyphony of formal resolutions within an autonomous aesthetic realm, epitomised, for me, by his many *Improvisations* from 1911 to 1913. These include shapes derived, for example, from Russian woodcuts illustrating the Apocalypse, with falling towers, angels with trumpets, and figures holding their heads to the sky from which New Jerusalem will descend. Rose-Carol Washton Long reads these veiled references as a mid-path between pure abstraction and recognition by which Kandinsky, 'hoped to make the spectator take part in the creation of the work by unravelling its mysterious, ambiguous images, to replace confusion with understanding'.[3] In 1911, it was possible to see the twentieth century as a new, revolutionary – for Kandinsky spiritual – age. After the outbreak of war in 1914, and through four years of industrialised slaughter when eighteenth-century infantry tactics were used in face of modern machine-warfare, this became a dream. Kandinsky moved from *Improvisations* to more formalised *Compositions*; elsewhere, modernism mutated into both abstraction and the psychically mediated figuration of Surrealism. By the 1930s, Europe was afflicted by the rise of Fascism.

That is the background to this chapter's reading of Herbert Marcuse's aesthetic theories, from his doctoral research on literature in the 1920s to his late writing in the 1970s. Like all members of the Frankfurt Institute for Social Research (the Frankfurt School), Marcuse was haunted by the failure of revolution in industrialised Germany in 1918–19, and the rise of Fascism and Nazi assumption of power in 1932. This does not *explain* Marcuse's turn to aesthetics, and a significant part of his work is in social theory and psychoanalysis, but it does contribute to his need to look beyond political practices for a means to liberation.

In this compromised scenario, art offers an imagined alternative realm of possibility; and, perhaps more importantly, it *refracts* the miserable reality (as he later calls it) to render that reality as if unreal, to negate it by juxtaposition. Marcuse writes, 'art is inevitably part of that which is and only as part of that which is does it speak against that which is'.[4] From that burden of estrangement, he adds, emanates 'a new consciousness and a new perception'.[5]

This is a position maintained, too, by Theodor Adorno: 'The appearance of the non-existent as if it existed motivates the question as to the truth of art. By its form alone art promises what is not… The unstillable longing in the face of beauty… is the longing for the fulfilment of what was promised.'[6] For Marcuse and Adorno, it is juxtapositions such as unreal-real, or social-aesthetic, which produce a creative ambivalence, again, an axis of tension between polarities along which, here, the work of theory is done.

Marcuse may seem outdated: he borrows from classical Greek thought and Kantianism, and tends towards a universalism which is untenable in post-modern discourses of pluralism and multiplicity. Yet Marcuse's optimism amid student protest in the 1960s, and rehabilitation of the aesthetic in his late work, remain interesting amid a renewal of protest and against the onslaught of economics under neoliberalism. In the last section of the chapter, I counterpose Marcuse's work – specifically his idea that a literature of intimacy, rather than political writing, is the last resort of freedom in times of terror – to Julia Kristeva's recollection of the sexual revolution of 1968, and her immersion after that in textuality as a revolutionary terrain. My aim is not to find direct similarities, let alone influences; more to reconsider the writing of each theorist by reading that of the other. But I begin with Marcuse's doctoral research on the German artist novel (*Künstlerroman*), completed in 1922.

# From the artist novel to affirmative culture

After the end of the war in 1918, Marcuse was a member of a soldiers' Soviet, and stood, rifle in hand, in Alexanderplatz, Berlin, defending the Social Democrat Republic. Armed far-Right gangs roamed the streets, and murdered the leaders of the Spartacus League (which became the German Communist Party), Rosa Luxemburg and Karl Liebknecht. The German Revolution failed. Marcuse returned to his studies, initially at Humboldt University, Berlin, then in Freiburg, to pursue doctoral research on the German artist-novel (*Künstlerroman*).

In the artist-novel, an artist or writer chooses between allegiance to, or alienation from, the existing society. Examples include Johann Goethe's *The Sorrows of Young Werther* (1774) and Thomas Mann's *Death in Venice* (1912). In general, the novel is a modern, bourgeois literary form, distinct from the classical epic which expresses 'the collective life of an entire people… born of the unity of the individual and community, subjectivity and objectivity… reality and form of life'.[7] In the novel, protagonists search for authenticity within or against society. For the artist, the price of the found self is exclusion when 'essence and longing' are incompatible with daily life.[8]

Marcuse looks to classical Greek culture as articulating the shared values of a society, and sees a return of this in the poetry of 'vagabond poets' (troubadours) in medieval Europe.[9] Bourgeois society produces a confidently self-aware subject but withdraws from conflict, in context of religious wars in which 'the subject viewed with disgust the completely debased, immiserated, raw, and hostile social environment that allowed for no fulfilment'.[10] Fear of conflict relocates anxiety to the opposition self-world. In Goethe's *Young Werther*, this leads to suicide; but in his later *Wilhelm Meisters Lehrjahre* (Wilhelm Meister's Apprenticeship, 1796), the protagonist is integrated into a social world which informs his creative work.

In his thesis in 1922, Marcuse adopts a Hegelian, dialectical structure of thesis, counter-thesis and synthesis. After describing cases of the genre he analyses contradictions, and alternative readings of those contradictions which reveal further contradictions. But the abiding theme remains the discrepancy of art and life: 'the integration of art and life could only persist as long as life is actually conceived of as the embodiment of Idea, spirit'.[11] He returns to this in an interview in 1978: 'Art and politics will never finally coalesce because the ideal society… presupposes an ideal reconciliation of opposites, which can never be achieved… The relationship between art and political praxis is therefore dialectical.'[12]

Marcuse sees the novel as inheriting the content of the epic in a new way 'no longer the direct expression of a kind of life, but… a sense of longing and striving'.[13] The novel has heroes and heroines, and its bourgeois readers struggle against the norms under which they live, replacing the (supposed) unity of the epic with aspiration:

> The rupture, the cleft, between what is and what could be, the ideal and the reality, has demolished the original wholeness. The progressive differentiation and diffusion of the nation into estates and classes, the expansion of social and cultural life, do not fit any longer into one strictly closed artistic form.[14]

The implications range from a critique of domestic life to the imaginative restructuring of society; and, in Marcuse's later writing, a reality ruptured by imagination to reveal radical alternatives.

In the artist novel, the protagonist 'finds it impossible to see even any potential satisfaction within the frame of the world's given conditions' and flees to a dream-world.[15] The message reiterated in the *Künstlerroman* – the self-aware artist either comes to terms with factors which constrain imaginative reality, or does not (as in *Death in Venice*) – is an opposition between art (or thought) and life, within a literary scenario. But in Germany in the early 1930s the conflict is transposed from the realm of fiction and theory to politics, when real life is under Nazi rule. As German, Jewish Marxists, the members of the Frankfurt Institute experienced this immediately and urgently.

After leaving Germany in 1932, first for Switzerland, then the United States, Marcuse begins to reflect on art's role, less as opposition, more as contributing to the status quo. In 1937, in 'The Affirmative Character of Culture' (Über den affirmative Charakter der Kultur), Marcuse says that beauty's permanence resides in unchanging Form, while practical life is inconstant, even if it retains traces of the ideal.[16] In bourgeois society, 'the view that concern with the highest values is appropriated as a profession by particular social strata disappears', to be replaced by a democratic universality.[17] But, in the money economy, 'competition places individuals in the relation of buyers and sellers of labour power'.[18] In Germany, culture functions as a unifying factor in a nation-state formed in the 1860s, elevating culture over everyday life and aligning it to a manufactured national destiny. This produces affirmative culture:

> That culture of the bourgeois epoch which led in the course of its own development to the segregation from civilisation of the mental and spiritual world as an independent realm of value that is also considered superior to civilisation. Its decisive character is the assertion of a universally obligatory, eternally better and more valuable world that must be unconditionally affirmed: a world essentially different from the factual world of the daily struggle for existence.[19]

Marcuse adds, 'To accusing questions the bourgeoisie gave a decisive answer: affirmative culture… [to] the need of the isolated individual it responds with general humanity, to bodily misery with the beauty of the soul, to external bondage with internal freedom, to brutal egoism with the duty of the realm of virtue.'[20] Affirmative culture is the balm of a heaven seen in art which leaves ordinary, and political, actualities unchanged. Or, as Marcuse puts it,

> Culture is supposed to assume concern for the individual's claim to happiness. But the social antagonisms at the root of culture let it admit this claim only in an internalised and rationalised form. In a society that reproduces itself through economic competition, the mere demand for a happier existence constitutes rebellion… The claim to happiness has a dangerous ring in an order that for the majority means need, privation and toil. The contradictions of such an order provide the impetus to the idealisation of that claim. But the real gratification of individuals cannot be contained by an idealistic dynamic which either continually postpones gratification or transmutes it into striving for the unattained. It can only be realised against idealist culture.[21]

In these conditions, beauty is displaced from ordinary life to aesthetic dreaming; its resolution of the contradiction between its promise of happiness and the conditions which deny happiness is resolved as illusion: 'the enjoyment of happiness is permitted only in… idealised form'.[22] Marcuse concludes, 'Bourgeois society has liberated individuals, but as persons who are to keep themselves in check.'[23]

Marcuse stayed in the United States, working for the US intelligence services until 1951, teaching at Brandeis University, then at University of California San Diego (where the Governor, Ronald Reagan, tried unsuccessfully to have him sacked). In his first widely read book, *Eros and Civilisation* (1956), he fuses Marxism and psychoanalysis, following Freud in arguing that the maintenance of a civilisation relies on postponement of an instinctive desire for happiness. He argues that immediate gratification of desires is revolutionary, portending an alternative to the consumerism in which desires are turned from real gratification (or need) to manufactured wants which keep capitalist markets moving.[24]

## Society as a work of art

In the 1960s, Marcuse engaged with student protests, speaking at campus meetings and conferences in North America and Europe. In his lectures, he used news reports and protest songs. During the Vietnam

War he coined the term 'Warfare State'.[25] Nearly forty years later, during the War on Terror, Susan Buck-Morss uses the term 'national security state' to describe the same 'wild zone of power, barbaric and violent, operating without democratic oversight'.[26]

In 1967, the year of The Summer of Love in San Francisco, the prevailing mood was optimistic. Tom Nairn and Jim Singh-Sandhu, participants in a student occupation at Hornsey College of art, London, recall that although 'the avant-garde role of the art student movement' was regarded as marginal by many, and seen as failing to 'conform to certain political schemata of the left',[27] there was a belief that protest could change the world.

Marcuse's 1964 critique of consumerism, *One Dimensional Man* [sic], was reissued in 1968. At Brandeis he taught a course titled 'The Welfare and the Warfare State'. Angela Davis, one of his students, recalls, 'When Marcuse walked onto the platform… his presence dominated everything. There was something… that evoked total silence.'[28] He was a prominent figure in the New Left, contributing to a revised Marxism in which the working class was no longer a revolutionary force – an argument elaborated by André Gorz in *Farwell to the Working Class*[29] – when students, young intellectuals and technocrats assumed that role.

This was the time of flower power. At the *Dialectics of Liberation Congress* in London in 1967, organised by alternative psychologists R. D. Laing and David Cooper, Marcuse gave a talk titled 'Liberation from the Affluent Society'[30] alongside Stokely Carmichael on black power, Allen Ginsburg on the demystification of consciousness, Paul Sweeny on the future of capitalism and Lucien Goldmann on Marxism and literature. The only female speaker was poet Susan Sherman. Vietnamese Buddhist monk Thich Nhat Hanh meditated silently. And the audience wore flowers in their hair.

Marcuse began, 'I am very happy to see so many flowers here and that is why I want to remind you that flowers… have no power', except that of men and women who 'take care of them against aggression and destruction'.[31] He reminded the organisers that the term 'dialectics of liberation' was redundant because 'dialectic is liberation'; and explained that the situation was unprecedented in looking to revolution in an *affluent* society.[32] Freedom is the antithesis to the unfreedom of consumerism; the politicised imagination evokes a world, not as it is, but as it might be. In this situation, when an affluent society's possibility of ease is denied, new, quasi-biological needs arise as if inherently. Student protest, meanwhile, seeks 'the rupture of history, the radical break, the leap into the realm of freedom – a total rupture'.[33]

For Marcuse, liberation is 'the construction of a free society... which depends... on the prevalence of the vital need for abolishing the established systems of servitude... on the vital commitment... for the qualitatively different values of a free human existence'.[34] A difficulty is that if the new requires a new consciousness in order to abolish the old society's regime, that consciousness emerges in the conditions it also prefigures. This 'vicious circle' haunts Marcuse in Berlin a few days after the Dialectics of Liberation Congress, in a lecture, 'The End of Utopia', at the student-organised Free University. He says, replying to a question from the audience, 'that is the circle in which we are placed, and I do not know how to get out of it'.[35] The key construct here is *qualitative* change as historical leap, not the result of a given trajectory, nor an incremental change, but a transvaluation of values, that is, a radical alternative to the prevailing way of apprehending the world. Marcuse seems to assume that this will happen spontaneously within capitalism's contradictions.

Marcuse argues in 1967 that in affluent, technologically advanced societies the prospect of liberation is no longer a utopian dream but a not-yet gained reality, suppressed by the dominant system. He continues, 'the result is a mutilated, crippled and frustrated human existence; a human existence that is violently defending its own servitude'.[36] To make the required leap requires a redefinition of socialism as 'the abolition of labour, the termination of the struggle for existence' to enable a 'liberation of human sensibility and sensitivity... as a force for transformation of human existence and of its environment'.[37] This means the refusal of the performance principle, and alignment to the pleasure principle by which life is characterised by living itself: a return to Eros in a society in which material needs are met, and the basic struggle for existence is replaced by pursuit of freedom in a convergence of work and play. In one way, thinking of Marcuse's earlier writing, this undoes the separation of the good, the true and the beautiful from practicality.

At the *Dialectics of Liberation Congress*, Marcuse introduces the idea of a society as a work of art as reclaiming the creative imagination as the guiding force of social formation, which of itself produces a new sensibility; and 'the terrible concept… an aesthetic reality – society as a work of art… the most radical possibility of liberation today'.[38]

As to how this happens, Marcuse is less precise, looking to politicised education, the student movement and the counter-culture as location of a new sensibility. He develops the idea in a paper, 'Society as a Work of Art', in Salzburg in August 1967. He stresses the separateness of aesthetics from ordinary life, arguing that art's artificiality is inherently transformative; and quotes surrealist Raoul Hausmann that art is 'a painted or moulded critique of cognition'.[39] And, when art is not subordinate to politics but politics is subordinate to imagination, 'art is rescued from its dual, antagonistic function' and its inherent truth and reality-to-come 'appear in this semblance' which fractures the status quo.[40]

Art carries a latent sense of freedom which enables it to interrupt routine. The precondition for this is autonomy: a critical, refracting distancing from actuality. Beauty is radical alterity. This is far from neoclassical ideas of beauty, but not without precedent: Rainer Maria Rilke writes, 'For Beauty's nothing but beginning of terror we're still just able to bear… Every angel is terrible.' (*Denn das Schöne ist nichts als des Schrecklichen Anfng… Ein jeder Engel ist schrecklich.*)[41] Beauty is the quality of a metaphorical space between desire and ideal 'in inseparable unity with order, but order in its sole *nonrepressive* sense'.[42] Marcuse cites Baudelaire's poem *Invitation au voyage*, with its refrain '*ordre, luxe et voluopté*' (order, luxury and sensuousness). I read this as a radical form of goodness, truth and beauty in which beauty departs from the affirmative role of bourgeois consolation (in the 1937 essay, above) to become radically disruptive. I return to this in Chapter 9.

In 1967, Marcuse argues that art preserves beauty in antagonistic opposition to reality; and although routinely suppressed in the affluent society, nonetheless,

> All the designs of creative imagination… transform themselves today into technological possibilities. But the prevailing order is mobilised against their realisation, because the content and forms of freedom possible today… are not reconcilable with the material and moral foundations of the prevailing order. Thus today the creative

imagination ... has become a social force for the *transformation of reality*, and the social environment has become the potential material and space for art.[43]

A society as a work of art interrupts the mechanisms of perception but equally supposes a sensuality infused with rationality. Marcuse concludes,

> For art itself can never become political without ... abdicating itself. The contents and forms of art are never those of direct action, they are always only the language, images, and sounds of a world not yet in existence. Art can preserve the hope for and the memory of such a world only when it *remains itself*.[44]

Returning to the difficulty of how new needs are produced in *An Essay on Liberation* (1969), written during the events of May 1968 in Paris, he proposes again that new biological needs arise inherently within the contradictory conditions of capitalism; and aligns beauty to the life instinct (*Eros*).[45] But the vicious circle remains:

> The rupture with the self-propelling conservative continuum of needs must *precede* the revolution which is to usher in a free society, but such a rupture itself can be envisaged only in a revolution ... which would be driven by the vital need to be freed from the administered comforts and the destructive productivity of exploitative society.[46]

But in Paris in 1968 the regime survived. The Left regrouped, but the new sensibility of the counterculture and student protest did not, alone, produce a new society. This does not as such invalidate Marcuse's argument, although it emphasises its status as theory rather than practice. Unconnectedly, Michel Foucault argues that repression produces resistance, and Henri Lefebvre proposes the idea of ephemeral yet transformative moments of liberation within the dulling routines of capitalism. Perhaps that is an exit from the vicious circle, if moments of a new society arise, and the memory is transformative inasmuch as it lingers, despite prevailing conditions, extending the horizon of the possible. For Marcuse, the failure of revolt in 1968 led to a more intense focus on aesthetics in face of the lack of real political change. Perhaps today's situation is not entirely dissimilar (hence this book).

# The aesthetic dimension

Marcuse begins *The Aesthetic Dimension* (1978) by justifying his interest in aesthetics by a lack of political change. Part of his aim is to establish that art contributes to the realisation of freedom by imaginatively refracting reality, so that the unreality of art is a new reality against which the existing reality seems fictional. Another part of his aim, from the title of the German edition – *The Permanence of Art* – is to explain why art evokes emotional responses regardless of the spectator's knowledge of the conditions of its production. This revises, or refuses, the Marxist aesthetic in which the conditions of production determine, as well as being echoed in, art's form. Art thereby spans an axis of polarities – the world as it is, and as it might be – wherein nothing is only as it seems: 'The world intended in art is never and nowhere merely the given world of everyday reality, but neither is it a world of mere fantasy, illusion, and so on.'[47] Reflecting debate in the 1960s and 1970s as to whether an unchanged self could change the world (other than in reproducing its tyrannies), he says, 'Liberating subjectivity constitutes itself in the inner history of the individuals... which is not identical with their social existence... [and] not necessarily grounded in their class situation'.[48] Love and hate are felt personally; that they permeate social life as well is not to say they are contained in class positions. Above all, Marcuse emphasises art's role of going beyond what is:

> The radical qualities of art... its indictment of the established reality and its invocation of the beautiful image (*schöner Schein*) of liberation are grounded precisely in the dimensions where art *transcends* its social determination and emancipates itself from the given universe of discourse and behaviour while preserving its overwhelming presence.[49]

Art reconfigures the categories through which reality is understood; it 're-presents reality while accusing it'.[50]

In modernism, aesthetic form is autonomous from perception, reasserting subjectivity and the force of evocation alongside, but ahead of, the sedimentation of the conditions of its production. This echoes Marcuse's work on the artist novel; but he also cites literary theorist Lucien Goldmann that the proletariat are subsumed in capitalist mechanisms of consumption, so that the negation of those mechanisms is external to 'progressive class consciousness'.[51] And he cites Adorno on art's 'uncompromising estrangement'.[52] He then admits the limits of a critically distancing aesthetic whereby 'art cannot change the world, but it can contribute to changing the consciousness and drives of the men and women who could change the world'.[53] I think the argument holds even without the reference to drives because it emphasises art's ability to evoke states of psyche combined with its refraction of reality, bringing into question the received realities (and codes of apprehension) of daily life. Whatever is imagined is part of human consciousness; 'inwardness and subjectivity may well become the inner and outer space for the subversion of experience, for the emergence of another universe'.[54] Art must remain art, nonetheless, its political relevance resulting from its autonomy.

There are two further issues. First, socialism remains one form of the envisioned better life, yet requires revision in order to address the contradictions of a late capitalist society where utopia is technologically viable but denied by a cycle of toil and compensatory consumption. Second, art cannot directly or adequately deal with a history which includes the Holocaust and the Vietnam War, 'because it cannot represent this suffering without subjecting it to aesthetic form… to the mitigating catharsis', yet, at the same time, art must recall such histories 'again and again' to preserve their memory as prevention of repeat.[55] Marcuse concludes,

> To the degree to which administered human beings today reproduce their own repression and eschew a rupture with the given reality, to this degree revolutionary theory acquires an abstract character. The goal, socialism as a better society, also appears as abstract – ideological in relation to the radical praxis which necessarily operates within the concreteness of the established society.
>
> In this situation the affinity, and the opposition, between art and radical praxis become surprisingly clear. Both envision a universe which, while originating in the given social relationship, also liberates individuals from these relationships. This vision appears as the permanent future of revolutionary praxis.[56]

It is the permanence of art as well, and resides in art's autonomy and in the vital subjectivity of a radical consciousness. Art has agency in transforming states not only of psyche but also of social and political consciousness. And that's it: what is possible today.

# A literature of intimacy

I could end there, with Marcuse's acceptance that, in the 1970s, radical social and political change was no longer imminent, in the way it seemed for a moment in 1968. Yet much of the above account of his aesthetic theories points to the radical alterity of art, or beauty, and I want to extend this, looking at his essay on French poetry under the Nazi occupation, begun in 1945 and revised in the 1970s.

In 'Some Remarks on Aragon: Art and Politics in the Totalitarian Era',[57] Marcuse argues that in a time of terror – the Nazi occupation of France – the last resort of freedom is not in political writing but in love poetry. He cites Louis Aragon and Paul Eluard, both poets active in Resistance writers' organisations, and reiterates the idea of negation: 'Art is essentially unrealistic: the reality which it creates is alien and antagonistic to the other, realistic reality which it negates.'[58] Art reveals the dream which the regime cannot allow, and does so in a form it cannot see:

> Sensuality as style… expresses the individual protest against the law and order of repression. Sensual love gives a *promesse du bonheur* [promise of joy] which preserves the full materialistic content of freedom and rebels against all efforts to canalise this *bonheur* into forms compatible with the order of repression.[59]

Marcuse introduces Baudelaire's poem *Invitation au voyage* (as he does in *The Aesthetic Dimension*), reading its sensuality as expressing an incipient sense of freedom. Then, citing Eluard's *Seven Love Poems in Wartime*, clandestinely published in 1942, Marcuse says, 'to these political poets and active communists, love appears as the artistic a priori… [the] counterblow against the annexation of all political contents by monopolistic society'.[60]

I have written elsewhere on the use of Eluard's poetry in clandestine literary magazines dropped over occupied France,[61] and my concern here is more general: that love poems carry a refusal of political repression in conditions of terror. At first, this may seem odd, or a retreat to the personal. But more is involved than the circumstance in which Eluard's poem *Liberté* was passed by a censor reading it, literally, as a love poem, bored by its repetitive iteration and not reaching the last line in which the object of love is named *Liberté*.[62] That is, Marcuse sees a liberating alterity in the literature of intimacy under terror, as if to say, a safe house in an occupied land. This is extended in formal terms in the use of traditional metre and rhyme, against the modernist tendency to free verse. Marcuse notes, 'nothing could be further from avant-gardism', while the poetry in question 'expresses a sensuality which does not allow the sublimation of the promise'.[63] So, 'in the night of the fascist terror appear the images of tenderness... calmness and free fulfilment' which offer a *qualitatively different* reality.[64] This is not affirmative culture but antagonism, estrangement, rendering real repression as if unreal, revealing,

> an awakening of memory, remembrance of things lost, consciousness of what was and what could have been. Sadness as well as happiness, terror as well as hope are thrown upon the reality in which all this has occurred; the dream is arrested and returns to the pat, and the future of freedom appears only as a disappearing light.[65]

This reconciliation of present threat in absent feeling is art's burden, its undeniable content as aesthetic reality, while the liberation of sensuality within a language of form insists on the inhumanity and inauthenticity of the regime. The essay ends in a paradox: 'Art may promote the alienation... and this alienation may provide the artificial basis for the remembrance of freedom in the totality of oppression.'[66]

Douglas Kellner summarises that the prevailing political reality is portrayed as destroying sensual life, which is the realm of harmony; love poetry, in opposition, 'presents totalitarian society shattering the ideal world projected in great poetry and art, and thus appears as that which must be negated and itself destroyed, as that which stands in the way of freedom and happiness'.[67] The promise of joy (*promesse du bonheur*) survives, the content of a latent hope and memory of moments of past realisation; indeed, it is indestructible, if in a parallel realm of aesthetic (but also personal) reality. If such poetry is personal in the experience of individual reception, perhaps it is not only personal but an instance of the transvaluation of values of which Marcuse spoke in London in 1967.

# An intimate revolution

Looking back to the events of May 1968 in Paris, in which she participated, Julia Kristeva argues for an intimate revolution, regarding 'the liberation of social behaviour' as 'the essential experience of '68'.[68] This, she adds, included group sex and hashish as a refusal of bourgeois norms; and is political because 'it began by striking savagely at the heart of the traditional conception of love'.[69] Further, '68 was 'a worldwide movement that contributed to an unprecedented reordering of private life'.[70] This has since been commercialised, but in 1968 sexual enjoyment appeared to be an aspect of living outside the reach of institutions and the market, resisting bourgeois norms and repressions, constituting free love in every sense.

This goes beyond Marcuse's concern for a *literature* of intimacy, since Kristeva refers to the revolutionary content of *acts* of intimacy. She also contributes to a feminist insistence that the personal is political. Nonetheless, Kristeva and Marcuse both revise Marxism through psychoanalysis (although Kristeva looks to Lacan while Marcuse, a decade earlier, looks to Freud). A further commonality is that while Marcuse looked to the universal quality of Form, Kristeva looks to universality in desire: 'my own... analytical experience taught me that desire, if it exists, is unalterable, infinite, absolute and destructive'.[71] These are coincidental comparisons; my juxtaposition of these thinkers between whom there is no documented influence is not a comparison as such, more, as said at the outset, an attempt to understand aspects of what each wrote in a slightly new way as a result of reading them together.

Nonetheless, there are some parallels. Kristeva looks back, against the post-structuralist grain, to the Hegelian concept of negation which was formative for Marcuse, and she draws on Adorno's aesthetic theory, again in common with, if after, Marcuse:

It is a type of German thinking I like a lot. But it is Hegel, and particularly the role he assigned to negativity, that has been emphasised in German philosophy. It is a fundamental aspect and today many sociologists refuse it. They tend to think of society as a calculation, as a programme, as a storage site of information.... I think this is wrong; without negativity, there is no longer freedom or thinking. One must consider thinking as a revelation, an exploration, an opening, a place of freedom.[72]

For both Kristeva and the Frankfurt School, the purpose of theory is to arrive at alternative scenarios to present unfreedom, extending Marxist praxis – the appropriate understanding of the past to gain insights into future possibilities for change – by relocating the question from areas such as class struggle and mass revolt to culture, and the norms, or codes, by which reality is apprehended, categorised and normalised in historically specific ways, and in ways which, in their selectivity, support (or affirm) the regime and its routines.

There are differences as well. Marcuse came from a prosperous German Jewish family, then fled Nazi Germany to remain in North America (when Adorno and Ernst Bloch returned to Germany after 1945). He was an established member of the New Left when he spoke at the Sorbonne occupation in May 1968 (also meeting the North Vietnamese peace delegation in Paris). Arriving in Paris from East-bloc Bulgaria, Kristeva had directly experienced Stalinism, and in May 1968 aligned herself to the cultural revolution of Maoism. Marcuse wrote a book against what he saw as the totalitarianism of state Socialism,[73] and was critical of Maoism. From their position, the Maoists were hostile to Marcuse, too, in his public talks. He was also an old man, aged sixty-nine in 1968, characteristically smoking a cigar and always retaining his German accent. In 1968, then, Kristeva, among the Maoists, and Marcuse, almost an elder statesman of theory, experienced the student uprising from equally engaged but otherwise different viewpoints. Marcuse went back to San Diego, his books unread in France till later.[74] Kristeva stayed in Paris, immersing herself in radical intellectual circles as well as a psychoanalytic milieu, contributing to the manifesto, *Théorie d'ensemble* (1968). After the failure of protest to dislodge the government, revolutionary activity moved to text.

Cecilia Sjöholm summarises Kristeva's position, 'the revolution is made into a question of text, not of political manoeuvres, and the goal … [is] "to articulate a politics logically linked to a non-representative dynamic of writing"'.[75] Kristeva went on to be an editor of the radical Left journal *Tel Quel*, which specifically saw text as revolt. I want to suggest a parallel here, between Kristeva's turn to text, and Marcuse's turn to aesthetics in *The Aesthetic Dimension*. In both cases, there is a perceived need to redefine the political, to widen and deepen its terrain and its means, so that future possibilities for change are found in new ways. Marcuse wrote of a new sensibility, then of aesthetics as the site of radical alterity. And Kristeva and the writers around *Tel Quel*, extend ideas articulated in daily meetings and discussions in May 1968 into critical textual practices. For Kristeva, 'to think is to revolt, to be in the movement of meaning and not the movement of the streets'.[76] Although someone wrote on a Sorbonne blackboard, 'structures don't go down to the streets',[77] in the 1970s, post-structural analyses were part of what was left (and Left) in a domain of always-present contingency and new subjectivities.

Kristeva defines the construct of revolt etymologically as 'return, returning, discovering, uncovering and renovating' in a 'necessary repetition when you cover all that ground', beyond which is a 'potential for making gaps, rupturing, renewing. Rebellion is a condition necessary for the life of the mind and society.'[78] The term 'life of the mind' is used by Hannah Arendt – on whom Kristeva wrote a commentary[79] – but for Kristeva is less an attribute of the human condition (a term tending to universalism), more contestational. Revolt assumes an intimate dimension, not in love poetry as it did for Marcuse, but through psychoanalytic insights:

> We have to get back to the intimate well-springs of revolt – in the deep sense of self-questioning and questioning tradition as well, sexual differences, projects for life and death, new modalities of civil society … re-rooting the self that takes us nearer to revolt … [and] in the psychoanalytic sense: Freud's insight means an invitation to revolt … all the better to reveal oneself (to create and re-create the self).[80]

Beyond the political Left and its strategising, 'revolt is a very deep movement of discontent, anxiety and anguish'.[81] Beside this, art and literature are contributions too often subsumed in the dominant society's cultural institutions and overwhelming productivism; nonetheless, Kristeva notes a 'concern for intimacy' cultivated in French literary experience as a counter to, 'globalizing liberalism'.[82] This is underpinned by an inherently liberating subjectivity, its articulation fusing Marxism and psychoanalysis in a permanently fractured subjectivity: 'The individual… experiences division, conflict, pleasure and jouissance in this fragmentation. This is the modern vision of psychic truth.'[83]

Marcuse saw the struggle in Freudian terms, beyond the performance principle,

> The struggle for existence… turns into the concerted struggle against any constraint on the free play of human faculties, against toil, disease, and death. Moreover, while the rule of the performance principle was accompanied by a corresponding control of the instinctual dynamic, the reorientation of the struggle for existence would involve a decisive change in this dynamic… A new basic experience of being would change the human existence in its entirety.[84]

He never entirely explained how the new sensibility emerges; if art fractures and refracts reality, and may make work playful, just as psychoanalysis is a means to revise Marxism, it remains necessary to ask how the miserable reality will change.

For Kristeva, art carries a radical desire which exposes society's mechanisms of conformity, the exit from which is the process of a deep subjectivity in (Lacanian) psychoanalysis; it is also, importantly, thought-as-revolt, when a latent desire for liberation is glimpsed in the constructs invented in writing itself. This revolt is continuous, always contingent, and means that the practice of writing is, in itself, inherently, liberating. Kristeva writes, 'the text's signifying practice thus retains the analytic situation's requirement that the process of the subject be realised in language'.[85] If psychoanalysis is a process of de- and re-constructing the subject, so writing is a process of doing this through words. The revolution in poetic language is not a set of literary devices (though they are implicated), nor an expression of Left politics in verse (to which Marcuse, too, would object); it is in itself a resistant practice when text is a zone of re-creating meanings in the intersection of different procedures of making text. In semiotics, writing 'involves both shattering and maintaining *position* within the heterogeneous *process*: the proof can be found in the phonetic, lexical and syntactic disturbance visible in the *semiotic device* of the text'.[86] After citing Mallarmé's poem 'A Throw of the Dice', Kristeva continues, 'as the text constructed itself with respect to an empty place… it in turn comes to be the empty site of a process in which its readers become involved. The text turns out to be the analyst and every reader the analysand.'[87]

Semiotics separates words (signifiers) from meanings derived within systems of difference, the latter always open to re-interpretation and reclamation. The subjectivity of 'experience-in-practice' is contingent; the subject is 'an excess, never one', breaking through a unifying enclosure, 'through a leap (laughter? Fiction?)'.[88] There is neither solution nor a sense of completion. An always-estranged subject feels solidarity with those others called strangers. Sjöholm summarises, 'emancipation… can only lie in the giving up of desire for unity, in the affirmation of conflict and alterity forming our lives and our minds'.[89]

Marcuse writes (quoted above), 'the integration of art and life could only persist as long as life is actually conceived of as the embodiment of Idea, spirit'[90] in his reading of classical Greek culture. He returns to this in an interview in 1978, stating 'Art and politics will never finally coalesce because the ideal society… presupposes an ideal reconciliation of opposites, which can never be achieved… The relationship between art and political praxis is therefore dialectical.'[91] Through different routes, he and Kristeva arrive at a scene of fracture and, at best, potential reconstruction. Putting together their different takes on intimacy, I wonder if Kristeva's extension of the idea into text is, in its way, an equivalent of Marcuse's idea that literature evades the regime, in certain conditions. But I am also reminded that Marcuse's essay on French poetry responded, in its 1945 origin, to particular historical realities, while Kristeva's turn to text implies a kind of universalism in the contingencies of writing and reading. Having said that, I am reminded in turn of Marcuse's reliance, in his early work at least, on the universalism of an Enlightenment which he sees as an incomplete project, which critical theory takes into a new stage (rather than junking it). What emerges, I think (and I am being purposefully tentative), is the importance of radically reconfiguring the means by which reality is understood and aligned to (or against) norms. From that, through the cracks, new insights might appear.

# Chapter 4
# States of exception

In the previous chapter, I reconsidered Herbert Marcuse's aesthetic theories, juxtaposing his argument for a literature of intimacy as freedom's last resort under terror to Julia Kristeva's view that verbal language is viable location of resistant intervention. In both cases, I read what may seem a withdrawal as a form of regrouping in Left cultural theory. In this chapter, I look to another writer from the milieu of the Frankfurt School, Walter Benjamin. There is an extensive literature on Benjamin,[1] so my focus is specific: his last work, *On the Concept of History* (Über den Begriff der Geschichte),[2] written in 1940 in face of Nazi persecution. In this series of short texts, Benjamin looks to a revised Marxism fused with Judaic Messianism for a radically new kind of history written from the position of the oppressed.

I situate *On the Concept of History* in context of Benjamin's doctoral research in the 1920s on German baroque drama, in which he raises the question of a state of exception (suspension of the law). He contests this obliquely with far-Right legal theorist Carl Schmitt, whose *Political Theology* was first published in 1922. The contention revolves around whether a state of exception is a means to maintain tyranny or to end it. The importance of history here is that its narratives are normally written by those in power, while 'criticism must penetrate beyond these predicates'[3] to envision a world reshaped via the forgotten history of the oppressed. This is a new beginning, like the moment of a Messianic redemption. It produces a new consciousness of the *now* in which past and future are distilled: 'for every second of time was the strait gate through which the Messiah might enter'.[4]

For Michael Löwy, *On the Concept of History* is 'the most significant document since Marx's "Theses on Feuerbach"' (where Marx says the philosophers have explained the world but the point is to change it).[5] That is reason enough to reconsider *On the Concept of History* now; but another is that the need for a break in the narratives of power may be as relevant under the regime of neoliberalism today as in Benjamin's time. To bring out this relevance, I juxtapose Benjamin's writing to Isabell Lorey's *State of Insecurity* (2015), in which she argues neoliberalism produces insecurities which embrace 'the whole of existence'.[6] As in Chapter 3, the aim of the juxtaposition is not to establish any documentable connection but to read both contributors as illuminating present as well as past concerns. Introducing *State of Insecurity,* Judith Butler says the present state of precarity 'can, and must be, undone through an activism of the precarious'.[7] Benjamin writes, 'it is our task to bring about a real state of emergency'.[8] I think there is common ground; the conditions differ and the means of intervention thus need to adapt, yet Benjamin and Lorey both look to a new kind of history, and a historical leap into a potentially new age.

# History turned upside down

Unpublished in his lifetime but sent in longhand to Hannah Arendt and Theodor and Gretel Adorno, *On the Concept of History* consists of eighteen one-paragraph theses and two appendices. It was written in 1940, in the catastrophe of the Nazi occupation of France. Fleeing Germany in 1932 as a Marxist and a Jew, travelling to Ibiza, Nice and then Paris, living in borrowed or rented rooms without most of his library, stripped of his German citizenship in 1939 and interned as a stateless person, history was real and urgent for Benjamin. Although granted a US entry visa, he lacked the necessary papers to exit France and was turned back at the Spanish border. Rather than face being sent to a camp again, he ended his life with an overdose of morphine.

I do not wish to romanticise Benjamin but the conditions are exceptional, and help explain why he moves from (an already revised but never rejected) Marxism to Messianism: the Jewish philosophy of redemption, a light shining from the end of history onto the present. In these conditions, when the Messiah always comes unexpectedly,

Benjamin imaginatively reconfigures history as a *real* state of emergency. But this does not occur in a vacuum. Benjamin recalls chance encounters in ordinary places, when everyday life seems to echo the chance juxtapositions of Surrealism, and his experiences of Expressionist theatre, and the use of montage in modernist film. The intersection of different realities conjures a latent utopia, as if buried in distant memories and revived by sudden, unexpected encounters which interrupt normality.

This idea – a latent utopia – is articulated by Ernst Bloch in *The Principle of Hope* (1959), and Bloch and Benjamin discussed such ideas in long conversations in Paris in the 1920s. Bloch (unlike Theodor Adorno and other contributors to the Frankfurt School) sees a glimpse of utopianism in popular fiction, and in medieval carnival when masters serve servants and the poor enjoy a life of ease: a world, and a narrative, turned upside down. Bloch comments on a painting by Pieter Brueghel, for example,

> This Land of Cockaigne exactly as the poor folk always imagined it to be. As an eternal Sunday, which is one because there is no sign of any treadmill, and nothing beyond what can be drunk, eaten boiled or roasted is to be found. A peasant, a knight, and a scholar in the foreground, the first two full and asleep, the scholar still with open mouth and eyes, expecting a roast pigeon or the piglet which stands at the back and already carries the carving knife with it.[9]

In similar vein, artist Conrad Atkinson once began a lecture with what he called an old Vietnamese proverb: you have to wait a long time on the hillside for a roast duck to fly into your mouth.[10] In a quite separate context, coincidentally supporting Bloch on popular fiction, Mikhail Bakhtin sees 'an extraordinarily flexible form of artistic visualisation … the discovery of new and as yet unseen things' in the nineteenth-century novel.[11] Elsewhere, Bakhtin refers to François Rabelais's literary rendering of carnival as using 'a parodic destruction of syntactic structures' to reconstruct truth by 'reducing the lie to an absurdity'.[12] Bakhtin writes on Rabelais, 'The terminus is not the laughter of the carnival mask but the nakedness that follows … the new form of seriousness that laughter brings into being'.[13] As Sigmund Freud is sometimes paraphrased, jokes are not a laughing matter.

There is no direct link between Bakhtin and Benjamin, and my point is simply that Benjamin's engagement with the radical otherness of the Messianic moment is not entirely new in 1940. For Tim Beasley-Murray, the most important connection between Benjamin and Bakhtin is in 'their different but analogous engagements with a world that is distinctively modern'.[14] He observes, too, that 'both display the ability to see signs of… future wholeness in the midst of an incomplete and fragmented world'.[15] Indeed, Benjamin wandered the nineteenth-century arcades of Paris, once used to display luxury goods but by the 1930s in decline, housing curiosity shops filled with the detritus of history. These are shops, engaged in commercial activities, yet in a warped time-frame, outside the mainstream of commerce under capitalism. Susan Buck-Morss writes in similar vein of Benjamin's fascination with the street stalls he saw on a visit to Moscow in 1927, in context of a state drive for production beside a residual public culture:

> Increasing the level of production is merely a means to an end of a society beyond scarcity that can fulfil not only material but aesthetic needs. The vibrancy of collective fantasy is a crucial indicator of the healthy development of these needs. Limited to an analysis of nonlinguistic expressions [because he did not speak Russian], Benjamin finds this collective fantasy in an unofficial form of popular culture, namely the non-essentials for sale from unlicensed vendors in the temporary stalls and markets that scatter colour on the snow-covered city streets: paper fish, picture books, lacquered boxes, Christmas ornaments, personal photographs, confectionery delights, and more.[16]

Benjamin himself mentions shoe polish, writing materials, handkerchiefs, dolls, stuffed birds and ladies' underwear. In these cases, offbeat and often pre-industrial commodities, seen in seemingly random arrays, become – in perception via a lens of imagined desire for a better life – a source of the latent utopian dream, if in reified form. As Buck-Morss adds, this experience leads Benjamin to be critical of the Soviet stress on productivism, and the limits imposed on cultural work. She remarks, 'the alternatives were power without freedom, or freedom without power. The potential of intellectuals to contribute to the creation of a truly socialist culture demanded both, and nowhere did they exist together.'[17]

Ordinary life was also, for Benjamin, a site of mass consciousness and the possibility of new visions of social formation. He writes,

> Streets are the dwelling place of the collective. The collective is an eternally wakeful, eternally agitated being that… lives, experiences, understands, and invents as much as individuals do within the privacy of their own four walls. …[Hence] glossy, enamelled shop signs are a wall decoration as good as… an oil painting in the drawing room of a bourgeois; walls with their 'Post No Bills' are its writing desk, newspaper stands its libraries.[18]

The street is revolutionary, a world turned inside-out when outdoor spaces are co-opted as domestic space; and a world turned back-to-front in time. Benjamin remarks, 'In the July Revolution [in Paris in 1830]… on the first evening of fighting… the clocks in towers were being fired on simultaneously and independently from several places.'[19] The hold of clock-time, as the product of industrialisation and the manufactured regulation of workers' lives, must be broken so that real (experiential) time prevails.

# Dialectics

The function of the dialectic mind is to see such new realities in everyday life, imaginatively reconfiguring possibilities within the contradictions of capitalism. These contradictions in themselves evoke a fracture in which another reality appears; and this replaces both the Idealist trajectory towards an absolute state (in Enlightenment, pure Reason), and class conflict (in Marxism) in the moment, or moment-of-becoming, which is a leap of sudden awareness. That awareness is subjective – in Marxist terms the subjective condition for change – but in Benjamin's dialectic it has a potential to be social as well, in a realisation that the regime – capitalism – is contradictory in promising the cornucopia of production while denying the utopian dimension of an end of scarcity, not least when scarcity is reproduced through market manipulations and conspicuous consumption. Marcuse argues this (Chapter 3), and I think it applies as much, if differently, to Benjamin's view of history as a lens determining the possibilities for future change.

In terms of practice, such as writing, Benjamin proposes an intervention within the means of production (the means which Soviet workers were called to take over). That is, rather than describing conditions, writing should change them. The context is the formation in France in 1934 of the Popular Front against Fascism, uniting Communist and Socialist trades unions and parties. In address to a Communist Party writers' event in 1934, notably, Benjamin says that literature must be *inserted in* the means of production.[20] Literature remains literature but expands the definition of what writers do. Citing the Soviet writer Sergei Tretyakov, who moved to a collective farm, Benjamin lists the following as the writer's tasks: organising wall newspapers, collecting funds, calling mass meetings, inspecting reading rooms, introducing radio programmes and sending reports to newspapers in Moscow. Against the objection that this is journalism, Benjamin says, 'I quoted Tretyakov's example… to point out… how wide the horizon has to be from which, in the light of the technical realities of our situation today, we must rethink the notions of literary forms or genres if we are to find forms appropriate to the literary energy of our time.'[21]

While it is easy now, after the end of state socialism, to set aside Benjamin's enthusiasm for Tretyakov, the significance of this paper seems, in face of the rise of Fascism in France, that the envisioned change is direct: not a call for or signpost towards, but acting in the here and now to announce the utopian moment. Dialectical materialism brings the Idealist trajectory together with the Materialist insight that people's values and deeds are conditioned by their environment, to insist on intervention in those conditions. Benjamin takes this to a stage at which the writer's role in a collective farm, or workers' in running the factory, *is* a utopian moment. That, in turn, constitutes a new history, as revolutionary as the announcement of Year One (in 1793) in the French Revolution.

# A new history

Benjamin writes to Theodor Adorno that *On the Concept of History* is 'a first attempt at pinning down an aspect of history that must establish an irremediable break' in the most familiar concepts of history.[22] The text crystallises elements of Benjamin's thought in the previous decades, such as his comment in the *Arcades Project* (Convolute J) on Charles Fourier's society of Harmony,

> [Work] would henceforth be conducted on the model of children's play… [as] the impassioned work of the Harmonians. To have instituted play as the canon of a labour no longer rooted in exploitation is one of the great merits of Fourier… the image of an earth on which… all places are worked by human hands, made useful and beautiful thereby.[23]

In the section on theories of knowledge (Convolute N), he says of the interruption of linear time, 'It's not that what is past casts its light on what is present, or what is present its light on what is past; rather, image is that wherein what has been comes together in a flash with the now to form a constellation'.[24] And, 'The dialectical image… emerges suddenly, in a flash… in the now of its recognisability … The concept of progress must be grounded in the idea of catastrophe.'[25]

Three ideas appear here: Fourier's inversion of work as play, the break in historical time and fracture as prerequisite for a new history. In Thesis VIII of *On the Concept of History* he states,

> The tradition of the oppressed teaches us that the state of emergency in which we live is not the exception but the rule. We must attain a conception of history that is in keeping with this insight. Then we shall clearly realize that it is our task to bring about a real state of emergency, and this will improve our position in the struggle against Fascism. One reason why Fascism has a chance is that in the name of progress is opponents treat it as a historical norm. The current amazement that the things we are experiencing are still possible… is not the beginning of knowledge – unless it is the knowledge that the view of history which gives rose to it is untenable.[26]

The normalised emergency is Fascism, to be ruptured by a *real* state of emergency, meaning a state of exception in which the power-over of oppression is ousted by the power-to of the oppressed. Esther Leslie notes that Benjamin 'perceives writing about the past as a form of avenging…. the rulers who have ruled need not always rule…. Progress, the continuation of business as usual, is catastrophic.'[27] The past becomes a potentially liberating story whence 'political practice demands that the kaleidoscope of concepts must be smashed. From the ruins other configurations emerge.'[28]

In the next thesis, Benjamin cites Paul Klee's drawing *Angelus Novus* (1920, Jerusalem, Israel Museum), which he bought in 1921 and kept with him in Paris:

> An angel looking as though he [sic] is about to move away from something he is fixedly contemplating. His eyes are staring, his mouth is open, his wings are spread. This is how one pictures the angel of history. His face is turned towards the past. Where we perceive a chain of events, he sees one single catastrophe which keeps piling wreckage upon wreckage and hurls it in front of his feet. The angel would like to stay, awaken the dead, and make whole that which has been smashed. But a storm is blowing in Paradise ... [which] irresistibly propels him into the future to which his back is turned while the pile of debris grows skyward. The storm is what we call progress.[29]

Again, there is a historical leap, aligned to a Messianic redemption which illuminates both past and present. For Löwy, this text 'sums up ... the whole of the document', being less a description of Klee's picture than 'the projection of his own feelings' onto it.[30]

Löwy sees a link to Baudelaire's poetry in the idea of a correspondence between the sacred and the profane. Baudelaire sees a correspondence between different sensory experiences, different times and spaces, and word-pictures and states of psyche. For Baudelaire, 'sounds, fragrances and colours correspond' in the evocation of a mood.[31] Löwy extends the idea as a correspondence, in a loaded sense of the word 'between theology and politics'.[32] The pile of wreckage on which the angel stands is a residue of progress *and* the ground of a new history. In 1940, this requires a real state of emergency. Miguel Absensour writes,

> To think of Fascism from the point of view of progress is to see it merely as an interlude ... or a relic destined to fade away and give free reign once more to progress ... To think of Fascism from the point

of view of the victims… of the state of emergency is to construct a permanent place for barbarism in history.[33]

A real state of emergency is now-time, the Messianic moment. For Löwy, Benjamin's fusion of Marxism and Messianism is not contradictory because he 'situates them in a relation of reciprocal illumination'.[34] Similarly, Leslie reads Benjamin's new history as emerging in the dialectical image, 'a sort of interruption in the continuity of historical narrative', creating a revolutionary instantiation of the struggle for the oppressed.[35]

# Now-time

The message of *On the Concept of History* is the reconfiguration of history as now-time: the fusion of Messianic time in which the latent hope of the oppressed is redeemed with that of Marxist class struggle. Richard Wolin, too, reads Benjamin as fusing dialectical materialism with redemption, so that the historical materialist's task is 'that of redeeming now-times from the oblivion of forgetting'.[36] He elaborates, 'in face of the boundless and irrepressible triumph of the forces of rationalisation' which erase all traces of the pre-modern, Benjamin feared that 'the all-important index of redemption which the past provides would also fall victim to the oblivion of forgetting'.[37] Christine Buci-Glucksmann, further, interprets *On the Concept of History* as combining Marxism with the Messianic content of Klee's image while retaining the model of dialectical materialism:

> Benjamin was compelled to bring into play *two languages* and *two worlds*. The one, political and Marxist, belonging to the dialectic as the site where the vision and praxis of the vanquished ceaselessly clash with the oppressive sovereignty of the rulers… [And] the complementary world of Kafka and Klee.[38]

Together, the two ways of reading history produce a three-way intersection of dialectical materialism, art and Messianism, which Buci-Glucksmann aligns to modernist art when it crosses into everyday life, fragmenting and redistributing images to recreate the moment of imaginative redemption.

# The exception

Buci-Glucksmann refers to Benjamin's reading of baroque tragic drama as a critique of an 'unreconciled history'.[39] To avenge the oppressed, the norm must be broken so that now-time reclaims lost memories. She reads this drama as a 'decadent, Saturnian history of mourning and melancholia',[40] wherein a new sovereignty emerges, revolving around the state of exception.

The exception is the fulcrum of German tragic drama, around which principalities fall, values are held hostage, and sacred and profane collide. Subjects (princes) holding absolute power collapse in doubt and inability to act in an already-ruined world, during the Thirty Years War (1618–48) between nominally Catholic and Reformist armies in central Europe. Benjamin's research on German baroque drama revolves accordingly on the uncertain relation of ruler and ruled, when the ruler is faced by external – or internal – threat. Benjamin argues that a new idea of sovereignty arose then, with new attitudes to tyrannicide and the position of the usurper. While the modern concept of sovereignty assumes supreme executive power, 'the baroque concept emerges from a discussion of the state of emergency, and makes it the most important function of the prince to *avert* this'.[41] Benjamin notes that the concept of the prince emerges in Reformist courts, while the classicising culture of the Renaissance lends the period a memory of stability. The ruler has 'dictatorial power if war, revolt or other catastrophes should lead to a state of emergency', but also enacts 'the ideal of a complete stabilisation, an ecclesiastical and political restoration'.[42]

These logics collide in German baroque drama, which juxtaposes 'the drama of the tyrant' to 'martyr-drama and pity' in a potential axis of tension:

> Seen in ideological terms they are the two faces of the monarch. They are the necessarily extreme incarnations of the princely essence. As far as the tyrant is concerned, this is clear enough. The theory of sovereignty which takes as its example the special case in which dictatorial powers are unfolded, positively demands the completion of the image of the sovereign, as tyrant. The drama makes the special point of endowing the ruler with the gesture of executive

power as his characteristic gesture… it was probably unusual for full robes, crown and sceptre to be wanting when the ruler appeared on stage.[43]

Audiences delighted in seeing the tyrant fall or enter madness 'destroying himself and his entire court'.[44] The dramas are thus cautionary critiques of power-over, exhibiting not only madness but also indecisiveness: 'the prince, who is responsible for making the decision to proclaim the state of emergency, reveals… that he is almost incapable of making a decision'.[45] For the audience, watching the values of the dynastic state played out on stage, the engagement is in the conflict between the timeless quality of office and the temporal failures of those who hold office.

Citing a play by Andreas Gryphius, Benjamin states, 'the sublime status of the Emperor [Charles I] on the one hand, and the infamous futility of his conduct on the other, create fundamental uncertainty as to whether this is a drama of tyranny or a history of martyrdom'.[46] The inept ruler is required, nonetheless, to avoid crisis:

> The function of the tyrant is the restoration of order in the state of emergency: a dictatorship whose utopian goal will always be to replace the unpredictability of historical accident with the iron constitution of the laws of nature. But the stoic technique also aims to establish a corresponding fortification against a state of emergency in the soul, the rule of the emotions. It too seeks to set up a new, anti-historical creation… which is no less far removed from the innocent state of primal creation than the dictatorial constitution of the tyrant.[47]

This is where Benjamin disagrees with Schmitt, whose *Political Theology* was published in 1922, three years before Benjamin completed his thesis (to be told the examiners found it incomprehensible).

Schmitt did not join the Nazi Party until 1933 but his position on sovereignty is key to his opposition to liberal democracy: 'Sovereign is he [sic] who decides on the exception', the latter defined as 'a general concept on the theory of the state' beyond emergencies such as a state of siege.[48] His focus on the exception follows a shift of values as a result of the 1914–18 war, from a neo-Kantian idea of the state as a universally rational political form and secular complement of Catholicism, towards a brutal reality in Germany's defeat and the fragile equilibrium of the Weimar Republic. In this situation, the state ensures the security of private lives, when religion no longer offers a universal truth and the state is no longer identified with the person of the sovereign. Except that the image of that sovereign who rules by divine right, who announces the exception, haunts Schmitt as his perverse utopian image in his construction of a modern legitimisation of power: sovereign is the person who decides both what is the exception and when to announce it.

Writing in 2005, Giorgio Agamben notes the categorisation of the political and the legal – one immediate, an outcome of power struggles; the other general, justifying or prohibiting the former – reflects the Nazi suspension of the Weimar Republic constitution:

> From a juridical standpoint the entire Third Reich can be considered a state of exception that lasted twelve years [1933–1945]… modern totalitarianism can be defined as the establishment, by means of the state of exception, of a legal civil war that allows for the physical elimination not only of political adversaries but of entire categories of citizens who for some reason cannot be integrated into the political system.[49]

Benjamin belonged to two such categories: Marxist and Jew. For Schmitt, meanwhile, liberal democracy, represented by Weimar, cannot stabilitise conflicting value systems. Georg Schwab summarises, 'sovereign authority not only was bound to the normally valid legal order but also transcended it… when a normal situation threatens to become an exception'.[50] While Article 48 of the Weimar constitution specifically allowed the exception as a temporary, pragmatic measure, Schmitt looks to a permanent sovereign dictatorship, 'the highest power, not a derived power'.[51] He asserts,

> It is precisely the exception that makes relevant the subject of sovereignty… especially when it is truly a matter of an extreme emergency and of how it is to be eliminated…. From the liberal constitutional point of view, there would be no jurisdictional competence… [but] if such action is not subject to controls… it is

clear who the sovereign is.… Although he [sic] stands outside the normally valid legal system, he nevertheless belongs to it, for it is he who must decide whether the constitution needs to be suspended in its entirety.[52]

Remembering Benjamin's theses on history, in which he writes that the state of emergency is, 'not the exception but the rule',[53] his understanding of the mechanisms of power-over seems a direct refusal of Schmitt's position.

Both relate to the situation in which they live but in incompatible ways. For Schmitt, 'all law is situational law. The sovereign produces and guarantees the situation in its totality.'[54] This is incompatible with the neo-Kantian state which he abandons after 1918, and which harks back to the 'natural law' of the baroque era which confounds 'the unity and order of the rationalist scheme'.[55] In another glance at a redundant past, Schmitt adds, 'the exception in jurisprudence is analogous to the miracle in theology'.[56] This historical break is opposed to that for which Benjamin calls; Schmitt sees a history which continues to oppress in the interests of the supreme stability which liberal democracy cannot provide.

Agamben notes that, in the civil war which followed the collapse of Fascism in Italy, after Benjamin's death, written laws become the 'defence of the constituted order'.[57] He concludes, 'a threshold of undecidability is produced', and with it, 'the aporias that every attempt to define necessity is unable to resolve'.[58] But the state of exception is not always conflated with necessity, or at least not from every position; its normalisation underpins the legitimisation of totalitarianism as defence against threats to the state's absolute control. That control, meanwhile, reflects a fear of disorder and awareness, necessarily repressed, that the basis of power-over is questionable. As Agamben says, 'not only does necessity ultimately come down to a decision, but that on which it decides is, in truth, something undecideable in fact and law'.[59] For Benjamin, questioning power's narratives is vital.

The sovereign announces what is justified by the situation, not by rational debate or by evidence. In doing so, as if appropriating the Messianic interruption for inverse ends, the sovereign separates the act of announcing the exception from the norm, while Agamben summarises, this 'introduces a zone of anomie into the law in order to make the effective regulation of the real possible'.[60] Citing the 'unbridled license' of carnival and Roman saturnalia in contrast, Agamben argues that the maintenance of the law depended then, in real terms, on exactly such exceptional, licensed and contained inversion when 'men dress up and behave like animals, masters serve their slaves, males and females exchange roles, and criminal behaviour is considered licit, or, in any case, not punishable… [in] a period of anomie that breaks and temporarily subverts the social order'.[61] Here, the exception is a measured, regularly introduced safety valve, lessening the prospect of revolt. For Agamben, 'the anomic feasts dramatize this irreducible ambiguity of juridical systems, and… show that what is at stake in the dialectic… is the very relation between life and law'.[62] But the state of emergency on which Schmitt writes is not contained; it reproduces the absolutism of pre-democratic societies while stripping them of religious and rational moderations and external comparison. That contributes to the mix of mythicised past and present power-lust which produced the fantasy of the Nazi thousand-year-Reich. In that way, *On the Concept of History* can be read as an immediate refusal of everything implied by Schmitt's absolutism.

As Bloch pointed out, Nazi culture appropriated elements of Left culture (its banners and songs, street marches and so forth) which it suffused with a fake medievalism (crowns in the Rhine, a sleeping Emperor under the mountain) in the cult of blood and soil. This produced a false public consciousness[63] in the aim of erasing the existing culture and social structure in a permanent historical shift. Benjamin knows this, which is why he calls for a real state of emergency – an authentic interruption in which the manufactured norm is suspended – although this is not inevitably a Messianic illumination.


# The Messianic moment

Benjamin's history of the oppressed collides with Scmitt's justification of the repression of freedom in the interests of power's continuity. But, looking back, Scmitt's assertions may be read as a response to his reading of Benjamin's essay on violence, published in 1921, a year before Schmitt's *Political Theology*. In 'Critique of Violence', Benjamin examines the relation of violence to law and justice. He rejects a simple justification by ends – the ends justify the means – because, 'the question would remain open whether violence … could be a moral means even to just ends', while the exclusion of this critique of means is 'a main current of legal philosophy: natural law'.[64] The appeal to natural law invokes a perceived necessity underlying legal formulations, and underpins Schmitt's case. Benjamin aligns this to social Darwinism – survival of the strongest (not what Darwin meant but widely used to justify white imperialism) – and via 'a short step' to a 'still cruder' doctrine of a legal philosophy, 'which holds that the violence that is … appropriate to natural ends is thereby also legal'.[65] An opposite view, he continues, is that violence is historically produced, from which 'the misunderstanding in natural law by which a distinction is drawn between violence used for just ends and violence used for unjust ends must be emphatically rejected'.[66] This separates a natural state, or norm, from a historically specific legal structure which reflects a society's values. But, within the norm, the state sees individual violence as a threat. In practice, the state constructs a norm whereby the general strike – an attempt, for Benjamin (as for Rosa Luxemburg) to escape the violent extortion of the employers – is such a threat: 'labour will always appeal to its right to strike, and the state will … take emergency measures'.[67]

Schmitt, despite his departure from Catholic and Kantian universalism, opts for a universal necessity of exception; Benjamin, in contrast, looks to the historically specific, temporally fractured moment when the disintegration of the norm occurs. These arguments reflect the situation in Germany after military defeat in 1918, when armed far-Right thugs roamed Berlin, and the Social Democrats made an alliance with the military command to maintain the Weimar Republic. Just as *On the Concept of History* reflects his situation in 1940, the essay on violence depicts it in 1921, when those events are recent memories. But he also writes, 'nonviolent agreement is possible wherever a civilised outlook allows the use of unalloyed means of agreement. … Courtesy, sympathy, peaceableness, trust … are their subjective preconditions.'[68] The complementary objective preconditions include laws which seek to crush the right, and must be opposed, and the compromises of liberalism and social democracy wherein means are justified by ends. For Benjamin, however, 'it is never reason that decides on the justification of means and the justness of ends: fate-imposed violence decides on the former, and God on the latter'.[69]

To summarise: the 1914–18 war broke Schmitt's faith in reason and God, leading him to a totalitarian theory of the exception. From an opposite position, Benjamin argues for a break in the cycle. His conclusion is enigmatic: 'all mythic, lawmaking violence, which we may call executive, is pernicious. Pernicious, too, is the law-preserving, administrative violence that serves it. Divine violence, which is the sign and seal but never the means of sacred dispatch, may be called sovereign violence.'[70] This prefigures arguments in *Dialectic of Enlightenment*, published by Theodor Adorno and Max Horkheimer in 1944, on the return of myth within rationalised modernity (a return of the repressed); and to the term 'administered world' as it is used in critical theory to denote the mechanisms by which unfreedom is made the norm. For Adorno, Samuel Beckett renders this administered world banal in his plays, the unreality of the stage casting the norm outside as more unreal, or unimagineable, than the imagined drama on the stage.[71]

In occupied France in 1940, the norm was real. Earlier, through the period of Weimar social democracy, Benjamin responds in one way, Schmitt in the opposite way. This is, in the most obvious reading, a contrast of Left and Right positions. But it is also a question of what can be understood from, or constitutes, history: a force for absolute power-over as, in effect, I suggest, a retreat from fear of uncertainties and change; or – for Benjamin – the imperative to reject that construct, to replace it with a Marxist-Messianism as the appropriate reaction to terror, inverting the exception in a moment of profound refusal. Perhaps, then, the key difference between Benjamin and Schmitt is that Schmitt is nostalgic for a pre-rational world while Benjamin is committed to a secular, revised rationality which is also infused with Messianism. As Löwy observes, while Schmitt reads modern ideas of the state as secularised theology, Benjamin writes, 'secularisation is both legitimate and necessary – on condition that the subversive energy of the messianic remains present'.[72] Löwy summarises Benjamin's alternative:

> It starts out from the hypothesis that each moment has its revolutionary potentialities. And in it an open conception of history as human praxis, rich in unexpected possibilities and able to produce something new, stands opposed to any kind of teleological doctrine that trusts in the laws of history or in the gradual accumulation of reforms on the safe and sure path of infinite Progress.[73]

Thinking of the arcades, each object in a shop window has its utopian afterimage, crossing from one time and space to another in which its meaning is re-created. Thesis XVIIa in *On the Concept of History* begins, 'In the idea of a classless society, Marx secularized the idea of Messianic time.'[74] If so, perhaps it can be reintroduced. But Benjamin locates the Messianic moment in the everyday, in stories rather than narratives, in the informal culture and tacit knowledges of ordinary life at the levels of individual *and* social consciousness.

It is not a matter of incremental progress, as in the compromises of Social Democracy. Nor is it the revolution of class progression, which has a Darwinist as well as Hegelian undertone. It is a spontaneous, sudden, unexpected, ephemeral yet transformative insight in which the world is renewed (or redeemed). These, at least, were the ideas which Benjamin wrote in his last work, which he carried in manuscript, with another unidentified (now lost) text, in his suitcase in September 1940, when he did not cross the Spanish border. More than eighty years on, does any of this matter? I think it does (or would not have written this book, in which this is the central chapter of the section on theory). Why? Because the issues have not gone away, just taken new forms in the totalitarianism of global capital and its recasting of liberalism (free trade) as neoliberalism (nothing is free except wealth accumulation).

# Precarity and power-to

Today, the state of emergency is again the norm in a perpetuation of insecurity as a control mechanism under neoliberalism. The function of the nation-state as protecting the people has been partly outsourced through privatisations, and the introduction of precarious employment (called flexible employment) is the new norm. Meanwhile, consumerism has moved from the competitive pursuit of new material goods with built-in obsolescence to services and what are variously called experiences and solutions, similarly empty of lasting satisfaction, in the immaterial economy. Lorey defines the consequent state of unease:

> Precarisation is not a marginal phenomenon... In the leading neoliberal Western industrial nations it can no longer be outsourced to the socio-geographical spaces of the periphery where it only affects

others. Precarisation is not an exception, it is rather the rule.… By way of insecurity and danger it embraces the whole of existence, the body, modes of subjectivation. It is threat and coercion, even while it opens up new possibilities of living and working.[75]

For Lorey, the question is where to find the cracks in this new system, how to glimpse an alternative in practices of self-empowerment which 'break through, refuse, or escape' from the norm.[76] I think this means that hope resides in the brittleness and propensity to leak of a system which presents itself as seamless and without alternative. But this system also defies stable definition. Neoliberalism has stolen the moment for its own purposes, taking apart the post-war Welfare State to introduce a brutalisation which is as unpredictable, ironically, as the moment of redemption. The new norm is uncertainty, non-normality. It is the sense of contingency which, in another context, permeated much postmodern theory, here turned nasty.

Quoting Robert Castel, who uses the analogy of a virus, Lorey elaborates,

> Without such state protection, people are constantly exposed to insecurity as if to a contagious epidemic… 'Like a virus that permeates everyday life, dissolving social ties and undermining the physical structures of the individuals… [with] a demoralising effect…' This reciprocal infection… constitutes states and societies which build on protection and securities, as endangerment.[77]

That was written in 2015, before the Covid-19 pandemic. The point remains that insecurity is the norm in the neoliberal state; it is no longer possible for the majority public to predict or to plan for the future, while the means of social security – welfare payments, regulation – are reduced, made difficult to access and render their recipients as marginal publics. At the same time, in Britain, far-Right populism constructs a hostile environment for refugees (or almost any foreigners) while the regime attempts to redirect responsibilities – from climate change to poverty, even Covid infection – to individuals. As Lorey says, again from Castel, the resulting fracture of the social fabric means that an increasing number of individuals – already less likely to identify with a social group, trade union or suchlike protecting entity, and set against each other – are regarded as superfluous, and hence relegated to zones of increasing instability. The margin is increased; the centre, if there is one, is increasingly the preserve of globalised elites for whom the state and the taxation which pays for public services are irrelevant.

Castel, Lorey notes, does not look to a reinstitution of the Welfare State but to 'a re-conceptualization of protection and security that is no longer oriented to groups and collectives, but more towards the pluralism of individuals'.[78] In the background, the disaffiliated – once called the underclass, then the socially excluded – may undermine the state which depends on precarity. I find Lorey's argument and reading of Castel persuasive, while the material conditions of the pandemic have emphasised and worsened patterns of inequality. I agree, too, that the insecurity which is the norm pervades everyday life. I would add that the privileging of certain mechanisms of knowledge – such as the use of algorithms in determining access to public benefits, or widely in digital sales platforms – marginalises not only the previously privileged knowledges of professional expertise but also the tacit knowledges and personal insights of ordinary life, which might otherwise refuse the norm or generate alternative social formations. And perhaps there is little prospect of real political change today, at least through representational politics. This leads me to another idea: that the new history which Benjamin foresees, and the rupture of precarity towards which Lorey looks, both require a transition from the continuity of power-over to the ephemerality of power-to. That might be found in direct action, as the emerging alternative to a politics of representation.

Direct action, I suggest, is, in practice, the end of instrumentalism: the means used are not directed towards an end, and therefore cannot be used (whatever abuses they produce) to justify that end. They *are* the ends, directly enacting the values of an alternative society. On the Zapatista movement in Mexico in the 1990s, John Holloway writes, 'Reality and power are so mutually encrusted that even to raise the question of dissolving power is to step off the edge of reality.'[79] The implication is not dissimilar to Benjamin's intention in writing, 'We must attain a conception of history that is in keeping with this insight. Then we shall clearly realize that it is our task to bring about a real state of emergency.'[80] Lorey, similarly, reminds me that bringing about an exception which inverts the structure of power-over remains the underlying need despite changes in conditions from 1940 to now (as

I write, in 2022). The previous model of class conflict is reconfigured according to a multiple axis of gender, race, sexual orientation and other categorisations in postmodernity; the dominant issues now are the climate crisis and global conflict; and the means of representation have moved away from liberal democracy and narrative to direct action and the cultivation of experiential knowledges and the stories which can be told at street level. What I think emerges from re-reading Benjamin beside Lorey today is that the task is, although in a quite different way, just as urgent as it was in 1940.

# Chapter 5
# Saying the unsayable

In the previous chapter I reconsidered Walter Benjamin's philosophy of history. I move now to Theodor Adorno, again with a selective focus. My point of departure is his remark on the difficulty of writing poetry after Auschwitz, which appears at the end of an essay on cultural criticism. I begin with it because it implicitly questions the capacity of culture to address the crisis of European history denoted by the generalising term Auschwitz. Adorno does not say poetry should not be written after Auschwitz, concluding that *cultural critique* is corroded. Monuments to the Holocaust – as critical public culture – tend to confirm this although new kinds of monument may offer an exit from the difficulty from the 1980s onwards.

After re-reading Adorno's essay and other work, I cite an anti-Fascist monument in Hamburg designed by Jochen Gerz, and Holocaust memorials by Peter Eisenman in Berlin and Rachel Whiteread in Vienna. I look back to the poetry of Paul Celan, and Samuel Beckett's drama, as cases of post-Holocaust literature when those events remained in living memory. Finally, from a recent theoretical framework, I cite Judith Butler's *Precarious Life* (2004), in which she says, 'there is a limit to discourse that establishes the limits of human intelligibility'.[1]

## Poetry after Auschwitz?

Towards the end of his essay 'Cultural criticism and society', Adorno says, 'to write poetry after Auschwitz is barbaric'.[2] He continues, 'this corrodes even the knowledge of why it has become impossible to write poetry today'.[3] His argument is, I suggest, tangential to the practice of poetry, and concerned with the difficulties of writing about culture in an end-game of values: 'cultural criticism finds itself faced with the final stage of the dialectic of culture and barbarism'.[4] That is, culture reflects the final, eroded stage of Enlightenment – the universal project of Reason – in a dissolution of human values; Enlightenment, after all, is the trajectory of a rationality aligned to human happiness and freedom. That is no longer a viable proposition after mass annihilation. The task of the cultural critic, still, is 'by virtue of its difference from the prevailing disorder', to go beyond that position, despite the cultural critic's immersion in a culture industry which affirms the dominant culture while itself needing, 'the difference in order to fancy itself culture'.[5] The cultural critic, like the Romantic poet relying on publication for a living, is thus compromised at the outset, while 'the free expression of opinion' is a myth of bourgeois individualism.[6] In the 1930s, the hollowness of the myth of culture was exposed in the Nazi imposition of its version of art appreciation; nonetheless, for Adorno, the underlying difficulty remains:

> The complicity of cultural criticism with culture lies not in the mere mentality of the ritic. Far more, it is dictated by his [sic] relation to that with which he deals. By making culture his object, he objectifies it once more. Its very meaning, however, is the suspension of objectification.... Even the enthusiasm for foreign cultures includes the excitement over the rarity in which money may be invested. If cultural criticism... sides with conservatism, it is because of its unconscious adherence to a notion of culture which, during the era of late capitalism, aims at a form of property which is stable and independent of stock-market fluctuations.[7]

The difficulty is capitalism, complicated by recent history – the stock-market crash of 1929 and extreme inflation in Germany – and the inevitable complicity of the critic in the culture industry which capitalism spawns. Against this, cultural criticism seeks authenticity, and cultivates a necessary distancing from actuality. This occurs when, 'the fact that every form of repression, depending on the level of technology, has been necessary for the survival of society, and that society as it is, despite all its absurdity, does indeed reproduce its life under the existing conditions, objectively produces the semblance of society's legitimation'.[8] As Walter Benjamin argued (Chapter 4), oppression becomes the norm.

All this is exacerbated by the history of Europe in the 1930s and 1940s, and the extreme history of the Holocaust, which is both irrational in Enlightenment terms, and a product of the industrial society which is one outcome of Enlightenment. A further complication is that the annihilated cannot speak, a function ceded to survivors likely to feel survivor guilt or a need for retribution. In *Negative Dialectics* (1966) Adorno comments, 'After Auschwitz, our feelings resist any claim of the positivity of existence as … wronging the victims; they balk at squeezing any kind of sense, however bleached, out of the victims.'[9]

Still, this history has contexts in European colonialism. It is beyond reason but not beyond enquiry. Gerhard Schweppenhauser writes,

> In the concentration camps it was not the historical-philosophical construction of the individual that was liquidated, but actual individuals. They were literally liquidated; but first they were de-individualized, reduced to mere numbered examples of species … In *Negative Dialectics*, Adorno illuminated this space from the opposite perspective: it is not the social expropriation of the individual's destiny but the expropriation even of his [sic] dying, destroying even the appearance of life's meaning as a coherent whole, that seals the loss of humane, autonomous subjectivity.[10]

The question is to what extent these events represented a degree of continuity in what was called European civilisation or culture, these terms having precise meaning in German as technical development and national spirit, respectively. Anson Rabinbach writes that the 1940s gave rise to, 'reflections on evil, or on how the logic of modernity … with its legacy of progress, secularism, and rationalism, could not be exculpated from events that seemed to violate its ideals'.[11]

Under Nazi race laws, people scripted for liquidation were first reduced to a sub-category of species, and denied human status. Joseph Goebbels stated, 'the Jews are the lice of civilised humanity'.[12] Zyklon B, the gas used to kill people in gas chambers, was a variant of Zyklon A, used to kill moths in textile warehouses. Peter Sloterdijk notes that *Sonderbehandlung* (special treatment), 'designated essentially the direct application of insect extermination procedures to human populations'.[13] From 1942 onwards, this was pursued through an infrastructure of administrative measures, and purpose-designed buildings and transport.

Further, just as the final solution killed not only Jews but also Roma, Sinti, Communists and homosexuals, among categories excluded from Aryan purity, it had precedents. Zygmunt Bauman writes,

> Ideational projects, and the technical resources that permit implementation of such projects, not only have been proved fully compatible with modern civilization, but have been conditioned, created and supplied by it. The Holocaust did not just, mysteriously, avoid clash with the social norms and institutions of modernity. It was these norms and institutions that made the Holocaust feasible.[14]

Bauman continues that the processes of mediation in modern societies (meaning, broadly, liberal democracies) were ineffective in preventing mass murder. He concludes, *'we live in a type of society that made the Holocaust possible…* '[15]

# Auschwitz after history

There was resistance even within Nazi Germany. But there is a history, from the European colonisation of other continents, the shipping of enslaved people as cargo, and the effective designation of labour as resource, which prefigures mass extermination. Looking at the late nineteenth century, Sven Lindqvist links imperial ideology to Social Darwinism:

> In the field of international law, this evolutionary ethic entails that the stronger are right. By displacing the lower races, man [sic] is only doing what the better organized plants do with the less well organized, and what more highly developed animals do to the less developed.[16]

Extending this distortion of Darwinism, Alexander Tille wrote in 1893, 'all historical rights are invalid against the rights of the stronger'.[17] Lindqvist continues that, in 1894,

> The Pan-German League paper *Alldeutsche Blatter*... stated that the conditions of life for the German race could be assured only through 'elbow room' stretching from the Baltic to the Bosphorous. In that process one should not allow oneself to be hindered by the fact that inferior peoples such as Czechs, Slovenes and Slovaks would lose their existence, anyhow worthless to civilisation.[18]

In 1904, the German colonisers of Southwest Africa commandeered the grazing lands of the Herero people, whom they forcibly sent to reserves; when the Herero resisted, the order was given to exterminate them. Most starved in the desert, their death rattles resounding, 'in the sublime silence of infinity'.[19] Any survivors were sentenced to hard labour in camps.

In a similar way, during the Boer War, British forces confined Boer civilians, mainly women and children, in camps where many died from malnutrition or disease. Then, turning to new technologies of aggression in 1917, the cost-effectiveness of air warfare was demonstrated by Squadron 221 in bombing the compound of Mohamed Abdille Hasan, the resistant ruler of Somaliland, killing his family and courtiers. Hasan surrendered two days later. The raid cost £77,000 – 'peanuts compared to what the army had asked for' – confirming the case for an air force on, 'economic considerations'.[20] Air warfare also provided entertainment. In 1927, the Royal Air Force carried out a mock bombing of a 'native village' in an air show near London.[21] Long before that, imperialism had normalised the relegation of non-white people to sub-human status to enable economic appropriation, and had established the supremacy of white culture in ethnographic museums and native camps with living inmates at World Expositions.[22] The difference in 1942 was that a colonial mindset was re-directed to people *within* a European nation-state, most of whom were assimilated.

## Culture after Auschwitz?

Citing, 'Adorno's much quoted maxim... that "to write poetry after Auschwitz is barbaric,"'[23] Monica Bohm-Duchen argues, 'it is no longer enough to reproduce the images of horror – the barbed wire, the crematoria, the skeletal survivors, the emaciated corpses – in a doomed attempt to re-create a sense of how it was'.[24] She adds that perhaps only survivors have the right to speak. But all representation is fraught, tending to normalisation and hence complicity, or to encapsulation in a history in which the events in question recede. But, for Anson Rabinbach, it is only distance which makes memories bearable; he comments on photographs of the destruction of European cities in the Second World War, 'a certain artificial distance, a wide-angle vision, is required'.[25]

There are images, such as photographs of the railtracks leading into Auschwitz; there are books, pictures and plays; and a thirty-six-page bibliography of texts on Holocaust dramas.[26] The question remains, 'How is it possible for me, for you, to speak at all about these things?'[27] James Young identifies three issues,

> First, memory-work about the Holocaust cannot... be redemptive in any fashion. Second, part of what a post-Holocaust generation must ethically represent is the experience of the memory-act itself. Last, the void left behind... demands the reflection previously accorded the horrific details of the destruction itself. For these artists, it is the memory-work itself, the difficult attempt to know, to imagine vicariously, and to make meaning out of experiences they never knew directly that constitutes the object of memory.[28]

In Germany, this history remained buried until the 1980s. This produced anti-monuments such as Horst Hoheisel's project to blow up the Brandenburg Gate, grind the stone to dust and bury it. That project was unrealised; but, working with architect Andreas Knitz, Hoheisel did insert a concrete memorial slab heated from below to body temperature in the grounds of Buchenwald. Young saw visitors touched by 'the human warmth embodied here'.[29] Or perhaps they found it uncanny.

# Anti-monuments

In 1983, Jochen Gerz and Esther Shalev Gerz entered a competition for a *Monument Against Fascism, War and Violence* in Hamburg. Their response was to design an anti-monument: a lead-coated column a metre square and twelve metres high, to be progressively sunk into a pit under a brick podium, in the suburb of Harburg, unveiled in 1986. An inscription on the column in German, French, English, Hebrew, Arabic and Turkish reads,

> We invite the citizens of Hamburg, and visitors to the town, to add their names here to ours. In doing so, we commit ourselves to remain vigilant.… it will gradually be lowered into the ground. One day it will have disappeared completely, and the site… will be empty. In the end, it is only we ourselves who can rise up against injustice.[30]

A steel-point stylus was attached, enabling people to sign the monument (like a petition). It was lowered periodically over the next seven years, visible now through a window in the podium. Young notes the aim was 'to provoke',[31] but the graffiti which covered it surprised the artists, ranging from tagging and lovers' hearts to racist slogans. A newspaper stated, 'the filth brings us closer to the truth than would any list of well-meaning signatures… like a fingerprint of our city'.[32] Visiting in 2010, I saw anti-Semitic graffiti on the explanatory text and images on the podium [Figure 5.1].

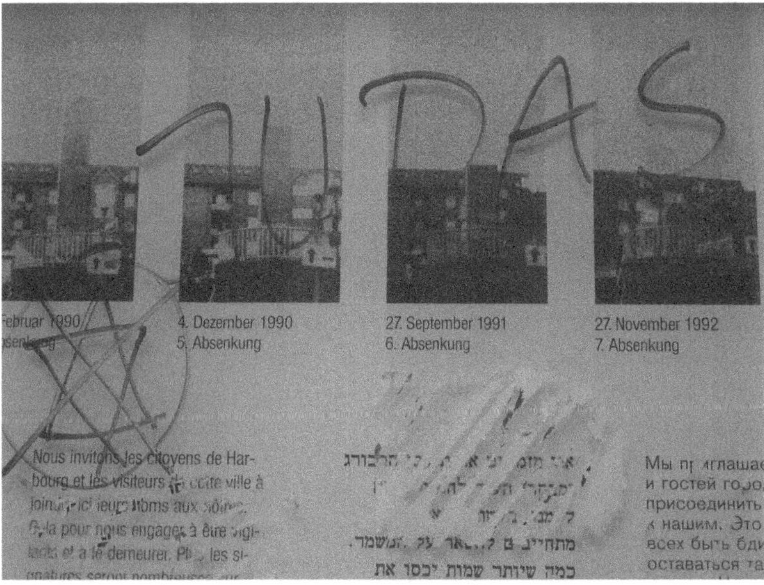


**Figure 5.1** Harburg, Hamburg, Jochen Gerz and Esther Shalev Gerz, *Monument against Fascism, War and Violence* (1986–1993): graffiti on the explanatory text, 2020

A second anti-monument is *Stones – Monument Against Racism*, Saarbrücken, undertaken by Gerz with a group of art students in 1990–3. They began by researching the 2,146 Jewish cemeteries which existed in Germany prior to the Nazi period, using this material to inscribe cobbles in the main square (in which the Schloss was the Nazi headquarters, and where deportees were collected). Students worked at night to remove cobbles and replace them with others dug up elsewhere, taking those removed to the art school for inscription with the name of a cemetery and the date of reinsertion on the unseen under surface. Gerz then announced the project, gaining official support after press controversy.

A more direct process of public response was used in *The Living Monument* at Biron, France in 1995–6. An existing Monument to the Fallen next to the village church was replaced by a structure of equal dimensions in concrete. This carried public memories silk-screened in white on red plaques affixed to its surfaces. The memories were collected through one-to-one interviews, then edited to a few lines. One states,

> I hope our children and grandchildren will experience no more wars. Wars like that in Bosnia will always exist. I hope they do not touch us. When I was young my parents refused to talk about the war… I remember the defeat: we escaped by car… Last year in Germany I saw Germans up close; I was surprised that they were friendly.[33]

Three years later, Rosana Albertini interviewed participants. One said, 'there are some of us, the ones who have been deported… who are still afraid to speak. It is too painful. I was scared myself… Rather than questioning us, he made us think.'[34] A person who hid in a cow shed for five days to avoid deportation said, 'There are no signatures… that's better.… the thoughts written on the monument are so personal… Mister Gerz pushed us to think about the war, about death. We had stopped doing that… it shakes the pit of your stomach.'[35]

In comparison, monuments at concentration camps tend to a repetitive vocabulary: at Treblinka, 17,000 irregular, granite slabs; at Majdanek, a massive, fractured slab on two supports; at Birkenau, a row of horizontal slabs on a cobbled street, inscribed in eighteen languages, 'four million people suffered and died here at the hands of the Nazi murderers 1940–1945', until the text was removed in 1989.[36] Cultural business-as-usual subsumes even these memories in its wider project, normalising history in the form of the monument which objectifies it. Perhaps Adorno (above) is accurate in his diagnosis. And perhaps the single street light lit all day on the site of the demolished Jewish ghetto in Lublin is more poignant than these forms in stone. I also recall my visit to the Jewish Museum, Berlin, designed by Daniel Libeskind: a series of displacements on an axis leading to an enclosed chamber in which a dim light from a high window illuminates a ladder on the wall, too high to reach. I went in. The door shut. My eyes adjusted to the dark. I realised I had not read the text outside explaining how to leave.

# An aesthetics of commemoration?

For Young, 'Memory is never shaped in a vacuum, the motives of memory are never pure… [if] the aim of some memorials is to educate… other memorials are conceived as expiations of guilt or a self-aggrandizement. Still others are intended as tourist attractions.'[37] Shelley Hornstein and Florence Jacoboeitz comment,

> In Germany, above all, it has become the essential imperative of the Holocaust memorial to remark on its own impossibility… and as such to unmark itself, so as to efface guilty traces of its own subsistence. A whole genre of anti-monuments has been catalogued… Habituated, one might even begin to suspect a certain grandiosity in such self-subversion… [and] question the longing for purity inherent in the work's own self-negation – the secret promise of the tabula rasa.[38]

And for Ziva Amishai-Maisels, the aesthetics of commemoration is inherently contradictory when art and the Holocaust, 'belong to two entirely different spheres which appear to be separated by an unbridgeable gap,' so that while art offers beauty and personal expression it is, 'powerless before the horror and cruelty of the Holocaust'.[39]

These remarks from an extensive literature imply that all Holocaust memorials fail. But I want to consider two more recent cases: the *Monument for the Murdered Jews of Europe* designed by Peter Eisenman (1998–2005) in Berlin; and Rachel Whiteread's *The*

*Nameless Library* (1996–2000) in Vienna. I also look for comparison at monuments to the Irish famine.

Working with sculptor Richard Serra, Eisenman designed a field of 4,000 concrete slabs of varying height, arranged in a grid over undulating ground. The labyrinth was seen as claustrophobic by the authorities, and the number of slabs reduced to 2,711 (by coincidence the number of pages in the Talmud).[40] Eisenman and Serra do not disclose their sources but Eisenman is on record as challenging Holocaust culture: 'I don't like the Holocaust industry. I don't like Schindler's List. I don't like anything that turns something so problematic into something so simple and easy.'[41] The grid on which the slabs are arranged may suggest a city plan, or a basic, abstract pattern, a reading enhanced by Rosalind Kraus's idea that grids indicate, 'modern art's will to silence, its hostility… to narrative, to discourse'.[42] That would be a turn to silence which represents the difficulty of representing such a history. Equally, thinking of Adorno's comments (above), the turn to minimal means in a period of Minimalist sculpture might consign memory to a cultural norm: another minimalist art-object, as site-general rather than site-specific (in one contention of the period) as it is culture-general in its reproduction of a museum and gallery commonplace.

On my visit, teenagers were using the *Monument for the Murdered Jews of Europe* as an adventure playground [Figure 5.2]. For Eran Neuman, it 'functions as the condition in which this play takes place, challenging both the bottom-up-visitor interpretation… and the top-down-authorities' tolerance toward the integration of daily activities into the context of Holocaust commemoration'.[43] Neuman reads the monument's design as allowing 'the appropriation of the Holocaust as an event that does not have a closed and tight signification',[44] but it may be the site rather than the memory which is appropriated.

Moving to Vienna, Whiteread is known for casting the interiors of things, notably a terraced house in London, *House* (1993). Invited to enter a competition for a Holocaust memorial in Vienna in 1995 she designed an inverted library interior. Rows of books cast in concrete fill the shelves, their spines facing inwards. Double doors lack handles. Steps bear the names of the camps to which Viennese Jews were deported. Viable associations include the Jews as the people of the book, the history of Jewish scholarship and hermeneutics,

**Figure 5.2** Berlin, Peter Eisenman, *Memorial to the Murdered Jews of Europe*, 1998

a tradition of sepulchres and the prohibition of religious images. In contrast to Eisenman's distributed monument, *The Nameless Library* at the renamed Judenplatz is a unified, solid presence. The plinth is inscribed in German, Hebrew and English in memory of the 65,000 Austrian Jews murdered by the Nazis between 1938 and 1945 [Figure 5.3].

The project was controversial. Could Whiteread, as a non-Jew and non-Austrian speak for murdered Austrian Jews? Then construction exposed the remains of a synagogue burnt in a pogrom in 1421, which campaigners saw as a more fitting memorial. Young notes, 'Austria's relation to its wartime past has remained... politely out of sight.'[45] On its unveiling four years after the intended date on the anniversary of Kristallnacht, when Jewish shops and dwellings were ransacked in 1936, Whiteread asked that the memorial should not be given an anti-graffiti coating. On my visit, I saw only flowers placed respectfully on the steps as small groups (mainly students) contemplated the *Nameless Library* in its large open site.

**Figure 5.3** Vienna, Rachel Whiteread, *The Invisible Library*, 1997

# The Great Hunger

Difficulties encountered in designing Holocaust memorials occur, too, in memorials to other extreme histories, such as the Irish famine of 1845–51, called the Great Hunger. Although caused by potato blight, it was a managed disaster: English landlords sold crops to English buyers, and cleared Irish workers from their estates. A million Irish people died. Many others migrated. Relief efforts were small, late and ineffective. Niamh Kelly sums up the situation in 1851: 'lack of sustenance had viciously extended to circumstances of eviction, forced and economic migration and abandonment of home in search for food and basic means of survival'.[46] In England, the Irish were seen as feckless inhabitants of a green and fertile land, and 'a parasitic encumbrance' on English landlords.[47] This predates Social Darwinism but is part of the same history of imperial exploitation, reducing a population to abjection, then naturalising it.

The *Famine Memorial*, Dublin by Rowan Gillespie (1997) shows five life-size human figures in bronze, one carrying a child, and a dog, all gaunt and anguished, making their way to the boats on the emigrant quay (on which it is sited). I could meet them if I went there but I could also meet bronze likenesses of James Joyce and Molly Malone elsewhere in the city, which suggests a general inadequacy of figuration to bear the content of crisis. In contrast, Mount St Anne's Retreat, Killenard, exhibits a preserved wooden cross made from a 'sliding coffin', the wooden box on a cart in which the dead were taken to common graves, 'during their passage from the wretched huts or waysides where they died to the pit'.[48] Like the street light in Lublin, the modest, incidental intrusion may be more effective than grand monuments which become... another public monument.

# Residual writing

The post-war period was haunted by mass death, from the deliberate wartime bombing of civilian targets to the use of atomic weapons at Hiroshima and Nagasaki in 1945. Bombing reduced entire city centres to rubble, with fatalities in six figures. A survivor of the raid on Hamburg in 1943, Hans Erich Nossack, writes, 'Since we no longer believe in ourselves, what are we still? Hollowed out by a night of depravity. So let's not speak of upright gait and creating!'[49] The dead were counted. Nossack responds,

> Why do they try to lie to the dead? Why don't they say: we can't count them! That would be a simple statement such as the dead, too, could understand. For otherwise it could be that, if they are not granted their right, they will gather one day around the monument from World War One, which was left standing along with the chimneys while three quarters of the city were laid waste.[50]

He recalls people in an unaffected suburb sitting on balconies drinking coffee. W. G. Sebald remarks that while no one expects ants to grieve when another anthill is destroyed, 'you assume a certain degree of empathy in human nature'.[51]

For Adorno, the devaluation of feeling in mass culture matches the unrepresentability of mass death: 'All mass culture is fundamentally adaptation... the pre-digested quality of the product prevails, justifies itself and establishes itself... as it constantly refers to those who cannot digest anything not already pre-digested.'[52] This expresses a fear of conflict which supports the scheme of compensatory leisure under capitalism. Mass culture is authentic only in purveying a mythicised happiness; 'only in this consummated conflictlessness does art wholly become one moment of material production and thus turn completely into the lie to which it has always contributed its part in the past'.[53] This emptiness, again, matches the inadequacy of Holocaust representation. It is only, Adorno says in *Aesthetic Theory* (1969), art which refracts reality's banality that refuses such compensation.

Adorno finds this in Beckett's drama. The bleak stage sets, the spare text, the loneliness of characters incarcerated in internal worlds, express this in a time of impending nuclear war. Robert Witkin comments,

> To perceive the loneliness of the human condition at the heart of a play by Beckett... is not a matter of communicating the feelings of those involved. We can see and feel the brokenness of life, its emptiness and isolation without concerning ourselves with what feelings the subjects themselves may claim to have or seek to communicate. It is the subjective process itself that is objectively modelled in such works.[54]

Beckett's characters are submerged in a gloom which is theirs, but more than theirs. They float or sink (ambivalently), in a solitariness which their words articulate without change. In *The End*, a character says, 'All I remember is my feet emerging from my shadow, one after the other.'[55] Another disembodied voice says, in *Worstward Ho*, 'On. Somehow on. Anyhow on. Say all gone. So on. In the skull all gone. All? All cannot go.'[56] The text consists of short passages with abrupt punctuation, like stage directions. Repetition and rhyme produce an uncanny familiarity.

In his play *Waiting for Godot* (1953), Beckett employs the same sense of an introjected void. Adorno emphasises the irony of an atmosphere which is, 'as crepuscular grey as after sunset and the end of the world', yet remains true to the 'circus colours' it exorcises while its anti-heroes are, 'inspired by clowns and slapstick cinema'.[57] He remarks, 'even artworks that incorruptibly refuse celebration and consolation do not wipe out radiance... this lustre devolves precisely on works that are inconsolable'.[58] In a sentence which echoes Beckett's austerity he says, 'Art emigrates to a standpoint that is no longer a standpoint at all because there are no longer standpoints from which the catastrophe could be named or formed.'[59]

It is simplistic to attribute Beckett's bleakness to the events of the 1940s. It is less so to say that he is informed by these conditions, as were his post-war audiences, although Beckett himself refuses to explain his work (characteristically saying it means what he wrote). Yet this is writing, in a late modern compositional technique. The text is mediated by external references but, equally, plays on the mechanisms of verbal language. For Joseph Anderton, Beckett's texts strip out externality, refracting context as content:

> This strategy of outlining the absence of context to reveal the salient conditions of production is conducive to a reading of testimony, particularly after recent philosophy and critical theory on Holocaust testimony and the manner in which contexts exceed representation ... Rendering relational forms incomplete through the burdensome peddling of them is key to the contextual significance and creaturely dimension of Beckett's form.[60]

Anderton argues that the failure of representation itself conveys the excess which cannot be represented. Hence, 'In terms of the Holocaust's demands on testimony ... the Beckettian memory suggests a form of remembrance in which the declared truth is less valid than the on-going process of remembering and failing to remember.'[61]

Pascale Casanova reiterates the picture of Beckett as embodying 'the prophetic, sacred mission assigned the writer by devotees of literature ... assimilated to a vague metaphysics, in a strange, solitary place, where suffering permits only a well-nigh inarticulate, shapeless language'.[62] But she does this to argue from an almost *opposite* position that Beckett's aim was literary abstraction. Citing a passage from *Worstward Ho*, in which phrases are clipped and semi-repeated, she says, 'If we overturn the prejudice of non-meaning ... we can bring out strict rules of composition and organisation'.[63] This implies an abstraction equivalent to Krauss's remark on the minimal grid (above). Casanova, indeed, situates Beckett's abstraction in such a context, citing Wassily Kandinsky's abstract paintings (which Beckett saw in private collections in Germany in 1936).

More specifically, David Lloyd investigates Beckett's interest in the work of the Romanian abstract painter Avigdor Arikha (a friend of

Beckett in the 1950s–1960s). Lloyd identifies a common element of living through extreme history, Beckett in the Resistance, Arikha having been deported to a labour camp in 1942: 'Like Beckett, but in very different ways, Arikha had lived intensely through the traumatic and destructive events of the Second World War and its aftermaths.'[64] But this argument needs to be tempered by Beckett's interest, too, in the figurative work of Jack Yeats, and Arikha's return to figuration in the mid-1960s, when Beckett wrote a text for an exhibition of his work in Paris in characteristic style:

> Siege laid again to the impregnable without. Eye and hand feverishly after the unself. By the hand it unceasingly changes the eye unceasingly changed. Back and forth the gaze beating against unseeable and unmakable. Truce for a space and the marks of what it is to be and to be in face of. Those deep marks to show.[65]

Depiction is a process of re-seeing, of revisiting *what it is to see*. It is a modernist position emphasising the medium of the glass, not the view. Beckett fractures the act of seeing; the residue which remains requires reassembly by the reader, for whom only brief, unhelpful hints are provided. For Lloyd, 'this is a gaze at gazing itself'.[66]

I said above that Casanova argues from an *almost* opposite position to the received reading of Beckett as articulating the post-war void. But she comes closer to a conventional reading at the end of her commentary: 'but to the very end … he would leave room for the most intimate and pathetic, for naked images which, like motifs, remain fleeting, fragile, and all the more poignant in that they are always on the point of fading'.[67] This echoes her idea that *Worstward Ho* is 'an ultimate, paradoxical, aporetic poetic art: trying everything, trying again, forging ahead as best one can, to the point where it is no longer possible … '[68] But, rather than reading this as a representation of futility, Casanova continues that once certain modalities are set in place they become compositional rules. That is, the form of the text is its content, revolving around ambiguity or contradiction: 'every time we encounter "said" we should read "missaid." The law of "somehow" involves the necessity of an unstable text that fixes, at the very moment it is written, its own laws of functioning.'[69] *Worstward Ho* 'refers to nothing but itself'.[70] Casanova concludes, again citing the model of abstract art,

The autonomy of each text is a kind of reiterated manifesto against the foundations of what had hitherto been regarded as constitutive of the literary... which Beckett's whole oeuvre shows to be nothing but the stamp of the profound conservatism of literature, incapable of ridding itself of the presuppositions of realism.[71]

Adorno, too, reads a unity of meaning and form when modernism goes beyond subjectivity, and argues that in *Waiting for Godot*, Beckett's 'consciousness was correct that the need for progress is inextricable from its impossibility. The gesture of walking in place at the end... reacts precisely to this situation.'[72]

# Non-redemptive meaning

Similar issues of iteration occur in the poetry of Holocaust survivor Paul Celan. His words are sparse on the page; broken sentences indicate the survival (or not) of meaning. Utterance is overstretched, but like music. Traces of metre remain to resemble wreckage; internal or half-rhymes – *Nichts* (nothings) and *steht* (stands); *grau* (grey) and *königsblau* (king's blue) – float meaning in a semi-void resembling the pictorial space of, say, Paul Klee's paintings.[73] As abstract sounds, the words instantiate a system of difference which I think is comparable to Beckett's use – as Casanova argues – of abstract motifs; but here they accompany traces of memory and narration. In an address on receipt of a literary prize, Celan explains that his writing is shaped by Hasidic stories (told in German by Martin Buber), and from the mix of languages used in the Hapsburg Empire:

> It, the language, remained, not lost, yes in spite of everything. But it had to pass through its own answerlessness, pass through frightful muting, pass through the thousand darknesses of deathbringing speech. It passed through and gave back no words for that which happened; yet it passed through this happening. Passed through and could come to light again...[74]

Words such as answerlessness clutch at meaning's straws. Language stays but at a cost, strewn about like chaff (the husk of grain).

Celan ended his life by drowning in the Seine in April 1970. John Felstiner notes, 'People have said that Celan took his own life… because valid speech in German was impossible after Auschwitz.'[75] Which brings me back to Adorno's remark on poetry after Auschwitz. But Adorno's argument is about cultural criticism when meaning is debased. Celan and Beckett demonstrate the possibilities to produce literature after Auschwitz. They also show that to do so requires a re-construction of the means of writing, yet within the cultural framework of late modernism, nor entirely against the expectations of that literature's publics. There is distancing and containment.

# Culture-critique

In 'Cultural criticism and society', Adorno addresses the cultural critic's dilemma faced with the polarities of authentic and mass culture, and of authentic and debased criticism under what he calls 'the prevailing disorder'; although critique is distanced, it remains subsumed within 'the very culture industry' which the critic seeks to leave behind.[76] The argument is that the separation of art from life is necessary for critique, but that this relies on the means (the culture industry) which are disparaged. Adorno writes as an academic, not a poet (but had been a composer), and complains 'the semblance of freedom makes reflection upon one's own unfreedom incomparably more difficult'.[77] Terry Eagleton notes, in a similar vein, 'an aesthetic thought is one true to the opacity of its object. But if thought is conceptual, and so general, how can aesthetic thought be other than an oxymoron?'[78] Eagleton reads Adorno's style of writing as 'a discourse pitched into a constant state of crisis, twisting and looping back on itself, struggling in the structure of every sentence'.[79] That is why the critic, like Beckett's characters, must go on. But now?

# Critical mourning

The destruction of the World Trade Center, New York on 11 September 2001 (9–11) raised questions as to how the 3,000 dead should be mourned. In context of the War on Terror by which the United States sought retribution, Judith Butler reflects,

> That we can be injured, that others can be injured, that we are
> subject to death at the whim of another, are all reasons for both fear
> and grief. What is less certain, however, is whether the experiences
> of vulnerability and loss have to lead straightaway to military violence
> and retribution.... if we are interested in arresting cycles of violence
> to produce less violent outcomes, it is no doubt important to ask
> what, politically, might be made of grief besides a cry for war.[80]

The cry for war reproduces the destructiveness of colonial conquest
which led to the call which Lindqvist relates (above) to kill all the brutes.
The brutes are re-categorised but the response unchanged. Yet, when a
group of demonstrators carried a banner, on the other side of the world,
saying that Americans should think about why the world hates them so
much, the super-power could respond only through a reproduction of
the violence which led to the question.

Butler notes that to say that the United States was somehow
responsible for bringing terror on itself unhelpfully encodes the
omnipotence which that state conventionally claims as a global super-
power. Instead, collective responsibility requires 'understanding of
the history that brought us to this juncture'.[81] Butler offers a point of
departure for such understanding, arguing that if 'U.S. imperialism is
a necessary condition for the attacks', it is necessary to address 'not
only how it is experienced by those who understand themselves as
its victims, but how it enters into their own formation as acting and
deliberating subjects'.[82]

Butler moves to the questions 'Who counts as human?' and 'What
*makes for a grievable life*?'[83] Since loss and vulnerability follow from
'being socially constituted bodies', and not from isolated individualism,
'one finds oneself fallen' as others fall.[84] This is mourning's non-
reversibility, entailing the realisation that the subject exists in relation
to, or mourns the separation from, other subjects. The difficulty is that
personal realisation does not always contribute to a political community
when the citizen's agency in producing social change is aligned to
the individualist autonomy which defines the modern subject. Butler
responds,

> Perhaps we can say that grief contains the possibility of apprehending
> a mode of dispossession that is fundamental to who I am. This...
> does not dispute... my autonomy, but it does qualify that claim

through recourse to the fundamental sociality of embodied life, the ways in which we are … implicated in lives that are not our own.[85]

Vulnerability, in other words, emphasises commonalities in human lives. But it insists on the shared, unsegregated, quality of vulnerability whereby no one is excluded from humanity, which is not the case under colonial regimes wherein 'violence is done against those who are unreal', whose lives 'are already negated'.[86]

Although Butler's reflections on mourning and subjectivity are her response to conditions after 9–11, I suggest that, first, the argument around colonialism is lent additional weight by its juxtaposition to this recent history; and, second, that a viable response is to recognise a common humanity in those whom violence and colonialism exclude. Butler approaches this via Emmanuel Levinas's writing on what he calls the face: the human-ness of others which is recognised intuitively but can be a point of departure for a discourse of subjectivity. The difficulty here is that a proliferation of faces debases recognition, whence the mechanically reproduced faces of news photography 'give a human face to Afghan women', but also to terror.[87] Then, if the spectator identifies with these images, it is 'as the unrepresented viewer, the one who looks on, the one who is captured by no image at all, but whose charge is to capture and subdue … the image at hand'.[88] That is the probably inescapable condition of the photographic image. Hence it is not surprising that the violence which is feared is pre-empted by violence which engenders the object of that fear. And this is personal-political:

> In the Vietnam War, it was the pictures of children burning and dying from napalm that brought the US public to a sense of shock, outrage, remorse, grief. These were precisely pictures we were not supposed to see, and they disrupted the visual field and the entire sense of public identity that was built upon that field. The images furnished a reality, but they also showed a reality that disrupted the hegemonic field of representation itself. Despite their graphic effectivity, the images pointed somewhere else, beyond themselves, to a life and to a precariousness that they could not show.[89]

Images of the gates of Auschwitz, usually with empty railtracks, offer an equivalent terrain beyond representation: absence as the effect of the industrialised annihilation of categories of population, when there is no one to remember, except survivors and perpetrators.

Such willing and non-willing participants feature in Claude Lanzmann's film *Shoa* (1985). Although epic in length – I have viewed three hours[90] – the film depicts passages of ordinary landscape where events occurred, and interviews with the seemingly ordinary people who undertook or witnessed them, including members of the special squads of prisoners who loaded corpses, or living bodies, from mobile gas chambers into furnaces. Some of them escaped, some survived; one was an administrator dealing with the railway network serving the camps, another a railway worker at Treblinka; others were local people who knew what was happening but justify their inaction through fear of reprisals. My lingering impression is the normality of these testimonies, laden with facts in a way which reminds me of Nossack's remark on the counting of bodies (above). But that is the crisis of representation. Veils of description, like aesthetic transposition, screen what can be said. I see no exit. Language is stretched to breaking point while retaining enough semblance … to be legible.

# Coda

As to memorials, the artist Mierle Laderman Ukeles gave a talk at a college on Statten Island in 2002. She was artist in residence at the New York Sanitation Department, and had been working on a large scheme for the rehabilitation of a landfill site there to which New York's waste was transported in barges. After 9–11, her office near Wall Street was unusable until specialist cleaning removed debris. The debris from Ground Zero (containing human ash) was moved in the same barges to become the uppermost layer in the re-opened landfill site, adding human remains to previous layers of garbage. After her talk, a questioner asked Ukeles what memorial to 9–11 she thought would be appropriate. She replied that some of the dead were nameless: immigrant cleaners without papers whom executives habitually ignore. She proposed that those executives should in future be kind to the nameless people who continue to work invisibly in other towers today.[91]

# PART THREE

# Critical practices

# Chapter 6
# After the statues

In Chapter 5, I investigated how culture represented the Holocaust, finding that while the conventional form of the public monument was inadequate to bear the burden of extreme history, alternative forms had emerged, while literature achieved a stretching of language to breaking point. In this chapter, I return to the problem of public representation, but looking at a wider history, beginning with the toppling of a statue of slave trader and philanthropist Edward Colston in Bristol in 2020. Public monuments, as a general category, represent the values which a society is required to maintain, personified by individuals to whom, where a plinth is used, members of diverse publics are required literally to look up. One question is whether the monument, as a formal type, is too integral to this relation of power-over to be able to carry alternative meanings. Another is whether the removal of statues is a legitimate act of social reformation (as happened, for instances, in Ireland during the struggle for independence, and in the East bloc after the end of state socialism in 1989). This leads to a further question, as to what else might appear in the public realm – which is by no means limited to public spaces – to convey the contested values of a democratic society of diverse publics today. But I begin in Bristol.

## Statues

A bronze statue of Edward Colston (1636–1721), designed by Irish sculptor John Cassidy, was erected in the centre of Bristol in 1895. While the figure is rendered conventionally in a neo-classical style, with flowing robes and a long wig, the plinth is supported by four dolphins in the Art Nouveau style of the 1890s. A plaque claims that Colston was a virtuous son of the city. In June 2020, the statue was pulled down by Black Lives Matter demonstrators and thrown into the river Avon in the nearby Harbourside district. Since then, Colston Hall has been renamed Bristol Beacon and a Victorian stained glass window in his memory has been removed from the church of St Mary Redcliffe. At the time of writing, debate continues as to the statue's future site, if it has one. One suggestion is that it be returned to the plinth in order to be toppled annually in a public festival. A majority opinion is that it be retained in a museum with suitable documentation of its history, contexts and demise. Of course, it could also be melted down and made into something else, such as street furniture.

Colston's statue has two histories: one as representing a local person in Bristol, the other as belonging to a general type of monument, among countless bronze likenesses of rich and powerful white men. This follows a proliferation of commemorative statues across Europe from the second half of the nineteenth century onwards. Many are now incidental, those whom they commemorate more or less forgotten unless brought to public attention by a new controversy. But there is also a recent, parallel genre of street-level figures, mainly from literature and popular culture. In Bristol, actor Cary Grant, by Graham Ibbeson, strides through Millennium Square; nearby, quaker William Penn holds a book; and poet Thomas Chatterton and Bible translator Edward Tyndale sit on benches, all by Lawrence Holofcener. Each is connected to the city. Chatterton, for instance, gained fame by claiming to discover a series of medieval poems in the tower of St Mary Redcliffe (he forged them, and, moving to London, died from an overdose of a drug used to treat sexually transmitted diseases: not an ideal role model for Bristol's youth). Nonetheless, these white male bronze images construct a canon of Bristol's famous people – virtuous sons of the city, as it were – to whom publics are at least figuratively expected to look up even though there are no plinths. Visitors take selfies next to them, as if star-dust rubs off.

Colston's statue did make people look up, to a supposedly virtuous benefactor. This is the message of the form of statue-and-plinth, a mode of representation which affirms a desired conformity among a nation-state's supposedly unified population. This is illusory, like the figurative visual language of representation (whether neo-classical or nineteenth-century naturalist). It is as fake as Chatterton's poems. And this is because, historically, most nation-states are composed of multiple publics following migrations – in Britain, from archaic movements of people retrospectively called Celts, to forced movements across the Atlantic and the post-war re-migration of their descendants to Britain (the Windward Generation, from the name of the first boat to bring them), and today's migrations from conflict zones – as well as being divided by wealth, gender, age and so forth. If publics (plural) are formed by common interest, most people belong to several. These complexities imply that historical representation is contentious, raising the question as to whose history is represented by and for whom. This is not the conventional function of the public monument, designed to erase or evade the social fact of difference.

Statues, then, stand for selective histories. As readings of history change, it is logical that statues are removed. Indeed, they are often torn down in revolutions when their currency as signs of an old regime is spent. Leaving aside the question of aesthetic value – in nearly all cases negligible, in my view – the issue is whether the form of the public monument is viable in contributing to changing public attitudes, or whether there are more effective ways to communicate in a public realm which extends beyond public spaces to institutions (such as art museums), the press and broadcast media, and now social media. In Chapter 5, I cited buried monuments in Germany which emphasised the difficulty, not the shared acceptance, of the history in question. Here, I move to the removal of Colston's statue before widening the discussion to other instances of the removal of public monuments.

# Colston's legacies

Colston was a slave trader, philanthropist and Bristol's Member of Parliament from 1710 to 1713. Born into a merchant family, much of his wealth derived from his membership (from 1680 to 1692) of the Royal Africa Company, founded by Charles II and granted a monopoly on trade in gold, silver, ivory and enslaved people from West Africa. During the period of Colston's membership, the Company shipped more than 80,000 enslaved people from Africa to the Americas, a quarter of them dying in transit, many thrown overboard to claim the insurance. In 1689, Colston donated part of his holding in the Company to the new monarch, William III, perhaps to secure its future under the new regime. Having no heir, Colston donated his wealth to schools, hospitals and alms-houses (although the source of his wealth was questioned even in the eighteenth century).

In the 1920s, when Colston's links to the slave trade were exposed, his status as a virtuous son of the city was challenged. The controversy surrounding his statue entered a new stage in 2015 with the launch of a campaign for a rewording of the plaque. Then, in May 2018, a red, knitted ball and chain was added to the statue's feet by Faith M. and, on 18 October that year, Anti-Slavery Day, a public artwork depicted the bodies of a hundred enslaved people laid out on the pavement in front of the statue, as if in the hold of a ship.[1] Also in 2018, a second plaque was made, seen as giving a more balanced account of Colston, but vetoed a year later by the City's new Mayor, Marvin Rees as inadequate. Finally, in 2020, anti-Colston protest erupted during the Black Lives Matter campaign after the police killing of George Floyd in Minneapolis. On 7 June, the statue was defaced with red and blue graffiti, pulled down, dragged to the water's edge, and thrown into the harbour. The police took a tactical decision not to intervene.

The statue was retrieved by Council workers on 11 June, and placed in storage. A year later it was exhibited at M-Shed, a city history museum, in horizontal position with its graffiti in place, beside placards used in the protest on 7 June and panels of background information [Figure 6.1]. In a survey conducted by M-Shed, many people supported the statue's removal. There was also a reaction by far-Right populists who block-booked tickets for the exhibition (required due to Covid-19 safety precautions), not to use them but to stop others doing so, and calling for the statue's return to its original site. Since then, the exhibition has closed and Colston's bronze likeness is again in storage. The plinth, too, remains empty, cleaned of graffiti but as unlikely to support Colston again as to have (with its plaque) a new occupant. Perhaps the vacancy itself is a statement [Figure 6.2].

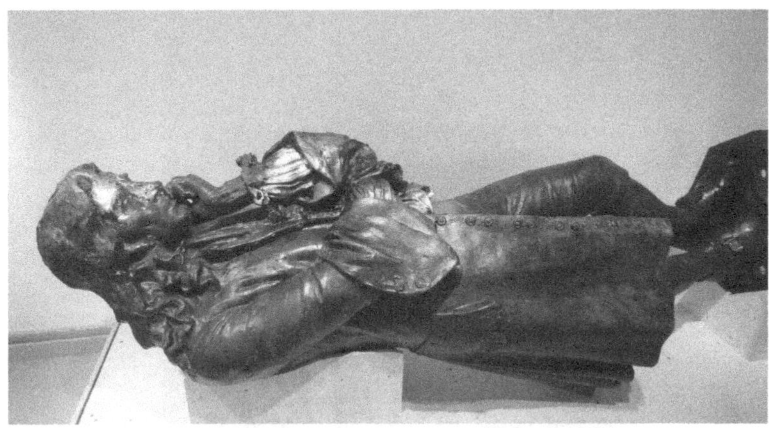

**Figure 6.1** Bristol, Colston statue exhibited at M-Shed, 2021

In 2020, British Home Secretary Pritti Patel described the removal of the statue on 7 June as 'utterly disgraceful', adding, 'it is not for mobs to tear down statues'.[2] This ignores a history of statues being removed from their plinths, such as a colossal Saddam Hussein in Baghdad on 9 April 2003, by US Marines who contacted foreign journalists to ensure coverage of the event by the global news-entertainment media. Another example was the destruction of a statue of Stalin in Budapest during the Hungarian Uprising in 1956, dragged across the tram lines, spat at and urinated on and broken up to mark what those involved hoped to be the end of tyranny, before Warsaw Pact troops crushed the uprising. I doubt commentators on the Right complained about those cases of de-accessioning.

Patel also ignores the history of words such as mob and riot, used by the authorities in the eighteenth and nineteenth century to dehumanise as well as criminalise people, mainly poor, who participated in public protest on issues from voting rights and Irish Home Rule to the unaffordability of bread (under the Corn Laws which fixed an artificially high grain price to benefit the landed gentry). Rees, speaking as a local black person and elected Mayor of Bristol, stated, 'I can't and won't pretend the statue of a slave trader in a city I was born and grew up in wasn't an affront', adding that Patel's remarks demonstrate 'an absolute lack of understanding'.[3] I would add that understanding

**Figure 6.2** Bristol, Colston statue: the empty plinth, 2021

involves both the specific history around Colston's representation in a public space, and the general function of statues as affirming structures of power-over and limiting efforts towards publics' power-to.

# Aftermaths

In 2020, Colston's was not the only statue to be removed from its plinth. In London, a statue of slave trader Robert Milligan was de-accessioned by Tower Hamlets Council, while around thirty other statues were removed across the city, and thirty-nine street and building names changed, following London mayor Sadiq Khan's call to no longer honour slave traders. In the United States, 170 statues of Confederate leaders have been removed since Floyd's death, although many remain.[4] Those statues were, typically, installed by elites who held power. As Walter Benjamin noted (Chapter 4), history is the victor's narrative.

There were cases of statues raised by public subscription (but not always as widely based as claimed). The bronze likeness of John Batchelor by James Milo Griffith, erected in the centre of Cardiff in 1866, for instance, commemorates a local Liberal politician, called the friend of freedom for his championing of radical causes. But this, like most statues, seems merely one of many now, at best a local landmark but largely disconnected in public awareness from the history represented. And there remains a massive under-representation of women and people of colour.

In Bristol, the question remains as to what should happen to the empty plinth. On 15 July 2020, sculptor Marc Quinn installed *A Surge of Power: Jen Reid*, a life-size bronze likeness of Black Lives Matter protestor Jen Reid with raised fist as 'a temporary public installation' on the plinth.[5] It was removed by the Council early the next morning but only after wide news and social media coverage. Reid, who briefly stood on the plinth on 7 June, states,

> I felt an overwhelming impulse to climb onto the plinth… Seeing the statue of Edward Colston thrown into the river felt like a truly historical moment: huge. When I stood there on the plinth I raised my arm in a Black Power salute. It was totally spontaneous… like an electrical charge of power was running through me. My immediate thoughts were for the enslaved people who died at the hands of Colston and to give them power. I wanted to give George Floyd power, I wanted to give power to black people like me who have suffered injustices and inequality. A surge of power out to them all.[6]

That is what Quinn sought to capture when a friend shared a picture of Reid (used in manufacturing the bronze figure): 'My first, instant, thought was how incredible it would be to make a sculpture of her… a moment I felt had to be materialized.'[7] The bronze was not intended as a permanent solution, simply an attempt to maintain public attention on the issue of institutionalised and systemic racism. If the work is sold, the profit will be donated to charities for black history and education nominated by Reid. Still, controversies continue. Robert Beckford, Professor of Black Theology at Birmingham University, writes, 'I'm worried that removing the symbols... is viewed as equivalent to anti-racist, institutional change.'[8]

Beckford alludes to removal as a cosmetic solution. There is a further issue in that systemic discrimination follows from the English national identity defended by Right-populists. It would be easy to say that this identity has no historical substance, is equivalent to an urban myth, because England is itself composite – merging populations from the pre-Roman to Saxon, Norman, Huguenot and other migrating groups up to present diverse ethnicities – but this does not mean the myth is ineffective. As Alex Niven writes, the manufacture of such an identity follows colonial conquests by which 'England was engaged in a radically countervailing campaign to make itself an inchoate, de-nationalized identity'.[9] He continues, 'the English un-nation is everywhere defined by a bizarre feeling of lack and emptiness', and that its driving forces, imperialism and capitalism, 'have always been such mysterious and immaterial entities so far as the majority of the population is concerned'.[10] Take away Empire, what remains? Not much except three devolved nations and the English reputation for alcoholism, football violence, deference to power and privilege, and racism. Making new public monuments is unlikely to change this.

# Should statues go?

The defacement and removal of public monuments did not, as said above, begin in Bristol in 2020. To look back further, two bronze equestrian statues of George II by Dutch sculptor John van Nost, made from the same mould, were commissioned in Ireland. One was erected on St Stephen's Green, Dublin in 1758, the other in Cork in 1760. The latter was gilded in 1781 to conceal surface deterioration, then moved to a new site in 1798. In 1862, after further deterioration and by then requiring wooden supports, it was toppled at night by unidentified individuals and thrown into the River Lee. A popular rhyme states,

> Vile George the First was reckoned
> Viler still George the Second
> No one ever said or heard

> A good word about George the Third
> When George the Fourth to Heaven ascended
> God be praised, the Georges ended.

The statue in Dublin was supported by an unusually high, three-tier plinth in an effort to deter vandalism. After the Battle of Waterloo in 1815, a proposal was made to replace it with a likeness of the Duke of Wellington, but that was erected in Phoenix Park. Nationalists argued for a statue of Daniel O'Connell, called The Liberator for his contribution to Catholic emancipation in the 1820s, but this, too, was unrealised. George II remained on his plinth. After the establishment of the Irish Free State, an attempt to blow up the statue in 1928 caused only superficial damage. But, on 13 May 1937, timed to coincide with George VI's coronation in London – the Georges had not ended – a larger bomb destroyed it.

I see no aesthetic loss, and would argue that it is logical to remove such relics of a displaced regime. Perhaps the act of removal, as part of a historical process of public agency, creates its own public memories; and, as in Bristol, an empty plinth has a certain eloquence. When a statue of Felix Dzerzhinsky, founder of the Soviet secret police (later the KGB), was removed from Lubyanka Square, Moscow, opposite the KGB head-quarters, in 1991, it was replaced by a bare stone from Solovki on the White Sea to remember the transportation of political prisoners to such remote camps. At the same time, after the dissolution of the Soviet Union, many Lenins, arm outstretched, his familiar peaked cap either on his head or in his hand (in one case both), were removed from their plinths and either put in storage or destroyed.

Although there were (mainly Western academic) objections to the removal of such statues as obliterating a history which should be remembered, Renata Salecl counters, 'no regime comes into power after a more or less violent upheaval without tearing down the pictures and statues of the previous rulers, especially if these rulers are perceived as totalitarian dictators'.[11] Citing the film *Disgraced Monuments* by Laura Mulvey and Mark Lewis (1992), which charted the removal of Soviet statues after 1991, Salecl notes that after the 1917 Revolution, most pedestals of Tsarist monuments remained while 'only the statue of the hero on top was changed'.[12] For Salecl, re-evaluations of the past have no need for the retention of public monuments which represent that past, concern for their preservation being no more than a nostalgic appropriation of history. Those who make this appropriation seem to think, she writes, that 'East Europeans are… not able to deal with their history in a civilised way', while the retention of monuments does not help dealing with 'the trauma' of those times.[13] I agree.

One response has been to exhibit statues in de-contextualised locations (which does not preclude the addition of contextual explanations). Colston's relocation to M-Shed is such a case. In the ex-East bloc the process has been, in a few cases, systematic. For example, in Budapest, and in a forest site in Lithuania, statues from the Soviet period are collected in outdoor museums. At Statue Park on the outskirts of Budapest, surrounded by electricity pylons, Lenin holds forth to air and trees, an object of photographic record, fixed in a vacant non-dialogue [Figure 6.3]. The trees seem to take the place of the white

**Figure 6.3** Statue Park, Budapest

walls of the modernist art museum, constructing the background as a value-free (in this case natural) screen which masks the world outside tourist-space just as the museum's white walls contain art-space. Lenin, it seems, is now part of the objectified array of goods offered for visual consumption in cultural tourism; postcards, CDs of Soviet music and other mementoes are sold in the shop. A similar array of post-Soviet nostalgia-kitsch is available at the forest park, called Stalin World, in Lithuania (where I bought a T-shirt and vodka glasses).

At Stalin World, founded by a millionaire who made his wealth from tinned mushrooms, there is enough space for each figure to occupy its own forest grove. The trees still act as equivalent to the white walls of the modern art museum, but there is no collective visual presence, only the isolation of statues on a boardwalk trail through the site, with periodic broadcasts of Soviet propaganda and songs from speakers on watch towers in the trees. A train previously used for deportations stands empty by the entrance, not an item of railway heritage so much as a marker, for those who recognise it, of oppression (when even the Lithuanian language was prohibited). The restaurant offers Soviet-style service; mushrooms are included in all main courses. There is a children's playground, so that families can stay all day. People have marriages there (illustrated in the site's own newspaper). But perhaps a major public for such sites is composed of Western academics and tourists such as myself, indulging in an *ostalgie* which ignores aspects of the real history obliquely represented there in a memory of a world in which there were, however imperfectly, two ideologies.

# A public realm?

Public attitudes change through processes of debate and confrontation rather than through the design of new monuments. A shift in British public opinion contributed to the ending of the slave trade in the 1830s. Today, a major realignment may be happening in response to both black history and the climate crisis. Public monuments play little part here, eclipsed by direct action and its distinct cultures. That does not deny a need to mark past histories, or to find ways of recognising the identities of marginalised social groups. But it does mean that shifts in how histories are understood, articulated in public debate, require more than the reproduction of the monument as a type of object.

An example is the Peterloo Massacre in Manchester in 1819. To begin with the facts: a peaceful meeting demanding an extension of voting rights in St Peter's Square, organised by the Manchester Patriotic Union, was charged by the mounted Manchester and Salford Yeomanry. Exits from the square were blocked by other units. The militia used sabres to cut down men, women and children, killing eighteen and wounding around 1,100. Afterwards, commemorative ceramics and textiles were sold to aid the families of victims. The event was reported in the press and in pamphlets such as *The Peterloo Massacre: A Faithful Narrative of the Events*, of which several print runs sold out at two pence a copy. The Prince Regent, future George IV, conveyed his support for the Yeomanry. The speakers, and the journalists who publicised the event, were prosecuted for sedition. Only recently, now that the event is called the Peterloo Massacre, could a memorial be made. The *Peterloo Memorial* designed by Jeremy Deller, and unveiled in 2019, consists of eleven concentric stone rings bearing the names of those killed. But I wonder if a stone monument is the best means of commemoration for radical histories, and whether performative means are more effective. For instance, Deller's 2001 filmed re-enactment of the Battle of Orgreave[14] – on 18 June 1984, during a national mine-workers strike – included 800 participants from the immediate locality and historical re-enactment societies. Through the film, the conflict between workers and a regime (under Mrs Thatcher) attempting to close industries with strong union representation continues in public consciousness. And, looking back to Peterloo, Shelley's poem *The Mask of Anarchy* was written when he heard the news of Peterloo, while living in Italy. Robert Poole writes, 'the cultural consequences of Peterloo were arguably as powerful as the political ones'.[15] Apart from Shelley's poem these included a plethora of satirical prints, cartoons and other verses circulated in popular editions.

To give another example, the Tolpuddle Martyrs – six members of an agricultural trade union transported to Australia in 1834 – are remembered by an annual Tolpuddle Festival organised by the Trades Union Congress. Rees spoke in the virtual event of 2021, beside folk singer Billy Bragg.[16] There is a Tolpuddle Martyrs Museum in the Memorial Cottages built in 1934, housing artefacts and documents; but while this offers (free) access to the history involved, the Festival is a living monument.

# New kinds of history?

Year One in the French Revolution indicated the revolutionary aspiration to begin history again, articulated in a public, performative culture (such as the procession to Marat's tomb, Chapter 1). Performative events offer an antithesis to monuments, their ephemerality being a refusal of the permanence of monuments which represents the claim to inevitability by which regimes sustain themselves via stone and bronze.

In Chapter 3, I cited Walter Benjamin's call for 'a real state of emergency', as the point of departure for a radically new kind of history.[17] Part of this is the refusal of linear narratives written from the viewpoint of the victors, which use a selective account to render history as if inevitable. An alternative is the sharing of stories, articulating experiences at street-level which convey, instead, a sense of co-presence. For modernist writers Blaise Cendrars and Guillaume Apollinaire, the suspension of linear time in tho fourth dimension – space-time, where/when everything happens simultaneously (Chapter 2) – creates a dimension in which not only are multiple sense-impressions reflected but also, perhaps, multiple possibilities are inherent.[18] Perhaps a different immersion in space-time, reconstructing the city through psychogeography, in course identifying traces of revolutionary pasts, occurs in Situationism in Paris in the 1960s.

The Situationists' predecessor, the Lettrist International, called for the closure of museums and distribution of their contents to bars and cafés across Paris. Simon Sadler writes of the Situationists as reading the city via alternative lenses, 'fascinated by buildings and places seemingly bypassed by religion, capitalism, and modernisation ... visible reminders of the relentless processes of history, of class struggle, of the contingency and impermanence of repressive regimes'.[19] The Situationists did not seek to replace old monuments with new ones, perhaps because they seemed uninteresting or irrelevant, but spent time wandoring the city, on foot or in taxis. This might seem like wasting time, which it was; but as a refusal of the regime of productivity, a purposeful purposelessness which undermines the norm of productivity in capitalism. Wasting time thereby becomes a form of revolt. The traces are few; a record remains in accounts from the time, and critical comment; it is easy to dismiss such practices as ephemeral, even wayward (and they were part-fuelled by wine), yet they contribute to a history of such practices of negation, each precedent widening the horizon of possibility. If praxis is the gaining of appropriate understandings of past conditions in order to produce insight on future possibilities for change, perhaps the Situationist *dérive* is a means of enacting such understandings to produce such insights. Or is this fanciful?

# New kinds of tactic

Benjamin wrote of a real state of emergency in which history is remade from the position of the oppressed. Similarly, a critical presence in the public realm is renewed by performative intervention (such as the events surrounding the removal of Colston's statue in Bristol). The ephemerality of such presences is a reflection of the always-incomplete processes by which a society determines its values. Just as importantly, I suggest, emerging cultures of direct action today enact communal values and collective aspirations able to give form to, rather than suppress, difference as a defining social condition in late (or post-) modernity. When statues require public emotional investment in values which are projected from a position of power-over, just as war memorials subsume personal grief in national memory, so the open, public enactment of alternative values (as in non-violent direct action) constitutes an alternative realm of social determination. Importantly, this refuses the instrumentalism by which power-over is maintained. For John Holloway, such self-determination is inherently rebellious, 'a ubiquitous moving against-and-beyond existing limits' whereby revolutionary theory and practice aim to 'distil or articulate this rebelliousness… refusing capital and projecting beyond it'.[20] In the next chapter, I review an exhibition containing the material traces of protest, and in Chapter 9 I look to the cultures of direct action. I end this chapter by suggesting that, just as Benjamin calls for a new kind of history, there is a need to refuse the norm of the public monument; to find new ways to enact the negotiation of the form a society takes, contingently and collectively.

Holloway asks, 'How can the world be changed without taking power?' and admits 'we do not know'.[21] He says of the Zapatistas in Mexico in the 1990s: 'such attempts are always contradictory and experimental, always in movement'.[22] This draws attention to a need to challenge instrumentalism, that is, the mechanism of determination from a position of power, when cause is power's will and effect is its application. Spontaneity, and the cultural forms of Simultaneity in the 1910s and Situationism in the 1960s, fracture this mechanism, if tangentially. Still, as Doris Sommer argues, 'the pleasure of art-making can be the energy that animates a politically possible project, for pushing impossibility past one and another checkpoint on a receding horizon, until the project achieves real political success'.[23] That would be utopian except that it is precisely what happens in alternative social movements and in cultural work which enacts (rather than signposts) alternative values.

# Chapter 7
# Exhibiting dissent

The previous chapter began with the overthrow of public monuments. In this chapter, I look more widely at protest cultures – their material traces in barricades, banners, badges and innovative technologies of occupation; and their social forms, such as communal living and collective decision-making – and at the overlap between political campaigns and art.

I begin by reviewing an exhibition, *Disobedient Objects*, at the Victoria & Albert Museum, London in 2014. This brought together objects representing the material culture of protest campaigns from the 1870s to the present. Protest culture is thereby reframed as cultural heritage, and the museum is reframed as a site of radical causes. I look at four cases of material from the exhibition, then cite Claire Bishop's writing on wider changes within art's institutions through participatory art. I move next to three recent examples of visual culture with a radical agenda, beginning with *Cloud Formations* by Forensic Architecture, exhibited at the Whitworth Art Gallery in Manchester in 2021. I discuss Eric Lesdema's collection of photographs, *Fortunes of War*, published with accompanying critical texts as a book in 2021; and end with *Freee Kiosk*, a participatory art project by Freee Art Collective in Northampton and other cities in 2016–17.

## Disobedient objects

*Disobedient Objects*, curated by Catherine Flood and Gavin Grindon, included exhibits such as a dock-workers' banner from the 1890s, suffragette china from 1910, a Black Panthers pamphlet from 1968, a photograph of anti-logging protest in New Zealand in 1978, anti-apartheid badges from the 1980s, coins stamped with the initials of para-military groups in Ireland during the Troubles, an image of the Women's Peace Camp at Greenham Common, dolls made by indigenous women in the Zapatista movement in Mexico in the 1990s, and documentation of climate crisis camps in the 2000s to 2010s. The curators say, 'exhibitions are moments of collective meaning-making. Bringing these objects and histories together… makes the museum a site for difficult questions.'[1] In one way, objects such as the miners' banner and suffragette china fit easily into the V&A's remit to conserve and exhibit material culture; in another way, as the curators say, protest banners and images of dissent stretch that remit. Four examples from the exhibition demonstrate the exhibition's temporal and geographical scope, and its crossing of conventional cultural categorisations.

To take the first example, the barricade is a temporary but material sign of insurrection. It was represented in *Disobedient Objects* by images from the 1848 Revolution in Paris and the Paris Commune of 1871. Used to block narrow streets in the city's working-class quarters, barricades were improvised constructions using paving slabs, furniture and such material as came to hand, but often supervised by skilled workers able to give them structural stability. Other improvised tactics included melting drainpipes to make bullet cases, with gunpowder made from lampblack and saltpetre scraped from walls; using shops as meeting places, and upper windows for sniper positions. In 1848, government forces devised a mobile barricade, ironically adopted by the Communards in 1871.[2] Bringing the story up to date, the exhibition also included a photograph of a barricade in protests against urban redevelopment in Gezi Park, Istanbul in 2013. In the catalogue, Marc Traugott writes that the barricade shows a capacity 'to operate not simply as a way of seeking refuge from physical assault but… as a means of claiming one's place in a revolutionary lineage'.[3] In other words, its material form is the outward sign of an immaterial (social, cultural and personal) alternative history.

Second, Occupy Wall Street began in New York in October 2011, spreading worldwide using social media and independent news feeds in a refusal of the soft power of consumer culture and, in a commitment to non-violence, the hard power of policing. The occupation of public spaces or buildings is a practical obstruction of business-as-usual, and a symbolic presence of a new society within the old. With Occupy it was a means of evolving effective methods of collective decision-making, and sustaining a new social formation. Occupy New York set up a General Assembly for open debate and decision-making, and became an equivalent of the state when volunteer doctors, nurses, psychologists and social workers offered free medical and welfare services. Occupy's material forms were, like barricades, improvised using found materials. Through the winter, heating was produced using cycle power. With time, Occupy sites around the world added improvised sheds and huts to their initial tent encampments. *Disobedient Objects* included a diagram for shelters made from wooden pallets, for example. But there were also immaterial initiatives, and the exhibition included documentation of the occupation of a television set designed to resemble the site of Occupy Zuccotti Park, on which the media company aimed to stage a re-enactment. Doubting the veracity of the media re-telling, Occupiers took over the set, asserting 'we are a movement not a TV plot'.[4]

The exhibition also showed images of climate camps in Britain, at Heathrow Airport (2007), Kingsnorth power station in Kent (2008), and Blackheath, London (2009), where metal and bamboo tripods were used to block approaches (adapting a prototype first used in anti-logging protests in Australia in 1989).[5] For Anna Feigenbaum, these camps are where 'disobedient design innovation' occurs. An anti-roads pamphlet says, 'Direct action is an evolving art form… innovate, improve and invent. Your imagination is the limit!'[6] Further examples of protest culture shown in *Disobedient Objects* included the use of circus and street theatre methods by the Clandestine Insurgent Rebel Clown Army (CIRCA), whose participants wore a mix of camouflage and circus costumes, using traditional clown tactics to ridicule policing methods and to defuse aggression.[7] Similarly, the anti-roads group Reclaim the Streets occupied a section of motorway outside London in 1996; the flowing skirts of dancers on stilts covered activists drilling holes in the road to symbolically plant trees.[8]

My third example from *Disobedient Objects* is a set of posters, maps and street signs made by *Grupo de Arte Callajero* (GAC) in Argentina from 1997 onwards. These marked the sites of detention centres under the military dictatorship which began with a coup in 1976, and the perpetrators' apartments. The signs resembled traffic signs, and the maps looked like public information (which they were, if unofficial), fly-posted around Buenos Aires for the thirtieth anniversary of the military coup. The maps carried the heading, in red, *Acqi Viven Genocidas* (Genocide Lives Here). Ana Longoni writes,

> A typical scene: on a day like any other in the late 1990s, somewhere in Buenos Aires, a group of young people are plastering the streets with posters... The posters show the face of a man who lives in the neighbourhood, giving his exact address, phone number and record: he is an army officer involved in numerous cases of illegal detention, torture and disappearance.... He is free, thanks to the so-called Pardon Laws.[9]

This is art as alternative politics, using graphic skills for political means. It remains art, but is outside the conventions of art's institutions. GAC were invited to show at the 2003 Venice biennale but Longoni notes that the invitation produced tensions within the group, and was eventually refused. She quotes Brian Holmes that 'the most interesting question within the artistic field then becomes: How to play the exhibition game in such a way that something real can actually be won.'[10]

My fourth example is a group of spoof newspapers: *Ignite*, produced by the London-based art-environment-democracy group Platform; and *Evading Standards*, by Reclaim the Streets [Figure 7.1]. *Ignite* appeared in December 1996 and November 1997, using the masthead of a defunct London free paper, *Tonight* and was distributed free to commuters at rail termini. It gave news on oil and pollution not carried by the mainstream press (at a time when printed newspapers were still a major form of news communication). Issue 1 carried the headline 'London company in dirty deal shock' over a story of the global oil company BP's links to the death of anti-oil protestors in Columbia; a side-column was headed 'Shell police accused of torture', and there was a competition to 'win a developing country', open to multinational companies.[11] Issue 2, titled *Smogbusters*, depicted a brown cloud consuming Canary Wharf, and included a recipe for smoked lungs. *Ignite 2* affirmed its status as art by acknowledging Arts Council funding, within Platform's *90% Crude* project 'a long-term investigation of the oil industry and transnational corporate culture' which asks how 'we might be living our lives in the first century of the next millennium'.[12]

**Figure 7.1** Spoof newspapers, *Ignite* and *Evading Standards* (author's collection)

Appearing shortly before the 1997 British general election, *Evading Standards* reflected a high level of voter cynicism by proclaiming, 'General Election Cancelled'.[10] A picture showed share traders in panic at falling prices (when trades were still done on the floor of the Stock Exchange). Produced for distribution at a march by striking dock workers, the copies were stored at a church in central London until, as a result of undercover police infiltration, they were seized. *Evading Standards* was hurriedly reprinted, with a picture of Labour leader Tony Blair selling burgers from a van. A two-page spread covered DIY media, economics and protest. The back page stated, 'The society that abolishes every adventure makes its own abolition the only possible adventure.'[14]

Reclaim the Streets produced the spoof paper using Platform's facilities, but Platform then disowned it, partly for legal reasons – *Evading Standards* mimicked the still trading *Evening Standard* (with a potential prospect of legal action) while *Tonight* had ceased trading and could not sue – but perhaps Platform were uncomfortable with the alignment of Reclaim the Streets to direct action.[15] Reclaim the Streets were, indeed, a single-issue campaigning organisation, part of the anti-roads protest movement of the 1990s; they used imaginative, performative tactics borrowed from visual and performance cultures – such as making a beach and setting out deckchairs in a London street, to stop traffic – but were not an art group. Platform, in contrast, began as and remained an art group, addressing political and (especially) environmental concerns. There is an overlap but also a gap. The contention over *Evading Standards* demonstrates this tension. Perhaps a benefit of the exhibition was that it put such tensions in retrospect.

# Institutional revolt?

With the opening of national museums in the nineteenth century, public access to culture was a means of defining and maintaining national identities. Today, museums are a sub-sector of the tourism industry. In both cases, inclusion in a museum collection or exhibition programme is evidence of status as part of a canon, while the cumulative cultural histories constituted by such canons contribute to what Herbert Marcuse called affirmative culture (Chapter 3), the conservative culture which reminds a society of what it is meant to remain. An exhibition such as *Disobedient Objects* redraws the definitions, challenging the idea as much as the content of a canon. This goes beyond efforts to expand museums' publics, although it may do that, by using material objects to draw attention to cultural and personal experiences of dissent. The curators of *Disobedient Objects* argue that while the material culture of non-privileged publics has been largely excluded from the history of collecting, 'objects have played a key role in social change alongside performance, music and the visual arts'.[16] Claire Bishop argues, too, that 'a more radical model of the museum is taking shape' which re-conceptualises 'the category of the contemporary'.[17]

Bishop cites the Museum of Contemporary Art Metelkova (MSUM), Ljubliana, Slovenia, designed by Groleger Arjitekti, located on a disused military base. Rather than looking to art as social balm, or being a repository of artefacts, MSUM exposes the violent disintegration of the Yugoslav Federation after 1989. Using digital archives and a documentary display, it accesses 'traditions that have historically proven to have emancipatory social potential'.[18] MSUM initiates critical engagement emphasising its local-in-the-global situation, not only in exhibitions but also through education programmes and a link to the activist group Anarhiv. For Bishop, MSUM indicates a critical turn within institutions parallel to a critical turn in participatory art. A desire to 'activate the audience' is 'a drive to emancipate it from a state of alienation induced by the dominant ideological order' under capitalism, totalitarian socialism or military dictatorship.[19]

Bishop cites Graciela Carnevale's project in *Ciclo de Arte Experimental* (Experimental Art Cycle) organised by Grupo de Artistas de Vanguardia (Avant-garde Artists Group) in Buenos Aires in 1968, during the military dictatorship. Carnevale prepared an empty room with a glass wall covered in posters; people were invited to enter as if to a gallery reception, but were locked in: 'I have taken prisoners… spectators have no choice; they are obliged, violently, to participate.'[20] After an hour, people started to remove posters but 'contrary to Carnevale's hopes, no one inside the gallery took action'.[21] Eventually, someone outside broke the glass. The audience escaped, some saying this ruined the work. Bishop comments,

> If European and North American participatory art is figured as a critique of spectacle in consumer capitalism and seeks to promote collective activity over individual passivity, then Argentinian artists… questioned this valorisation of first-hand immediacy, and combined this with opposition to the US-backed dictatorships, in which peaceful protest was abolished, and social trust shattered in a climate of constant suspicion.[22]

Out of context, Carnevale's gesture seems extreme. Yet, as if informed by Theodor Adorno's negative dialectics (Chapter 5), it refracts the oppression perpetrated by the regime while re-contextualising it as art. Without that re-categorisation I wonder if such a gesture might be seen merely as coercive; but I wonder, too, to whether that ethical consideration should apply in the same way within the art world as outside it. The work was re-produced as an exhibit in *Documenta 12*, Kassel in 2007: art playing the exhibition game (in Holmes's terms, above). Bishop contrasts Carnevale's project to the work of Brazilian theatre director Agosto Boal, in which actors enter ordinary places such as a restaurant to voice lines which provoke verbal exchanges. After their initial intervention, all is unscripted improvisation, a micro-society in formation (exhibiting its reactionary as well as progressive attitudes).

Apart from the ethics of intervention, another issue is whether the uncomfortable aspect of projects such as Carnevale's is commodified in art institutions through repeated staging. For instance, *La Monnaie Vivante* (*Living Currency*) curated by Pierre Bal-Blanc at Tate Modern in 2007 included Tania Bruguera's *Tatlin's Whisper #5* (2008): mounted police demonstrated crowd control tactics inside the Turbine Hall. The living currency here is the human body. For Bishop, the project shows how 'individual drives are subordinated to economic and social relations', within 'the entertainment industry's laws of transmission and reception'.[23] Tate Modern is an apt setting, seeking a competitive edge in the art world by staging edgy events. Esther Leslie writes, 'Tate is a brand that niche-markets art experience. Its galleries are showrooms. However, this is still art and not just business. The commodity must not show too glossy a face.'[24] Hence the spectacle of controlled risk. Leslie adds, 'the gallery invites a user-friendly hit-or-miss approach through its patronage of levelled values and jolly relativism'.[25]

Outside London, *Fracking Futures* by the art group HeHe (Helen Evans and Heiko Hanson) was exhibited at the Foundation for Art and Creative Technology (FACT), Liverpool, in 2013. Its aim was to critically refract the issue of fracking at a time when new licences were issued by the British government in the economically depressed North-West region. HeHe installed a semblance of a fracking site in FACT's ground-floor gallery, as a 'temporary, experimental drilling site for hydraulic fracking'.[26] It included a reduced-scale drilling rig. Floor tiles were ripped up and tremors felt. Dirty water bubbled in pools. A shaft of flame marked a periodic release of gas amid the noise of drilling. A sign stated that FACT was attempting energy self-sufficiency by exploiting reserves of shale gas under its site.

In fact, British law does not give property owners rights to mineral extraction; nonetheless, the explanatory statement continued (in another use of spoof tactics),

> HeHe have begun initial exploratory tests to extract shale gas through an innovative process known as fracking… Great care has been taken to ensure this process is safe and pose no threat to local ground water or the atmosphere. The operation… is being carried out with maximum transparency whilst maintaining audience safety.[27]

*Fracking Futures* used a theatrical suspension of disbelief to engage spectators in the issues surrounding fracking. Reports in the local newspaper *The Echo* accepted the invitation to believe: 'Liverpool residents and local businesses were said today to be reeling with a sense of shock as it was announced that fracking could take place in the centre of the city.'[28] One member of FACT's staff is quoted (anonymously, 'in a pub conversation') as being told to wear a hard hat to work: 'not the reason I came to work in the arts'.[29] FACT Director Mike Stubbs is quoted, too, as committing the organisation to carrying out risk assessment and public consultation in response to concerns raised by *The Echo*.

A mass protest at a fracking site at Balcombe, Sussex, in which Green Party MP Caroline Lucas participated, gained widespread media coverage and contributed to the withdrawal of the fracking company. But other licenses remained active, especially in the North-West. Fracking Futures did not aim directly at ending shale gas exploration so much as putting the issue in the public mind, using the semblance of neutrality often associated with technology and professional expertise as a device for public engagement.

## Cloud Studies

Forensic Architecture's *Cloud Studies,* shown at the Whitworth Art Gallery, Manchester in 2021 and Visual Carlow, Ireland in 2022 [Figure 7.2], brings public issues and documentary evidence into public focus through digital technologies. Forensic Architecture is a multi-disciplinary research agency investigating human rights violations imposed by states, police, military forces and companies. Based at Goldsmiths College, University of London, it collaborates with grassroots activists, legal teams, NGOs, and media organisations 'to carry out investigations with and on behalf of communities and individuals affected by conflict, police brutality, border regimes and environmental violence'.[30] *Cloud Studies* uses videos supplied by local activists, and computer-aided graphics and multi-image visualisation, to depict traces of toxic pollution resulting from aggression by state and corporate powers. A voice-over describes events in a tone which is descriptive, calm rather than judgemental. By exposing evidence accessibly as well as in forensic detail Forensic Architecture invites the spectator's engagement. The presentation on a wide screen takes around an hour, and traces the toxic effects which turn air into an assault weapon in locations from the Middle East to South-East Asia and elsewhere.

**Figure 7.2** Forensic Architecture, *Cloud Studies*, installation, The Bombing of Rafah, 2015, 3-channel film, model and print, installation, Whitworth Art Gallery, Manchester University, 2021 (courtesy of Forensic Architecture)

The exhibition occurred during the Manchester International Festival, whose website stated:

> Tear gas clouds spread poison where we gather, bomb clouds vaporise buildings, chemical weapons suffocate entire neighbourhoods and air pollution targets the marginalised. Our air is weaponised. Our clouds are toxic. From Palestine to Beirut, London to Indonesia and the US-Mexico border, Forensic Architecture investigates, explores and exposes how power reshapes the very air we breathe in this urgent and compelling exhibition.[31]

Incidentally, Peter Sloterdijk argues in *Terror from the Air* (2009) that new weapons of terror make the basic means of survival more explicit while 'new categories of attack… expose… new surfaces of vulnerability'.[32]

*Cloud Studies* is part of a long-term work of investigation into 'herbicidal warfare, tear gas, forest fires, oil and gas pollution and bomb attacks'.[33] It is politicised, but not aligned to any specific interest. Nonetheless, specific events require responses, in this case incidents in Gaza and Sheikh Jarra in May 2021, on which Forensic Architecture and the Whitworth Art Gallery agreed that the following text should be displayed on a sheet of paper by the entrance to the exhibition:

> While working on this exhibition, Forensic Architecture witnessed with horror yet another attack by Israel's occupation forces on Palestinians…. The ferocity of bombing produced man-made environmental disasters, with underground explosions leading to artificial earthquakes under Gaza City. At the same time, the targeting of agricultural storage facilities produced massive airquakes, with clouds of toxic fumes covering entire residential areas…. We honour the courage of Palestinians who continue to document and narrate events… and to struggle against this violence, apartheid and colonisation.[34]

This, with other aspects of *Cloud Studies* such as the depiction of herbicidal warfare in Gaza, produced an objection from a group of pro-Israeli lawyers that the project was anti-Israeli. The original statement at the exhibition entrance was removed, and a statement from the Jewish

Representative Council of Greater Manchester & Region was displayed beside a response from Forensic Architecture in a glass case outside the exhibition. After thousands of letters of protest, the Whitworth reinstated the original statement by the door. In 2022, the University terminated the museum Director's contract. More than a hundred academic staff signed a letter in protest, and twenty-three artists withdrew from British Art Show 9, staged in various venues (including the Whitworth) in Manchester.[35]

While *Fracking Futures* provoked through theatre, *Cloud Studies* exposed inconvenient and politically charged realities using a medium, video, which attests to veracity. For Matthew Fuller and Eyal Weizman (Director of Forensic Architecture), 'aestheticisation… is dialogic and collective, just like an emotion is relational and justice is assembled'.[36] They continue, 'Crucially, aesthetics also pertains to the intellect. It implies the ability to perceive. This can include the ability to recognise pain… to sense this in the political sphere.'[37] This, I felt from seeing *Cloud Studies* twice, was the case.

# Everyday conflict

The camera offers veracity. Of course, images are also contextualised and framed within specific narratives. Playing on how images are read, Lesdema's photographs and edited collection of critical essays in *Fortunes of War* illuminate 'the relationship between the human organism and its regulatory paradigm'.[38] The images range from peopled to empty spaces, long shots to close-ups, many of them enigmatic. But on close examination, empty spaces are not empty so much as replete with the traces of human intervention: the wreck of a tank on an expanse of sand, material traces of conflict in wasted places. Such presences render the scene uncanny, or the ordinariness of a scene emerges as bordering on the banal in its de-contextualised state. Each image implies a wider scope: 'detailed visual fractures' which express 'a seizure, a whole being divided'.[39] The remoteness of the lens as medium – a distancing in which the viewer is complicit – and the reproducibility of the photograph are means to dis-connection: the gaze facing what it cannot comprehend. Yet these are human-made conditions, as are the categories of perception they affirm. The outcome is 'a lack of isotopy: a term used in linguistics to consider a text as a coherent entity'.[40]

This emphasises the need for active interpretation. For Alfredo Cramerotti, who works in particle physics, 'we do not really know what happens when something materialises; what we can know is only how physical aspects of reality affect one another', and 'cultural form is also a matter of interaction'.[41] I take this to mean less that the spectator completes the image by reading it, more that the process of reading is always incomplete.

*New Greenham Common* (1997) shows an interior wall bearing a painted, one-dimensional, shadow-like image of a bomb falling through the ceiling, surrounded by fragments. Light falls on the floor, exposing a spreading pattern of dark against a pale surface. Is it a trace of carnage? Looking again, it is a flower-pattern on the carpet [Figure 7.3]. But the image is loaded, almost banal in its simplicity yet highly complex in the associations it evokes.

The building depicted is on the now disused US airbase of Greenham Common, where the Women's Peace Camp protested against the presence of nuclear-armed bombers from 1981 onwards. The missiles were withdrawn in 1991, and the site reverted to its pre-war status as parkland in 1997. The cold-war era control tower is now a visitor centre. The photograph draws on those histories, distilled into an image which combines reality with portent, and echoes of recent images of conflict scenes. To me it conveys the brittleness of society's hold on the valuing of life. After all (as it would have been), the bombs stored at Greenham might have been used, or the base hit in retaliation to a nuclear strike. And there are suppressed reports of a nuclear accident in 1958.[42] Returning to the image, the interior space, denoted by the carpet and what may be heating pipes on the wall, resonates with media images of the aftermath of bombing in civilian areas in Syria, drone attacks in Iraq and Afghanistan, and (as I write in March 2022) scenes of war crimes in Ukraine. The question is not where the conflict happened, more how all this is normalised.

For Andreas Philopoulos-Mihalopoulos, the distancing of the photographic medium is the message 'obliquely, yet relentlessly, haunting the bodies and the spaces between those bodies'.[43] Or, perhaps, haunting the absence of bodies in an everyday space which might have once been inhabited. Philopoulos-Mihalopoulos continues,

**Figure 7.3** Eric Lesdema, *New Greenham Common* (1997), c-type colour print from, *Fortunes of War* (courtesy E Lesdema)

Every single image booms with the question, planting in the viewer the compulsive urge to find the conflict… We are captured in search, in our turn performing what we unconsciously do anyway: ewe populate space with conflict and its violence, and we position ourselves in relation to it, whether this might be in the deep end or at a distance, taking sides or blocking the conflict rom our view.[44]

In this way, the photographic image shifts from recording the past, frozen in time, to hinting at the future: 'We anticipate future sadness, solitary death, ecological disaster, resource depletion… we have always been complicit with the waves of refugees, the unequal power distribution, the unjust emplacement of human and non-human bodies.'[45]

Those remarks locate the images in the realms of global capital, which is as distributed as cyberspace. Other images in *Fortunes of War* are identifiably from Europe and North America. Together, they shape the grid of perception. For Nicolette Barsdorf-Liebchen, *Fortunes of War* depicts a daily life 'peopled by ourselves: liberal, somewhat naïve perhaps, polite and acquiescent, purposeful or placid, in hapless self-delivery to unmentionable forces invisibly sequestered in plain sight'.[46]

# Not agreeing

Finally in this chapter, I move to the work of Freee Art Collective (Dave Beech, Andy Hewitt and Mel Jordan), and its critical position within, but extending the boundaries of, the art-world. Hewitt and Jordan, working as Hewitt+Jordan before joining Beech to form Freee, write, 'We do not see our role as offering cohesion for a largely self-interested, middle class cultural sector… [but] to reveal the inequalities within cultural systems.'[47] In the same text, titled *I Fail to Agree* (2004), they say,

> We try to emphasise that art and cultural systems are not benign; they are a significant part of society and are deeply affected by political and ideological agendas. We believe in the possibility of art having some agency in the development and support of democratic systems. The dominance of advanced capital makes it all the more vital to maintain art as a space for thinking and for contesting authority.[48]

The exhibition *Futurology* at the New Art Gallery, Walsall in 2004, and the accompanying publication (cited above), ask what the de-industrialised Black Country in the West Midlands could be like twenty years on. For many cultural agencies and local authorities, the desired future would have been summed up in the term 'urban regeneration', often, since the 1980s, *culturally-led* regeneration. The New Art Gallery is an example of a new cultural institution in an architecturally significant building, in a regeneration area. It has touring exhibitions, houses a collection and supports emerging local artists. While exhibiting in the new gallery, Hewitt+Jordan argue that little other than property values tends to be regenerated in urban regeneration schemes; they insist, 'Within the new cultural settlement, in which art is dominated by two massive emerging economic structures, namely culture-led regeneration and biennale style art fairs, art production has become a highly visible constituent of the enlarged culture industry of a global economy.'[49]

This responds to the subordination of art to the redevelopment sector's need to make a visible but cosmetic splash rather than addressing the deeper causes of uneven economic benefit, or the social implications of the immaterial economy and flexible employment. But it is, I suggest, also an updated form of arguments made by Theodor Adorno from the 1930s to 1960s, in effect that the function of the culture industry is to maintain capitalism. Adorno writes, 'the more industry exhausts what has already been perverted into commodities in the very name of culture, the more the omnipresence of culture proclaims itself'.[50] How do engaged art practices negotiate that minefield?

# Kiosks

Besides projects such as *Futurology*, Freee's work includes staged photographs for billboard display (one of which I discuss in Chapter 8), group recitals of manifestoes, badges, T shirts and football-style scarves bearing politicised messages, gallery installations including staged photographs and texts, and participatory events. One staged photograph, *Protest Drives History* (2008), depicts Freee holding a large orange banner stating those words, against wind and rain beside the dark waters of a quarry.[51] The resulting image has been used in various venues; and an exhibition at International Projects Space, Bourneville, Birmingham in 2007 included a large, wall-mounted text:

> The concept of public space, beloved of lonely myopic law-abiding right-on gushing morons, can only imagine the public as a mass of bodies.
> The concept of the public realm, preferred by shifty-piss-guzzling half-witted busy-body nerve-wracked self-serving technocrats, can only imagine the public as a mass to be administered.
> The concept of a public sphere, in the radical tradition of Critical Theory, imagines the public producing itself through the politicised acts of cultural exchange.[52]

A text on a gallery wall addresses spectators, and Freee regard gallery-goers as a potentially politicised constituency. But I want to focus here on their use of kiosks, extending from art-space to a potential public sphere whereby a public is not inherited (as in the case of gallery goers) but produces itself ephemerally, extending to several publics during the course of a project. Such a public changes, and elicits no expectation of coherence or consistency. Freee write,

> We started making kiosks which became structures in which we could activate conversations … Kiosks are more public, more intimate and more approachable than shops. They have a sociality that shops lack, by taking away the commercial profit-making utility of the kiosk we can capture its social dimension. The kiosk shows how socialism exists inside capitalism, trapped in financial exchanges we can see glimpses of a world of public exchange.[53]

Freee set up a series of kiosks as hubs for public articulation of values in 2016–17, in *The Medium Project* curated by Catherine Hemelryk for NN Contemporary Art, at York University for an arts and humanities research event, in Cardiff for *Cardiff With Culture: Visioning the City*, and at the Gallery, Milton Keynes. The first kiosks were simple wooden frames, with posters attached and a table for papers, badges and so forth. The design was significantly enhanced at Milton Keynes with expertise from the group FAT (Fashion Architecture Taste), made to resemble a glass-sided bus shelter on steps. Slogans are displayed on the glass, and a longer text on the steps. The kiosk houses activities such as badge making and collective manifesto readings as well as informal gatherings [Figure 7.4].

There are several, overlapping associations. The kiosk in the ex-East bloc was where people congregated to buy everyday items. Walter Benjamin saw decorative objects indicating an unsanctioned imagination in kiosks in Moscow in 1927 (Chapter 4). In British railway stations they were once ubiquitous as newsagents but are now mainly coffee outlets. And kiosks sell lottery tickets throughout Europe. Transposed to art, the form of the kiosk asserts a social presence. But social and political processes have their own aesthetics: the wit of verbal play on received conventions, of finding commonalities within the space of difference. For Freee, 'kiosks draw people in not exactly like the offer of a cup of tea … but they are our version of conviviality.'[54]

**Figure 7.4** Freee Art Collective, *Kiosk*, Northampton (courtesy Freee Art Collective)

The term 'conviviality' was used in urban design in the 1990s to evoke an ideal of liberal democracy as a space of informal communication and shared values, reflecting a notion of the classical Greek agora. One offshoot of this romancing of public space was the spread of small piazza-lite sites in urban redevelopment schemes. The aim may have been to foster nice conversations about the meaning of life, or how to run the world, as if people were waiting for such a site in order to be democratic. In reality, most of the seats in the nice piazzas belong to global fast-food chains. This is public-sphere-wash, and technocratic social management. Freee reclaim the space of a *potential* commons for a radical, as they see it a necessarily untidy, exchange.

In a dialogue with Charles Esche, Freee say they try to generate 'techniques of dissensus'.[55] Rather than encourage consensus, Freee use the kiosk as where people can disagree: 'the idea of neoliberalism comes out of liberal democracy and an idea of consensus – or populism – and forgets to think about dissensus'.[56] Free reject the mechanism of gallery-based education as liable to incorporation in cosmetic solutions to socio-economic issues. Instead, they see their pursuit of politics as 'an extension of the avant-garde idea of turning the aesthetic subject into a critical subject'.[57]

# Saying no

A century before *Kiosk #1* in Northampton, the Dadaists used performative disruption and non-coherence at the Café Voltaire, Zurich to subvert the values of a society of bourgeois nationalism, colonialism and industrialism, which produced the war in 1914. Works cited above by Carnevale and Bruguera do this in extreme ways in art-spaces. This constitutes, I suggest, a reconfiguring of the political sphere, if limited by an institution's policies and its public image (often as carefully crafted as the exhibits). Forensic Architecture fractures that institutional grid. And Freee recognise Jacques Rancière's argument that 'the essential work of politics is the configuration of its own space. It is to make the world of its subjects and its operations seen … the manifestation of dissensus as the presence of two worlds in one.'[58]

The work of art-politics is incomplete, just as single-issue campaigns are ephemeral: 'art promises a political accomplishment that it cannot satisfy, and thrives on that ambiguity'.[59] For Freee, all this means 'not giving up and always thinking there's an alternative'.[60] The constraining mechanisms by which power-over is maintained are not insuperable; human agency has the potential to rewrite the script of human futures.

This chapter has considered a few of many extant ways in which a refusal of the destructive norms of late capitalism is effected or leaves material traces in contemporary culture. I have not tried to weave the threads together in a pattern; to do so would be against the spirit of the work discussed. Nor do I wish to prescribe what artists or curators should do: that would put me in a position of power-over, writing a meta-narrative when the need is instead to find alternative scenarios and tactics whence power-over is replaced by power-to. Often, the means, such as occupations, street theatre, badges, placards and kiosks are ephemeral, as was the barricade. Similarly, receiving a spoof newspaper at a railway station may spark responses among a few commuters, even if most of the papers are discarded. This is not a limitation: the experience of being present among others of like mind is transformative. The traces of an alternative world, built according to alternative values, contribute cumulatively and collectively to the tipping point at which public attitudes shift towards a new norm. For Adorno, this means the alerting to opposition, against conformity and monopoly capital's elimination of objection:

[Art] transfigures the world into one in which conflict is still possible rather than revealing it as one in which the omnipotent power of production is beginning ever more obviously to repress such a possibility. It is a delicate question whether the liquidation of aesthetic intrication and development represents the liquidation of every last trace of resistance or rather the medium of its secret omnipresence.[61]

The question then is how alternative means of opposition refuse the instrumentalism which is the motif of power-over.

# Coda

At a seminar in the Geography department at the Open University several years ago I raised the question, how do societies change? It was dismissed as naive, which it is (but I see purposely naïve questions as open-ended and provocative, aware that societies change anyway, all the time). My interest was in how what seem to be minor (localised, small-scale) interruptions or shifts of frame contribute to wider changes in public attitudes by setting new precedents, and by being imaginative or witty. Such initiatives are often appreciated among Left audiences but seen as marginal due to their scale. Asking if they can be scaled up to the scope of a metropolitan city, however, is the wrong question. The benefit is not in a potential replication or standardisation on a grand scale, or as a formula, but precisely in their rooting in local conditions and engagement of local people. Art can help by lending visual means or drawing public attention to such projects; but its role is also to reshape the categories and codes through which realities are apprehended and comprehended. In that way, the process of social change resembles that of verbal language, always poised between its rules and the everyday uses which contravene but also change those rules.

This is the aspect of verbal language which informs Charles Darwin's theory of evolution. As Elizabeth Grosz writes, Darwin is interested in 'language's capacity to sustain, even require, ongoing change while maintaining its systematicity and integration, its correlated growth... at any given moment of time'.[62] This implies continuous renegotiation, not the pursuit of a trajectory: Grosz explains, 'Darwin provided a model of time and development that refuses any pre-given aim, goal, or destination… He refuses anything like the telos or directionality of the dialectic.'[63] For culture, this means institutions are re-moulded by their uses, beyond divides between the museum and the street, or art and the cultures of protest.

# Chapter 8
# Revolution is sublime

I ended Chapter 7 with a discussion of the use of kiosks as hubs for public engagement by Freee Art Collective (Dave Beech, Andy Hewitt and Mel Jordan). I begin here with another of their projects, *Revolution Is Sublime* (2009), a staged photograph. I examine the image, then situate it in relation to two related works by Freee, *Protest is Beautiful* (2006) and *Protest Drives History* (2008). I consider the manifesto which accompanies *Revolution Is Sublime*, intended for participatory readings, and move to a reconsideration of beauty and sublimity, citing Friedrich Schiller and Edmund Burke. I ask whether aesthetics offers an exit from the binds of an unfree society (for instance, in Schiller's idea of play), and whether art offers an alternative to the alienated labour of capitalism (drawing on other writing by Beech). Finally, looking for a transgression of capitalism's regime, I turn to *Bank Job* (2019) by artist Hilary Powell and film-maker Daniel Edelstyn, in which a gold-painted van was blown up and £1.2 million of debts cancelled. Coincidentally, *Revolution Is Sublime* and *Bank Job* are both set in Walthamstow, East London.

## Revolution is sublime

*Revolution Is Sublime* is a staged photograph suitable for billboard reproduction and gallery exhibition. In a secluded garden in Walthamstow, the artists carry a large circular mirror bearing the text Revolution Is Sublime [Figure 8.1]. The mirror is plastic, lighter and less fragile than glass, but the poses suggest weight as the artists manoeuvre it into its sylvan setting.

**Figure 8.1** Freee Art collective, *Revolution Is Sublime* (2009), staged photograph (courtesy Freee Art Collective)

In one way, the image is economical: set in a shallow space, with one central figure group; in another way, it is complex, everything in it appearing the result of deliberation, like the site, setting up a dialectics of figure-ground, image-text and culture-nature. The foliage suggests the forest glade of neo-classical art where nymphs appear and myths are re-played, in a genre of figure-in-landscape. But this is not Nicolas Poussin's Roman Campagna, but an early-twenty-first-century, post-industrial edge-land beside the river Ching, the gravel bank and shallow water of which occupy the lower part of the image. Above, the figures occupy the centre, trees and sky the top. The scene's balanced asymmetry is articulated by the text on the mirror but its meaning is ambivalent, as much framed by its natural surroundings as those surroundings are lent additional loading by the text.

If the image's composition alludes, perhaps obliquely, to neo-classical painting, art is multi-valent, and the image is also poised between twenty-first-century London and an aesthetic realm of imaginary reality, a juxtaposition heightened by photography's claim to realism. Whichever way I look at it, I return to the three dialectical dualisms: figure-ground, image-text and culture-nature. Or perhaps the photographic medium adds a fourth, real-artificial. Thinking freely, I take the trees to represent nature's cycle of growth and decay, admitting that nature is a cultural construct. I read the three figures in contemporary casual clothing as locating the scene in the present and the mundane, but equally representing their agency to intervene in the conditions of their lives (and in art). Another dialectic emerges: cyclic-linear (historical) time; but I also recall Walter Benjamin's observation that, in the 1830 Revolution in Paris, revolutionaries shot the public clocks which imposed linear time and regimented the working day. Does agency require that time, too, or does the image say that cyclic time is linear time's alterity? Of course, it is a fine day: Jordan is wearing sunglasses.

I cannot speak for the artists, and am projecting my own critical inheritance onto the work. What lingers is how the image engenders potentially creative dualisms. Not only cyclic-linear time, or nature-culture, but also structure-agency, and the stasis-dynamism of the flowing river and the photograph fixed forever. But why do they carry the mirror to a secluded woodland, not a gallery or public place? Is it to hide it, or to enlist the resurgence of nature in support of revolution?

In neo-classical thought, nature is the realm of both beauty as delight, and the sublime as licensed danger. Nature exhibits growth and decay as inseparable phases of a natural cycle, and the sublime is a defence against the inherent intimation of mortality. Returning to the image, the artists, not in Arcadia but in Walthamstow, venture into the margin of a green, peri-urban site. Beech and Jordan hold the disc from behind; Hewitt faces into the scene as if – a gesture from Romantic art – inviting the viewer to join them. A low-left patch of light is one point on a diagonal which intersects the mirror on route to light on the trees, top-right. The mirror rises slightly from this diagonal, reflecting the artists' faces at its edges. In contrast to this naturalness, the inscription alludes to permanence in a system of meanings in which each term is defined in relation to another. The sublime is non-beautiful; and all the terms are carried, literally and metaphorically, by the artists.

I may be over-interpreting the image. Jordan says, 'we always said we never laboured over these works but we were aware of what might happen in the image and what we might do with it'.[1] But I know that Freee used cardboard cut-outs to test poses and angles before the photograph was taken.[2] Besides, pictorial analysis is a means of entering the drama which the work initiates. For instance, diagonals in Romantic painting convey the dynamism of a changing world. In *Revolution Is Sublime*, the way the inscription rises suggests human agency; and perhaps the message of natural decay, as leaves fall and the water in the river runs away, challenges the maintenance of neoliberalism as much as, in the eighteenth and nineteenth centuries, it questioned the permanence of imperial power.

# Changing the world...

As said above, *Revolution Is Sublime* is the third in a sequence of staged photographs, with *Protest Is Beautiful* and *Protest Drives History*. In *Protest Is Beautiful*, the artists hold a banner on which artificial sunflowers state the title. There are two versions, one in a sun-lit meadow, and one on a blue background. For me (an art student in London from 1967 to 1971), the image is reminiscent of flower power; but that reminds me, too, that Herbert Marcuse said that flowers alone have no power, only that of the people who 'care for them against aggression and destruction'.[3] In *Protest Drives History* (on which I write elsewhere),[4] the artists struggle to hold another banner against wind and rain, by the dark waters of a quarry (Bayston Hill, Shropshire, the largest quarry in England). The artists stand, refusing to give in to the elements (although the weather was not predicted in planning the work).

I am not sure if protest does *drive* history, rather than being one force within it (the others being the state and capital); but the image reminds me of histories of refusal, and the need to challenge narratives of power, incidentally part of the message of Leo Tolstoy's *War and Peace* (1869). Here in the wind-swept quarry, protest insists that history is not inevitable but *produced*. At a more mundane level, the banner is orange because that was the colour of the roll of canvas available in the market at a price within the project's budget; the letters are blue because that is the complementary colour: another axis, sublime-mundane.

For Kim Charnley, Freee's work represents 'a self-conscious interrogation of the legacy of the revolutionary project of the avant-garde and its translation into contemporary art'.[5] An implication of this position is that radical artists relinquish the art world's institutions (such as the art market and its informal but strong links to public sector museums). That removal from art's institutions would lead to self-marginalisation except that the point is to refuse the normalisation of those structures, using art's agency to create alternative scenarios. In this way, modernism's autonomy is politicised, taking over the means of art's production and distribution (reception being the work of engaged spectators). Charnley points out, too, that Freee's work is informed by the idea of a public sphere developed by Jürgen Habermas, 'said to include institutions including the press, the arts, and education, where ideas and issues … are debated'.[6] For me, Habermas's model is idealised, like a university department on a good day, yet the *idea* of a public sphere remains a vital aspiration, and one to which Freee's work contributes. In any case, as Charnley notes, protest is integral to a real public sphere: 'protests articulate demands that then become part of the deliberation that shapes the polity'.[7]

# Is revolution sublime?

The mirror from *Revolution Is Sublime* was exhibited with the large-scale photograph in the exhibition *The Peckham Experiment*, curated by Jo David and Rachael House, at Camberwell Art Space, London in 2009 [Figure 8.2]. The photographic image is reflected in the mirror. A manifesto published alongside the work, begins,

> Revolution is sublime, but the work of the revolution will be mundane. When a socialist government is in power we will hand over all the key organisational decisions to the workers. The rich and powerful will not simply applaud and stand to one side while the workers take over … we will have to establish a state that backs up the workers and the poor while undermining and penalising the rich and powerful.[8]

The text goes on, conjuring the internal and external conflicts of the Bolshevik Revolution of 1917, that emancipation begins in 'the confiscation of the landed estates, the introduction of workers' control of the workplace and the nationalisation of the banks', and control of all monopolies.[9] Then workers will use modern technology to realise a life of ease in which they work for themselves and provide for all. Military measures will deal with 'exploiters'.[10]

**Figure 8.2** Freee Art Collective, *Revolution Is Sublime*, installation view (courtesy Freee Art Collective)

Part of Freee's practice is to organise public readings of manifestoes. Participants say aloud all or part of the text, as they see fit. These are small-scale gatherings, and enable dialogue in a situation poised between private and public scales. Perhaps with this in mind, this text includes an update for the twenty-first century in referring to 'carers both paid and unpaid! Unemployed and exploited people!' who are invited to take over the means of production and distribution: 'the road to the victory of socialism... over all exploitation, over all poverty and debt!'[11] The Paris Commune is cited as a precedent: 'initiative, independence, freedom of action and vigour from below'.[12] Everyone will enjoy 'the best food available' and have beautiful clothes.[13] I hope they buy them from Oxfam, not new.

I read the manifesto as suspended between the histories of revolution – the organised mass overthrow of the state – and a post-industrial Left re-grouping, after the revolutions of the eighteenth, nineteenth and twentieth centuries did not produce free societies, or really-existing Socialism. The revolutionary past of crowds carrying banners, singing revolutionary songs and overthrowing the regime is encapsulated in history now. Yet the public readings of the manifesto may contribute towards an emerging, radical contemporary realm of agonistic politics. In such a realm, instead of following a predetermined model of the new (as in the leadership of the Party), the future is yet to be determined, just as the process is always incomplete.

Within the open-ended, multiple contestations of that process of social formation, a refusal of work undermines a system built on productivity. This informed Situationism in Paris in the 1960s, when purposeless wandering refused productivity (Chapter 7); and the Holy Monday – everyday as holiday – as depicted in Georges Seurat's *Bathers* and *Sunday at the Grande-Jatte* (Chapter 1). Elsewhere, Beech discusses this refusal under the heading of autonomy, citing André Gorz to effect that work is 'an historical tendency with radical implications, not least because this implies both a "disaffection from work" and an abandonment of the traditional trade union demand for higher wages'.[14] Citing Kathy Weeks, Beech concludes,

> The refusal of work is a political slogan that has the potential to unite communists, anarchists, socialists, libertarians, bohemians and aesthetes insofar as it promises 'to reduce the time spent at work, thereby offering the possibility to pursue opportunities for pleasure and creativity that are outside the economic realm of production.'[15]

A related demand appears in Franco Berardi's idea that alienation now takes the form of a 'progressive mentalisation of working processes', again leading to a call to refuse to work.[16] This can be set beside Isabel Lorey's argument (Chapter 4) that the conditions of precarious employment under neoliberalism bind those afflicted in coercive subjection, requiring an exit outside the system. To re-enliven cooperation is thus revolutionary. Beech summarises, from Berardi and Paolo Virno, that the 'micropolitics of work… proposes that cognitive workers are alienated by bringing their personality to the workplace'.[17]

That has implications for art when a premium is put on individuality, as in the importance of the signature, a privileging withdrawn in collective production. And in contrast to bourgeois individualism, the art produced in the years immediately following the Bolshevik Revolution merges image and text, art and political slogan, idealism and expediency. In the conditions of war-Communism, Tim Clark writes, 'Every statement of fact is haunted by questions of motive, origin and ideology. What for one set of experts is a chain of improvised expedients, patched together from day to disastrous day, is for another a process driven from start to finish by certain political imperatives.'[18] Clark cites a propaganda board by El Lissitzky: 'It was because War Communism was both chaos and rationality, both apocalypse and utopia… that it gave rise to the modernism we are looking at,' which re-maps reality via visual and verbal language; as El Lissitzky said, 'do not map the world, transfigure it… take the mood of euphoria and desperation, and finally synthesise the two terms'.[19] Clark adds, 'Modernism thrives on situations of signifying collapse, of situations where… a transvaluation of values is about to take place.'[20]

That distinctive phrase, a transvaluation of values, was used by Marcuse in London in 1967 at the Dialectics of Liberation Congress (where he addressed flower-power). I do not know if Clark was there but Marcuse says,

> To give sensitivity and sensibility their own right is, I think, one of the basic goals of integral socialism. These are the qualitatively different features of a free society. They presuppose… a total trans-valuation of values, a new anthropology. They presuppose a type of man [sic] who rejects the performance principles… who has rid himself of the aggressiveness and brutality that are inherent in the organisation of established society… [and] who is biologically incapable of fighting wars and creating suffering… who has a good conscience of joy and pleasure, and who works, collectively and individually, for a social and natural environment in which such an existence becomes possible.[21]

In *An Essay on Liberation*, Marcuse looks to 'the rebellion of the young intelligentsia' for whom imagination is political action.[22] This aesthetic reality, or 'society as a work of art',[23] returns my attention to *Protest Is Beautiful*. Forty years after flower power, Freee (quite independently, born later) re-create that optimism, standing in the sunlit meadow to insist on what the banner says colloquially and philosophically. Protest *is* beautiful; revolution *is* sublime; and protest prefigures revolution, to portend both delight and fear as situations shift unpredictably.

# Sublime anticipation, aesthetic play

The reactions of philosophers to the French Revolution of 1789 were ambivalent. Romantic poets saw the end of tyranny and a terrifying violence. Burke felt both wonder and awe. Aware of civil unrest, foreign wars and social divisions in Georgian Britain, he retreats to a realm constructed by beauty and the sublime to escape those conflicts. Burke castigates revolutionary violence in *Reflections on the Revolutions in France* (1790), but this extends from arguments made earlier in *Philosophical Enquiry into the Sublime and the Beautiful* (1756). There, he affirms a hierarchic social structure as a natural order in which subjects enjoy subjection. Jason Frank interprets Burke's theory as 'an affective device for the naturalisation of order and rank in human society'.[24] Burke sees an unchanging nature as providing relief from history's vicissitudes, while sensory experience offers the universal basis for aesthetic appreciation. This reflects the rise of the natural sciences, and a search for a secular basis (in place of religious explanations) from which to investigate reality. But Burke rejects Kantian abstraction:

> Whenever the wisdom of our Creator intended that we should be affected… he [sic] did not confide the execution of his design to the languid and precarious operation of our reason but he endowed it with powers and properties that… captivate the soul before the understanding is ready either to join with them or to oppose them.[25]

For Burke, beauty is associated with procreation, the society of others and sympathy; the sublime with the pains of solitude, fear and self-preservation. Burke seems to be captivated by self-preservation. That is why he neutralises horror within the aesthetic, as 'delightful horror'.[26]

Burke means delight in a specific way, as enlivening or character-building, building a 'sense of fortitude', not as mere pleasure.[27] This excess beyond intellect is his way to cope with fear: no one drowns in a painting of a storm at sea.

Licensed danger informs the design of eighteenth-century landscaped parks, with Roman, Greek or Egyptian ruins, and shaded grottoes. Contrasting with long vistas, these enclosing spaces offer not just shade but a glimpse of mortality. Christopher Woodward stresses the latter,

> Ladies were expected to shiver with horror as the path disappeared into a cold, dark grotto with a waterfall thundering in the invisible distance. Emerging into a gentle valley grazed by sheep they paused on the steps of a classical temple, and a gentleman in the party might be moved to declaim Virgil's *Georgics*.[28]

Simon Pugh challenges such a regression to an archaic past against present emergencies, 'The simulated regression to a primitive age does nothing to question the permanent crises that were beginning to be recognised as a feature of capitalism.'[29] All of which was both informed by and the intention of Burke's character-building aesthetic of fortitude, affirming the ambivalence of an art which inherits a history of being haunted by the fear of conflict.

Burke was a reactionary defender of hierarchies, rejecting ideas such as the social contract. For him, aesthetics upholds tradition:

> Always acting as if in the presence of canonised forefathers, the spirit of freedom, leading in itself to misrule and excess, is tempered with an awful gravity… By this means our liberty becomes a noble freedom. It carries an imposing and majestic aspect. It has a pedigree and illustrious ancestors. It has its bearings and its ensigns armorial. It has its gallery of portraits, its monumental inscriptions… [30]

That sounds like a baronial house with its array of portraits. But he was spellbound by the French Revolution, 'suspended, by our astonishment at the wonderful spectacle… what spectators, and what actors! England gazing with astonishment at a French struggle for liberty and not knowing whether to blame or applaud!'[31] But his reaction to the

Terror in 1793 produces his reconfiguration of the sublime in terms of subservience and patriotism, or joyful coercion. As Mary Woolstonecraft pointed out, this was present in his earlier writing, too, but secondary then to the sublime as the appearance of immensity in nature. In the end, Burke falters in face of 'the contagious sensibility of beginning anew'.[32] Thomas Paine, author of *The Rights of Man* [sic] (1791), saw Burke's sublime ideal as a ridiculous intrusion on political thought. Yet for Burke, in Frank's reading, 'the self-regarding spectacle of a people – at once actors and spectators, beholding their own democratic capacities for wilful innovation and being further enlivened by the sight, was the threatening essence of the radical democratic sublime'.[33]

For Schiller, in a very different response to the same conditions around 1793, aesthetics is not a retreat but a means *to address* the violence of revolution. *On the Aesthetic Education of Man* [sic] is, as published, a revision of a series of twenty-seven letters to his patron, Prince Friedrich-Christian of Schleswig-Holstein-Augustenburg. Schiller is, like Burke, critical of Kant's *Critique of Judgement* (1790), with its balancing act of sensibility and rationality. In place of this he established Reason as the basis for human freedom, ideally reflected in the liberal (bourgeois) state. But, in the second letter, Schiller says, 'The course of events has given the spirit of the age a direction which threatens to remove it … from the art of the Ideal.'[34] This is his reaction to the execution of Louis XVI: 'I haven't been able to look at the papers … I feel so sickened by these abominable butchers.'[35]

Schiller's desire for freedom in the rational state which the Revolution initially articulates is mediated by a fear of disorder. In the fifth letter he says, 'arbitrary rule is unmasked and … can no longer … maintain the appearance of dignity', while 'there seems to be a physical possibility of setting law upon the throne, of honouring man [sic] … as an end in himself, and making true freedom the basis of political action'.[36] So far, he coincidentally echoes Burke. But a further problem takes him in a new direction as art soars beyond reality, 'for Art is a daughter of Freedom, and takes her orders from the necessity inherent in minds, not from the exigencies of matter'.[37] Art, thus positioned, is the manifestation of an imagined reality, parallel to but separate from ordinary reality. It is accessed, not by perception, but in mental (inner) sight.

Despite the title, the letters do not offer a pedagogy; their purpose is 'a sober exploration of problems which have become the focus of... the human sciences today', located at an intersection of physiology, psychology, philosophy and aesthetics, and of intellectual and moral insights 'gained through bodily exploration of the physical environment'.[38] That is, the human mind awakes, 'out of the long slumber of the senses',[39] to find the inner force of intellect in which everyone has an inherent ideal, the archetype of a human being, so that it is life's task to be 'in harmony with the unchanging unity of this ideal'.[40] In the ninth letter, Schiller asserts, 'Art cannot falsify.'[41] He accepts that art is subject to the 'spirit of the age', yet, 'truth lives on in the illusion of Art, and it is from this copy, or after-image, that the original image will once again be restored'.[42] Art goes ahead: 'before Truth's triumphant light... the poet's imagination will intercept its rays, and the peaks of humanity will be radiant while the dews of night still linger in the valley'.[43] This is more radical than Burke's aesthetic retreat. Although expressed in Romantic terms, Schiller's letters offer precedents for the modernist avant-garde: art carries an imagined reality, an idea not incompatible with Marcuse's fusion of Idealism and a revised Marxism in *The Aesthetic Dimension* (1978):

> The world intended in art is never... the given world of everyday reality, but neither is it a world of mere fantasy, illusion and so on. It contains nothing that does not also exist in the given reality... the world of a work of art is unreal... But it is unreal not because it is less, but because it is more as well as qualitatively other than the established reality.[44]

Or, as Schiller says, a dynamic state enables social organisation by reconciling divergent interests; an ethical state makes this morally necessary; and an aesthetic state 'can make it real, because it consummates the will of the whole through the nature of the individual.... Beauty alone can confer... a social character.'[45]

Reading Schiller's letters on aesthetics anachronistically through the lenses of Dialectical Materialism and critical theory, I could say he politicises aesthetics by introducing a vision of a better life. Reconsidering this, I borrow Schiller's model of reconciliation to read – instead of dualism – a creative axis of meaning between aesthetics and politics, where the work of theory is done, gaining and conveying insights towards informed practices. But the question is how art intervenes: leading the led, as with the avant-garde? Or...

# Revolutionary art?

One idea is that art is a model of non-alienating labour, from which other forms of labour learn. Beech argues against this, saying, 'art's hostility to capitalism… has precapitalist roots in the aristocratic scorn of… manual labour', developing from the elevation of painting and sculpture within the hierarchy of the liberal arts.[46] The divide between work and pleasure is, for Beech, collapsed under Communism, while Berardi's idea of a refusal of work is a pre-instantiation of that collapse. Beech notes that Berardi's idea has informed cultural activism within market conditions; and concludes that although post-capitalism does not merge art and work within the processes of production, mediation and marketing, still, art may yet be aligned to 'a hostility to capitalism… rooted in the rejection of capital accumulation as the rationale for living'.[47] I would add, citing Free Art Collective as example, that co-production in artists' groups enables art-work to be revolutionary in, at least, rejection of the bourgeois premium on authorship. This may be a more helpful insight than saying art is non-alienating labour, when mainstream art production is either subservient to art's institutions, or has become a new sub-category of blue-chip investment.

Cooperative art-working rejects the Romantic notion of the lone artist, who is in reality part of a system of production and distribution. As a collective, Freee exert their cultural agency in systems of verbal meanings and political allegiances, and via open-ended, participatory processes of articulation. This extends artists' efforts to take over the means of distribution which began with non-juried (Independent) salon exhibitions in Paris in the 1880s, and led to the Secession movements in Vienna, Berlin and Munich in the 1890s, a tendency more recently renewed in the utilisation of redundant industrial buildings as artist' studios.[48]

# Dualisms and paradoxes

*Revolution Is Sublime* depicts three figures in a landscape. The juxtaposition of figures and landscape runs through Neo-Classical and Romantic art, constructing a dualism of agency and ordering. The diagonals in Romantic painting upset that equilibrium, as they do in *Revolution Is Sublime*. But *Revolution Is Sublime* is not sited in a landscaped park but, as said, in a post-industrial urban edge-land. This may signify a distancing of revolution as mass uprising – the working class no longer drives change, and the solidarity which once grew in factories is denied by the immaterial economy and precarious employment – when other kinds of tactic, such as direct action, replace the model of class conflict. In a Romantic way, the text on the mirror disrupts the landscape background; yet as edge-land, like weeds in a pavement, that background paradoxically operates as a limitation of human agency in the conditions of complexity which characterise post-industrial societies.

The mirror in *Revolution Is Sublime* is held in place through a balancing act of experience and aspiration. Revolution is distanced but not abandoned, almost as an image of ancestral figuration. Marcuse opens *The Aesthetic Dimension* by saying that reality can be changed only through radical political praxis; and that a concern with aesthetics as a realm of fiction, 'where exiting conditions are changed and overcome only in the realm of the imagination'[49] requires justification. But he also holds that art addresses a truth and experience which are 'essential components of revolution'.[50]

This aligns to Schiller's emphasis on play. For Schiller, play is *the* imaginative act, the re-framing of reality as something beyond appearances which shapes the, 'spirit of imitation', while realizing that semblance is 'autonomous'.[51] Extending from this, freedom exists in the realm of imagination, but,

> The poet transgresses his [sic] proper limits, alike when he attributes existence to his ideal world, as when he aims at bringing about some determinate existence by means of it. For he can bring neither … to pass without exceeding his rights as a poet (encroaching with his ideal upon the territory of experience, and presuming to determine actual existence by means of what is merely possible) or surrendering his rights as a poet (allowing experience to encroach upon the territory of the ideal, and restricting the possible to the conditions of the actual.[52]

The dilemma resembles that of art's aesthetic and social dimensions in critical theory. There is no resolution, only the introduction of a third polarity denoted by imagination as a play 'of freely associated ideas'.[53] Then, 'from this play … which is still of a wholly material kind, and to be explained by purely natural laws, the imagination, in its attempt at a free form, finally makes the leap to aesthetic play'.[54] The reasoning is a little slippery, and supported by analogies such as 'uncoordinated leaps of joy turn into dance'.[55] Yet the point remains that there is a way to exit the bind of material conditions. Or, as Marx later said, to change the conditions which constitute this bind. Schiller, moreover, sees play as transgressing the categories of normality. He worries, post-1793, that it can be chaotic; hence a need for rational moderation;[56] but asserts, 'beauty provides us with triumphant proof that passivity by no means excludes activity'.[57] In the 1960s, play was taken up as a radical idea by artists designing adventure playgrounds. Now, in a period of direct action, how does art realise that radical leap?

# Bank Job

Freee's manifesto (above) states, 'Revolution is sublime, but the work of the revolution will be mundane.'[58] Taking mundane to pertain to ordinary lives, not as a pejorative term, I turn to *Bank Job*, a project intervening in financial markets, producing a film and a book, and seen by Powell and Edelstyn as undermining capitalism. The background is the financial services crash of 2008, when bundles of unpaid debt advanced by unscrupulous lenders to people who could never pay (called sub-prime mortgages) were sold on as assets below face value. In 2008, they lost their currency. Edelstyn writes that by over-valuing such bundles, dealers 'aided and abetted the banks in selling junk debt to investors, making profits out of mortgages that were financial time bombs. The scale of the banking fraud was epic and unprecedented.'[59] To prevent the disintegration of the global banking system, very large sums of public money were used to bail out private-sector financial institutions. Edelstyn continues that the crisis entrenched the power of the financial sector while 'diminishing that of the state and in turn people'.[60] Although sub-prime mortgages have largely disappeared, the sector of dubious debt has grown in payday lending whereby people who do not have enough money for necessities are forced to borrow at exorbitant rates from lenders who capitalise on poverty, multiplying the debt in interest. Powell and Edelstyn opposed this scenario by opening an alternative bank in Walthamstow, with help from a wide network of contributors and supporters.

*Bank Job* has been called 'a kind of art-installation-meets-community activism project'.[61] It combines these aspects with film-making, deriving insights from previously filming debt resistance activism in Los Angeles and New Yok, and the Rolling Jubilee Fund which bought and cancelled $3.8 million worth of student debt. Powell and Edelstyn returned to London to begin scripting and producing a film in which a golden Ford transit van containing paper signifying £1.2 million worth of debt is blown up on waste-ground in sight of Canary Wharf.

The site for the alternative bank, Hoe Street Central Bank (HSCB), on Hoe Street, was aptly a building previously housing a branch of the Cooperative Bank. Powell, Edelstyn and a group of collaborators set up a press and printed their own money, sold as art, as a means to buy and cancel the debts of local people. Their notes bear the faces of a local community youth activist, a local head teacher, a local food bank organiser, and a family providing hot meals to local people in need. Powell and Edelstyn write, 'we were using and adapting the tools of our age, combining analogue and digital to create something of beauty and use', while combining 'beauty, art and activism'.[62] They remember people's reactions when asked to buy banknotes, which had limited circulatory value:

> The reasons people bought the banknotes were diverse, from wanting to be part of a 'bailout of the people by the people' (the tagline of the Rolling Jubilee), to contributing to the local causes, loving the banknotes for what they symbolised, as art – and a fusion of it all. We were at times shocked and upset when people understood their donation as solely a donation or at best an exchange for our bit of paper.… Exchanging sterling for HSCB currency was to join the Bank Job and that was what we wanted.[63]

After selling a substantial quantity of notes at face value, Powell and Edelstyn moved to production of more elaborate, higher-denomination bonds using traditional letterpress, screen printing and foil block techniques. Each gold-edged bond entitled the purchaser to its ownership as art, an invitation to see the explosion of the van, and a fragment of the van melted down as a coin, as well as a chance to make history. Using the proceeds, Powell and Edelstyn purchased £1.2 million worth of debt owed to payday lenders in postcodes E17, E11, E10 and E4 (in the neighbourhood of the Hoe Street Central Bank). These debts were cancelled. Those affected were informed by hand-written letters in white envelopes, not the brown-envelopes of bureaucratic or business communications. They also channelled £20,000 to the community projects whose organisers are featured on the notes. Powell and Edelstyn recall,

> We bought up a package containing the debt of 411 people averaging £2,960 each… This was all very quiet, involving spreadsheets, General data Protection Regulation, phone calls and meetings. Due to the delinquency (old, lost, deemed unruly) of the debt we were not overrun with individual stories that could counter some of the shame and stigma surrounding debt, but we'd also been very wary of highlighting the debtor… and consolidating narratives of the debtor as other, as sinner to be redeemed or saved.[64]

And,

> We wanted to make this symbolic destruction of debt visceral and real in an exploded, expanded sculpture to shake the foundations of both capital and art, and provoke deep questioning of our current debt-fuelled economic system. This was financial education and it was time to drop the niceties. Out came the balaclavas and pitch alternators that led to comedy rather than menace.[65]

The controlled explosion took place in May 2019. Fragments of gold-painted metal flew. Debris settled. Charred bits of the paper by which capitalism maintains its power drifted in the wind, like chaff.

Five months later, Powell and Edelstyn participated in Extinction Rebellion's occupation of public spaces in Westminster. In the book *Bank Job*, they cite Katherine Flood and Gavin Grindon, curators of *Disobedient Objects* (Chapter 7), on the importance of material culture generated by social movements as 'responding to powerful enemies with more powerful images and stories'.[66] Powell admits that 'the secondary debt markets aren't going to disappear… but [*Bank*

*Job*] raises awareness of the absurd corruption of the whole system, and looks at the bigger picture'.[67] That might align to Adorno's idea of art refracting reality as absurdity; it also echoes Lorey's arguments in *State of Insecurity*. When Powell and Edelstyn say, 'we are living in a state of emergency' as the pandemic reveals the deficiencies of neoliberalism and 'the political, public language around the pandemic is full of images of war',[68] they allude to a corrosion of values. Against this, artists interrupt routine by evoking imagined worlds.

But capital seeks revenge. For *Bank Job*, this took the form of a requirement, after extensive negotiations, to vacate the building in Hoe Street when new owners sought to monetise their asset. The owners saw the artists' appeals to funding bodies as political interference in a property deal: 'we were in a catch-22; with no deal secured, we were unable to launch a fundraising community share offer or secure other organisational support'.[69] Meanwhile, a local petition said, 'the Rebel Bank is indeed much more than a building; it's an intervention in social imagining that is just the beginning of greater, positive things to come.'[70] Powell and Edelstyn comment,

> The bank… lived on in the spirit of resistance and resilience it had come to embody.… From its beginning this was an experiment in 'What If?' What if, in the shells of every recently vacated bank across the country… there erupted flourishing scenes of economic education and cultural action for a just future?[71]

That is revolutionary, like the abolition of office and property in Abbot Joachim of Fiore's announcement of the Third Age in Calabria in 1200.[72] It is also, mundanely, part of the work of creating a new society to which art-work (as verb) is integral. Revolution is sublime but can be critically reconfigured in new tactics and new terrains of wonder. Awe, like shock, is reserved for those who maintain power-over.

# Chapter 9
# Beauty is convulsive

Throughout this book I have argued that art refracts reality, enabling glimpses of imagined alternatives. Here, I draw on theoretical insights presented earlier in the book – Herbert Marcuse's claim that love poetry is the last resort of freedom under terror (Chapter 3); Walter Benjamin's call for a new kind of history (Chapter 4); and Theodor Adorno's view of aesthetics as creating a dialectic of reality-unreality (Chapter 5) – to read beauty as radical alterity, interrupting the norm and convulsively heightening reality. In brief, Doris Sommer argues, citing Friedrich Schiller and the Russian Constructivist artist Viktor Shklovsky, 'Art is disarming technique.'[1]

My focus is on performative interventions between, or fusing, art and political campaigning. The context is a period, since the 1960s, when non-violent direct action becomes a new kind of politics in response to the failure of representational politics to deal with urgent issues from social injustice to the climate emergency. I would say, too, that single-issue campaigns not only gather unlikely coalitions according to a common concern, but also, importantly, constitute an incipient new society within the old by enacting the values they hold and for which they campaign. Examples include anti-roads protests in the 1990s, Occupy in 2011–12, school climate strikes organised by Greta Thunberg, and Extinction Rebellion since 2019. All these campaigns were (or are) ephemeral, yet each is a moment in a new kind of social, cultural and political formation; each widens the horizon of the possible, and does so in part through an aesthetics of being-there. For participants this is transformative. For spectators, the memory lingers.

In this chapter, I consider four examples of performative, collective practice between politics and aesthetics, which I read as contributing to a shift in awareness among the publics they attract. They are Liberate Tate, who opposed Tate's sponsorship by the oil industry; the Women in Black who silently demonstrated against men's violence; Red Rebel Brigade, who use street theatre tactics at Extinction Rebellion occupations of public spaces; and Little Amal, a large-scale puppet who progressed from Turkey, through Europe to Britain in 2021, representing countless refugees from conflict zones. In each case, I begin by describing the work, then draw on the voices of those concerned to elaborate its meanings.

# Liberate Tate

A naked man lies in foetal position on the floor of the Duveen Gallery (the main hall) at Tate Britain, London. Two figures dressed in black carry oil cans bearing a green and yellow logo reminiscent of the global oil company BP. They pour the contents of the cans, a black liquid looking like oil (actually molasses), over the man. He remains on the floor for eighty-seven minutes. People watch, captivated by the theatre of this unadvertised event. The guards are taken by surprise, too, because, on one hand, Tate regularly commissions live-art events in a programme including 'social and political debate',[2] while, on the other hand, the artists did not inform the curators in advance (nor ask a fee for their appearance). The walls display images of female bodies in an exhibition, *Single Form,* sponsored by BP.[3]

This is *The Human Cost*, staged by Liberate Tate in April 2011 on the first anniversary of the Deepwater Horizon oil spill, which killed eleven oil workers and spilled five million tonnes of oil into the Gulf of Mexico. The work's eight-seven-minute duration represents the eighty-seven days it took to stop the spill. I was not present but imagine the performance elicited a theatrical suspension of disbelief among spectators. It also ignored the boundaries between live-art and political action, and between an institution called a Temple of Art at its opening by the Prince of Wales in 1897 and the potential public sphere of politicised opinion and exchange. A photograph of *The Human Cost* appeared the next day on the front page of the *Financial Times*. Art activist Mel Evans writes, 'the tender, tragic image of the performance has been shared thousands of times globally',[4] arguing that art brings distant events into the gallery as a public arena, with a visceral presence.

For BP, sponsorship of the arts buys respectability. Julian Stallabrass writes, 'BP hopes that the subliminal association of its brand with the transcendent values still commonly linked to art will act as a counterweight to the torrent of filth – pollution, environmental devastation, political corruption and violence – which its business continually produces.'[5] Similarly, James Marriott, of the art-environment-education group Platform, sees BP's sponsorship of Tate as transactional, 'an integral part of engineering the social and political circumstances that will best ensure the long-term security of those investments in oil and gas projects'.[6] Members of Liberate Tate knew this because most of them worked in the cultural sector.

Liberate Tate emerged within the ambience of Platform, alongside Art not Oil (which stages theatrical interventions in museums and theatres), during and after a workshop on art and activism. The organisation described itself as 'an art collective exploring the role of creative intervention in social change', aiming to end Tate's deal with BP.[7] The focus on sponsorship was specific, an effort to deprive BP of the respectability which underpins its public image in context of wider campaigns to question public attitudes to oil (and other fossil fuels).

In another work, *The Gift* (2012), Liberate Tate played on understandings of modernist art and design. A hundred participants carried a 16.5-metre white wind turbine blade over the bridge to Tate Modern, depositing it in the Turbine Hall as a donation to Tate's collection of modern art and design. The blade's huge, whale-like form arrived unannounced to achieve maximum impact and spectacle, juxtaposing an element of renewable energy production to the redundant fossil-fuel power station which houses Tate Modern. Evans recalls,

When the security staff attempted to block the blade on entry, performers beguiled them with the calm determination that comes with the knowledge that a plan is safe and good and will take as long as it takes, and as the final piece was put into position the crowds gathered at every balcony began to cheer. The blade lay across the full width of the space like a beached whale; a polished bone-like object holding sadness and beauty, lay on its side as an offered alternative to oil: use me instead.[8]

Pure white, its form follows function to epitomise a machine aesthetic. The turbine blade in the Turbine Hall was an evidently modernist aesthetic object, its function related to but refracting its site, previously housing commissions including Ai Weiwei's *Sunflower Seeds* (2011) and Tania Bruguera's *Tatlin Whisper #5* (Chapter 7), making the turbine blade an obvious candidate as a new acquisition for the collection.

Despite its appropriateness but predictably, the offer of *The Gift* was refused by Tate's Trustees. Liberate Tate then contacted Tate's members, asking them to urge the Trustees to reconsider their decision. Hundreds wrote supporting letters. Despite the importance of Tate's members – many are categorised as opinion formers, and, in a transactional world, their subscriptions are a significant income stream – the Trustees refused to change their minds. Still, the documentation is part of the work (archived at Tate). Eventually, Liberate Tate won a court case forcing Tate to say how much it received from BP, who ended their sponsorship. Liberate Tate then disbanded, having demonstrated the efficacy of a campaign shaped by aesthetic awareness and inside knowledge of the sector.

# The Women in Black

The Women in Black appeared in Jerusalem in January 1988 when Israeli Jewish women, supported by Palestinian women, marched against the Israeli occupation of the West Bank and organised vigils to remember people killed in the conflict. Dressed in black, the women stood silently for an hour in the afternoon in a prominent site, carrying placards demanding the end of the occupation. Their demonstration of stasis, as an act of public mourning and a refusal of the norm of male violence, was subsequently adopted by many groups of women worldwide. In Belgrade in October 1991, to take a prominent example, Women in Black Against War (*Zene u Crnom Protov Rata*) demonstrated against violent ethno-nationalism in ex-Jugoslavia, specifically resisting the regime in Serbia and generally calling for an end to injustices perpetrated by racism, sexism, militarism, imperialism and capitalism.

Athena Athanasiou writes that against 'war fever and nationalist mobilisations', and a state requiring the 'unambiguous loyalty of its gendered subjects', Women in Black refused the tide of gendered nationalist fervour.[9] She quotes Women in Black Against War's first public statement,

> The work of women in peace groups is presupposed; it is invisible, trying, women's work; it is part of 'our' role; to care for others, to comfort, aid, tend wounds, and feed. The painful realisation that the peace movement would… also follow a patriarchal model caused a serious dilemma for feminist-pacifists. We wanted our presence to be visible, not to be seen as something 'natural', as part of a women's role. We wanted it to be clearly understood that what we were doing was our political choice, a radical criticism of the patriarchal, militarist regime and a nonviolent act of resistance to policies that destroy cities, kill people, and annihilate human relations.[10]

The Women in Black were denounced by the regime, and attacked by far-Right groups. Vigils were suspended during NATO bombings of Belgrade in 1998 but resumed in 2000. Since then, groups have formed in many countries, although their vigils were put on hold due to the global Covid pandemic.

Athanasiou describes the presence of the Women in Black as a 'polyvalent network of resistant and dissident solidarities within an already multi-layered landscape of anti-war and anti-regime civil opposition'.[11] To me, their importance is in the interruption of routine to create a moment in which the state of mind which produces both domestic and inter-ethnic violence is challenged. They maintain that 'male violence against women in domestic life and in the community, in times of peace and in times of war, are interrelated'.[12] That state of mind equally explains ecological destruction; and Women in Black have begun to 'reflect beyond our own needs to the needs of the health of the planet and all humanity'.[13]

When the Women in Black say 'the war industry is at war with the eco-sphere',[14] they echo Marcuse's words in 1972, 'the genocidal war against people [in Viet Nam] is also ecocide in so far as it attacks the sources and resources of life itself… monopoly capitalism is waging a war against nature'.[15] Marcuse's aesthetics rely on an Enlightenment universalism, but the Women in Black adopt a feminist-pacifism situated in a post-structuralist refusal of meta-narratives. This opens a space, in discourse and literally in their public presence, where attitudes and values, agencies and structures, can be renegotiated: an *agon* – an open, active public realm of contestation – as component of an emerging public sphere.

Interviewed by Athanasiou, Judith Butler argues, 'the norms against which we struggle are social norms, and they govern us precisely as social creatures'.[16] Hence a subject (citizen or self) emerges only among others through forms of collective presence, struggling against the norms by which masculine aggressivity and the mindset of conquest are enforced. The emphasis on a process of becoming-through-others occurred previously in Hannah Arendt's construct of natality, as the gaining of a mature self only through perceptions of others and others' perceptions of the self (as denied by race laws to Jews in Germany in the 1930s).[17] Butler re-states this in the conditions of 2013 as a self which 'comes into being, and can only come into being, on the occasion of relations with others… in and as the relation itself'.[18] Elsewhere, Butler writes of the multivalency in which social bonds are produced, whence words such as 'I' and 'you', 'we' and 'they' are implicated in 'an ambivalent social bond' which challenges aggression.[19]

# Public mourning

The Women in Black stand silently, dressed in black as the colour of mourning, enacting the value of nonviolence which articulates a radical alterity in a violent society. The sight of their silence interrupts the routines by which conflict is normalised, in which women are assigned secondary roles (as in caring for the wounded), and where business-as-usual is a potentially crushing norm. Butler and Athanasiou argue,

> The predicament of being moved by what one sees, feels and comes to know is always one in which one finds oneself transported elsewhere, into another scene, or into a social world in which one is not the centre. And this form of dispossession is constituted as a form of responsiveness that gives rise to action and resistance, to appearing together with others, in an effort to demand the end of injustice.[20]

There is a long history of public contestation via mourning, as in Greek tragedy. Gail Holst-Warhaft observes on Aeschylus, in context of classical theatre's incorporation – during the formation of a hierarchical, male-dominated state – of rites of mourning traditionally carried out by women in public sites,

> Tragedy … does more than reflect the conflicts surrounding funerals. By appropriating the language, music and gesture of traditional women's lament and employing them in public performance, tragedy's deep play involves the audience in an *agon* that provides men with an outlet for the potential violence of grief while denying women any public role in the artistic ritual drama they customarily controlled. In the earlier dramas, the curved tiers of marble seem unable to contain the fearful power of women's lament, and tragedy paradoxically threatens its own existence as a public Athenian institution.[21]

In classical Athens, public drama was political, an instantiation of the *agon* but at a point at which society began to relegate such activities to specific sites and audiences. While, that is, it is nice to see classical Athens as the birthplace of democracy, it was a society dependent on slave labour and the conquests which procured enslaved people, in which only free-born Athenian men owning a specified wealth could participate in the Assembly (*pnyx*). There was public mixing in the market (*agora*) surrounded by covered walkways, but only between men who had sufficient leisure for public affairs. In this period of formalisation of spaces and functions, as Holst-Warhaft notes, public acts of mourning were both contained in their allotted fora, and potentially subversive as reminders of a society in which women's voices carried a provocative tone. The Women in Black reclaim that role, both in the street and in their silence which reclaims the silenced voices of women in the conditions of patriarchy and the nation-state. For Athanasiou, Antigone is 'a figure of ambivalent and fractious complexity', who reiterates *and* subverts the norm by passionately 're-enacting the inextricable link between injured engagement with regulatory norms'.[22]

I want to introduce one further lens on this instantiation of subversion. Marcuse argues that the new sensibility he sees in student protest in 1968 'has become a political force',[23] and situates this, through literary references, in a realm of beauty, serenity and nonviolence. He sees, too, a new sensibility as the prerequisite of radical change, identifying it in student protest and the counter-culture of the late 1960s. I wonder if it has reappeared in another form today, adapted to present conditions and public issues, in the work of Liberate Tate and the Women in Black. In the beautiful, transgressive eruption which rejects the violent, coercive norm as it collapses the categories of art and politics, an alternative society begins to appear, as vision but also as reality. I find this, too, in the work of Red Rebel Brigade.

# Red Rebel Brigade

Red Rebel Brigade was devised by Doug Francisco and Justine Squire, from Bristol's Invisible Circus, in response to Extinction Rebellion's uprising in April 2019. The troupe dress entirely in red: red gowns, red gloves and red headscarves adorned with red cloth roses. Their faces are painted white. They move in 'a slow-motion mime show'.[24] Red, they explain, resonates with spectators as the colour of blood and passion, or in mundane terms of stop signs, in a 'mournful and engaging spectacle… symbolic of the rebellion itself'.[25]

Red Rebel Brigade describe themselves as 'an international performance artivist troupe dedicated to illuminating the global environmental crisis', in support of groups 'fighting to save humanity and all species from mass extinction'.[26] Their website states,

> Red Rebel Brigade symbolises the common blood we share
> with all species,
> That unifies us and makes us one.
> As such we move as one, act as one and more importantly feel
> as one.
> We are unity and we empathise with our surroundings, we are
> forgiving,
> We are sympathetic and humble, compassionate and
> understanding,
> We divert, distract. Delight and inspire the people who watch us,
> We illuminate the magic realm beneath the surface of all things
> and we invite people to enter in, we make a bubble and calm
> the storm, we are peace in the midst of war.
> We are who the people have forgotten to be.[27]

Unlike other groups around Extinction Rebellion, Red Rebel Brigade avoid arrest. They face but do not aggressively confront police lines, and rather than sit down to block roads they move slowly across them in a choreographed progress. The effect is 'sombre and mournful… like Greek chorus, Buto dancers, Victorian funeral mourners'; the message is 'Change, the possibility to change, delivered with love and understanding'.[28]

Red Rebel Brigade refer to the chorus of classical Greek theatre, an analogy worth pursuing in terms of political form (as with Athanasiou, above). In Greek tragedy, the chorus act out the polarising forces of the plot and its implications for the audience, creating an *agonistic* realm of contested allegiances. Sophocles's *Antigone*, for instance, poses the demands of state and kin as incompatible: Antigone is denied permission to bury her brother Polynices, killed fighting the tyrant Creon, so that his body will be eaten by dogs and birds. Tradition demands its preservation in burial. The state denies it. This matters because, as said above, tragedies articulate a society of changing attitudes, to which they contribute in the turns of the plot. Contradiction morphs into paradox, and such turns elicit audience responses. For instance, Holst-Warhaft notes that the antiphonal chorus of lament in *Antigone* appears at the end, after Antigone's death; and that her burial lament opens with a hymn to Eros (Life). This creates 'an antagonism between her and the chorus that is never resolved'.[29] Faced with incompatible allegiances, the audience are swayed to and fro, an effect enhanced by the familiarity of the dramatic form. Holst-Warhaft adds, drawing parallels between Greek tragedy and the surviving culture of women's laments in Greek villages, 'Antigone's lament for herself is displayed before an audience whose response to laments must always have been induced by an art of poetry and song… familiar with Antigone's… means of expression through funerals of their own dead.'[30] Looking at Red Rebel Brigade, the comparison with Greek tragedy adds a lens of dramatic contestation, the chorus moving in a space-between just as the red-dressed players move between public and police.

There are few direct parallels between classical Greek society and post-industrial Europe, nor between today and the baroque era in which Benjamin examines another tragic drama (Chapter 4). Yet there is continuity in the need for a performance expressing the potential for social transformation, for the public acting out of opposition, in a dualism resolved by either the violent elimination of one force, as in war, or through process of social and cultural becoming, which are open-ended, often messy, and offer no total coherence but only a prospect of permanent renegotiation. The contested allegiances of tragedy are, in this frame, mutually inextricable elements of an axis of Eros-Thanatos, lyric-lament, and protagonist-antagonist (the latter exemplified by the chorus).

# XR and post-representational politics

In April 2019, Extinction Rebellion occupied four sites in London for ten days, including Oxford Circus and Waterloo Bridge. I visited Waterloo Bridge. There were people sitting in circles to discuss issues, a speaker on a small stage, a vegan food stall and rows of trees in pots. It felt like a student campus occupation, with a benign ambience. People strolled freely over the bridge, either from interest or on their way somewhere (including, that day, a few police officers who exchanged friendly greetings with protestors). Food coordinator Momo Haque writes, 'people joined us off the street, coming in their lunch breaks, returning at the end of their working day… regular passers-by, inspired by what they saw'.[31]

I read these occupations, like those of Occupy in 2011–12, as an emergent new society living a radical alternative to a society based on the destructive norms of capitalism. They are there because the representational politics of the nation-state and liberal democracy fail, producing catastrophes from the Iraq war to global heating and species extinctions not as anomalies but as the default position under capitalism. Thunberg described the COP 26 climate conference in Glasgow in 2021 in which the representatives of nation-states met as blah, blah, blah. Instead, the school strikes initiated by Thunberg, and events organised by campaigns such as Extinction Rebellion, bring the climate crisis to the urgent attention of citizens who find their governments wanting. Direct action is a means to open a space in which alternatives are articulated, but where they are, equally, given form, demonstrating the possibility to live at least for a while according to the values of life. The commitment to non-violence is in itself a radically alternative means towards new social formations.

British Green Party MP Caroline Lucas argues for 'a paradigm shift in the way the world is structured and the way we live our lives', and quotes Thunberg, 'If solutions within the system are so impossible to find, maybe we should change the system itself.'[32] Extinction Rebellion uses theatrical tactics to challenge the system and, as said, to act out an alternative to it. For instance, at Oxford Circus a pink boat carrying the words TELL THE TRUTH was used as a speaker's platform. It was photogenic, reproduced frequently in print, broadcast and social media; and, I suggest, the transformative effect of these occupations for those present is, in itself, in being there, among others of like mind and sensibility. That accords with Butler's comments (above) on struggle, and is articulated by participants James and Ruby when they recall, 'creating a show and a traffic-stopping photo opportunity got us plenty of global media coverage… but it couldn't really capture the emotion and community around this roadblock'.[33] Since 2019, police tactics have become more hostile. *The Guardian* reports that in London in 2021, 'police officers smashed windows on the bus and wrestled with those on board, putting activists in headlocks and throwing punches at them'.[34] But the report also asks if Extinction Rebellion has lost momentum, with fewer participants and a less visible presence. Well… campaigns come and go. The coalitions of individuals, groups and interests which they unite are ephemeral, but Extinction Rebellion has, in two years or so, put the climate emergency ahead of the economy, immigration and crime for the British public.[35] For those not present, the visual impact of media images evokes alternative kinds of history, an alternative world. George McKay argues that such non-violent direct action 'contributes to construction of self: protest is about conditions and events *out there*, but it is also about *inner* values and responsibilities'.[36] And when John Jordan says 'Direct action introduces the concept of play into the straight, predictably grey world of politics,'[37] this hints at Schiller's belief in play as a life-affirming society (Chapter 8).

# Little Amal

As conflict continues in the Middle East, and pressures of economic failure and climate change afflict much of the global South, refugees travel to Europe in increasing numbers in life-threatening conditions.

The numbers produce far-Right hostility. In Britain, the increase in small boats crossing the Channel is used as an excuse to tighten border controls, after the introduction of a hostile environment for asylum seekers and economic migrants alike, an effect heightened after the UK's departure from the European Union.

Against grand themes such as national identity, adopted by the far-Right, refugee's stories are immediate and personal. *Little Amal*, a larger than life-size puppet, travelled from Turkey via Greece, Italy, France, Switzerland, Germany and Belgium to Britain in 2021. The project was developed from Good Chance Theatre's play *The Jungle* (2015), based on the refugee camp called the Jungle in Calais, a pejorative name denoting the marginalisation of refugees. The puppet, *Little Amal*, was made by Handspring Puppet Company, previously producers of the horse in the play *War Horse*.[38] She represents the hundreds of children in the camp at Calais, and by extension hundreds more in transit across Europe: 'She walked for all the children… forced to undertake

**Figure 9.1** Little Amal meets Alice, Oxford 2021 (photo courtesy Valerie Holman)

extraordinary journeys under life-threatening conditions. Little Amal walked so that we didn't forget them.'[39]

*Little Amal* was welcomed by communities along the route. Arriving in Oxford on 26 October 2021, she met Alice (from Lewis Carroll's *Alice Through the Looking Glass*), in the Garden of Live Flowers. Amal brought a bag of memories from Syria, both happy and sad. As these spilt out around the city, Alice helped her find them, moving from the Botanic Gardens through the city centre to Merton Fields[40] [Figure 9.1]. Two kinds of Beauty meet: blond Alice, an English beauty of sweetness, innocence and light (although Alice has to make her own navigations through dark forces in her parallel universe), and the emotive pathos of Amal, a refugee with memories of a better life in a land with its own beauties, refracted in present memories of conflict and loss. *Little Amal* then moved to the climate conference in Glasgow, and found a new home in Manchester. The small boats still cross the Channel (and the Mediterranean). There is no end to crisis, only the hope that wars will end because one day people refuse to fight them, and refugees will be regarded as citizens in their adopted countries.

# Coda

None of this is a society as a work of art – in Marcuse's terms (Chapter 3) – yet the projects reviewed in this chapter prefigure an immanent revolution, not the imminent revolution of marches, banners and the overthrow of states, but a complex, multiple, uneven, ephemeral moment of becoming. New Jerusalem does not descend from a gilded sky, and was always separated by a chasm from the world of ordinary life. Incipient social formations are created in acts which articulate really existing alternative values, and live them. For centuries, the dominant narrative of white, men's military and economic conquest and coercion has been maintained as a strategy of power-over: 'what men [sic] want to learn from nature is how to use it in order wholly to dominate it and other men'.[41]

I have argued throughout this book that the dwindling of political hope in terms of the conventions of representational politics necessitates a new kind of politics, equivalent in its way to Benjamin's new kind of history. And this, I think, validates a concern with aesthetics because beauty is the radical Other to routine, and to the culture industry's maintenance of business-as-usual. It is interruption and fracture, the straw that breaks capitalism's binds. Non-violent direct action and its performative appearances enact and give form to such alternative ways of apprehending reality; and this is, immanently not imminently, present not tomorrow, an incipient new society within the old. Revolution is sublime. Beauty stops you in your tracks. The work of revolution is mundane and extraordinary. I leave it there for now.

# Notes

## Introduction

1   Olusoga, D., 2022, quoted, Gayle, D., 'Four Cleared of Toppling of Edward Colston Statue,' *The Guardian*, 6 January, p. 1.
2   The revolutionary calendar was backdated to the Autumn equinox, 1792.

## Chapter 1

1   Saint-Simon, H. de, [1825] 1975, 'The Artist, the Scientist and the Industrial: Dialogue,' *Opinions littéraires, philosophiques et industriels*, trans. Taylor, K., *Selected Writings on Science, Industry and Social Organisation*, London, Croom Helm, p. 280.
2   Saint-Simon, 'The Artist, the Scientist and the Industrial: Dialogue,' p. 281.
3   Saint-Simon, H., [1825] 1975, 'Physiology Applied to the Improvement of Social Institutions: Supplementary Notes,' trans. Taylor, K., *Selected Writings on Science, Industry and Social Organisation*, London, Croom Helm, p. 275.
4   Rancière, J., [1988] 2011, *Staging the People: The Proletarian and His Double*, London, Verso, p. 24.
5   Rancière, *Staging the People*, p. 26.
6   Ibid.
7   Soboul, A., [1958] 1962, *Les Sans-culottes parisiens en l'an II*, cited in Clark, T. J., 1999, *Farwell to an Idea: Episodes from a History of Modernism*, New Haven (CT), Yale, p. 16.
8   Clark, *Farwell to an Idea*, p. 18.
9   Ibid., p. 18.
10   Ibid.
11   Ibid., p. 34; 36.
12   Benjamin, W., [1940] 1977, 'Theses on the Philosophy of History,' *Illuminations*, London, Fontana, p. 263.

**13** Lowy, M., [2001] 2016, *Fire Alarm: Reading Walter Benjamin's 'On the Concept of History*,' London, Verso, p. 88.

**14** Rancière, *Staging the People*, p. 24.

**15** Clark, T. J., 1973, *Image of the People: Gustave Courbet and the 1848 Revolution*, London, Thames and Hudson, p. 113.

**16** Courbet, G., Courthion, P., 1951, *Courbet raconté part luis-même et par ses amis*, Paris, in Clark, *Image of the People*, p. 109.

**17** Illustrated, Clark, *Image of the People*, p. 62, fig. 21.

**18** Clark, *Image of the People*, p. 48.

**19** Ibid., p. 49.

**20** Proudhon, P.J. [1849] article in *Le Peuple*, 19 February, quoted, Clark, *Image of the People*, p. 49.

**21** Proudhon, P. J., [1865] 1970, *Du Principe de l'art et de sa destinastion sociale, Selected Writing*, ed. Edwards, S., London, Macmillan, p. 215.

**22** Proudhon, *Selected Writings*, p. 216.

**23** Clark, *Image of the People*, p. 17.

**24** Ibid., p. 114.

**25** Ibid., p. 98.

**26** Rancière, [1975–81] 2011, *Staging the People*, p. 23.

**27** Courbet, G., [1854] 1978, letter, Toussaint, H., 'The dossier on "The Studio" by Courbet,' *Gustave Courbet 1819–1877* [exhibition catalogue], London, Royal Academy of Arts, p. 254.

**28** Toussaint, 'The dossier on "The Studio" by Courbet,' pp. 249–280.

**29** Ibid., p. 266.

**30** Chevreul, M. E., 1855, *The Principles of Harmony and Contrast of Colours, and Their Application to the Arts*, London, Longman, Brown, Green.

**31** Collini, S., 2019, *The Nostalgic Imagination: History in English Criticism*, Oxford, Oxford Universityb Press, pp. 77–101.

**32** Nochlin, I., 1968, 'The Invention of the Avant-Garde,' *Avant-Garde Art*, eds. Hess, T. J. and Ashbery, J., New York, Collier, pp. 13–17.

**33** Nochlin, 'The Invention of the Avant-Garde,' p. 17.

**34** Clark, *Image of the People*, p. 155.

**35** Ibid., p. 156.

**36** Ibid., p. 33.

**37** Ross, K., 2015, *Communal Luxury: The Political Imaginary of the Paris Commune*, London, Verso, pp. 27–28.

**38** Benjamin, W., [1935] 1997, 'Paris – The Capital of the Nineteenth Century,' *Charles Baudelaire*, London, Verso, p. 174.

**39** Harvey, D., 1989, *The Urban Experience*, Baltimore (MD), Johns Hopkins University Press, pp. 200–228.

**40** House, J., 2004, *Impressionism: Paint and Politics*, New Haven (CT), Yale, p. 111.

**41** Leighton, J. and Thomson, R., 1997, *Seurat and the Bathers*, London, National Gallery, p. 119.

**42** Leighton and Thomson, *Seurat and the Bathers*, p. 117.

**43** Smith, P., 1997, *Seurat and the Avant-Garde*, New Haven (CT), Yale, p. 77.

**44** Argüelles, J., 1972, *Charles Henry and the Formation of a Psychophysical Aesthetic*, Chicago, University of Chicago Press, p. 85.

**45** Argüelles, *Charles Henry*, p. 103.

**46** Smith, *Seurat and the Avant-Garde*, p. 79.

**47** House, J., 1980, 'Meaning in Seurat's Figure Paintings,' *Art History*, III, 60, September, pp. 345–356.

**48** Clark, *Farwell to an Idea*, p. 105.

**49** From census, Charle, C., [1990] 2015, *Birth of the Intellectual 1880–1900*, Cambridge, Polity, p. 234, Table 1.1.

**50** Charle, *Birth of the Intellectual*, p. 66.

**51** Herr, L. 1888–1889, 'Le Progres intellectual et l'affranchissement,' [ms], quoted, Charle, *Birth of the Intellectual*, pp. 66–67.

**52** Mallarmé, S., quoted, Huret, J., [1882] 1982, *Enquete sur l'évolution littéraire*, Vanves, Thot, p. 78, in Charle, *Birth of the Intellectual*, p. 79.

**53** Bowness, A., 1979, 'Introduction,' *Post-Impressionism* [exhibition catalogue], London, Royal Academy of Arts, p. 9.

**54** Harvey, *The Urban Experience*, p. 229.

**55** Figes, O., 2019, *The Europeans: Three Lives and the Making of a Cosmopolitan Culture*, London, Penguin, p. 194.

**56** Denisoff, D., 2007, 'Decadence and Aestheticism,' *The Cambridge Companion to the Fin de Siecle*, ed. Marshall, G., Cambridge, Cambridge University Press, p. 38.

**57** Rancière, J., [2000] 2004, 'The Distribution of the Sensible: Politics and Aesthetics,' *The Politics of Aesthetics*, London, Continuum, p. 19.


# Chapter 2


**1** Clark, T. J., 2013, *Picasso and Truth: From Cubism to Guernica*, Princeton (NJ), Princeton University Press; *Farwell to an Idea: Episodes from a History of Modernism*, 1999, New Haven (CT), Yale; Cottington, D., 1998, *Cubism in the Shadow of War: The Avant-Garde and Politics in Paris 1905–1914*, New Haven (CT), Yale; Spate, V., 1979, *Orphism: The Evolution of Non-Figurative Painting in Paris 1910–1914*, Oxford, Oxford University Press.

**2** Williams, R., [1988] 1997, 'The Politics of the Avant-Garde,' *The Politics of Modernism*, London, Verso, p. 52.

**3** Williams, 'The Politics of the Avant-Garde,' p. 49.

**4** 'August Strindberg,' www.sweden.se/culture-traditions/august-strindberg [accessed 20 May 2020].

**5** Denisoff, D., 2007, 'Decadence and Aestheticism,' *The Cambridge Companion to the Fin de Siecle*, ed. Marshall, G., Cambridge, Cambridge University Press, p. 32.

**6**   West, S., 'The Visual Arts,' *The Cambridge Companion to the Fin de Siecle*, ed. Marshall, G., p. 145.

**7**   West, 'The Visual Arts,' p. 148.

**8**   Shattuck, R., 1969, *The Banquet Years: The Origins of the Avant-Garde in France 1885 to World War I*, London, Cape, p. 9.

**9**   Figes, O., 2019, *The Europeans: Three Lives and the Making of a Cosmopolitan Culture*, London, Penguin, p. 114.

**10**  Billington, M., 'The troll in the drawing room,' *The Guardian*, 15 February 2003, on-line www.theguardian.com/stage/2003/feb/15/theatre. artsfeatures [accessed 20 May 2020].

**11**  Williams, R., [1988] 1997, 'Theatre as a Political Forum,' *The Politics of Modernism*, p. 85.

**12**  Williams, 'Theatre as a Political Forum,' p. 86.

**13**  Strindberg [1895] letter to Gauguin, quoted in Boudaille, G., 1964, *Gauguin*, London, Thames and Hudson, pp. 208–209.

**14**  Williams, 'The Politics of the Avant-Garde,' p. 49.

**15**  Ibid., p. 50.

**16**  Williams, R., [1986] 1997, 'Language and the Avant-Garde,' *The Politics of Modernism*, p. 74.

**17**  Mansbach, S. A., 1999, *Modern Art in Eastern Europe: From the Baltic to the Balkans, c. 1890–1939*, Cambridge, Cambridge University Press.

**18**  Wood, P. ed., 1999, 'Introduction,' *The Challenge of the Avant-Garde*, New Haven (CT), Yale, p. 18.

**19**  Gleizes, A., 1918, 'The Abbey of Créteil: A Communistic Experiment,' *The Modern School*, (New Jersey), 5, number 1, October, pp. 300–315.

**20**  Clark, *Farewell to an Idea*, pp. 181–183.

**21**  Gleizes, A. and Metzinger, J., 1912, *Du Cubisme*, Paris, Figuiere, section 2, quoted in Cottington, *Cubism in the Shadow of War*, p. 159.

**22**  Cottington, *Cubism in the Shadow of War*, p. 161.

**23**  Delaunay, R., 1913, letter to Franz Marc, quoted in Cottington, *Cubism in the Shadow of War*, p. 179.

**24**  Spate, V., 1976, *Simultaneity* [exhibition catalogue], Cambridge, Kettles Yard, n.p.

**25**  Spate, *Orphism*, p. 208.

**26**  Ibid., p. 212.

**27**  Kandinsky, W., [1911] 1977, *Concerning the Spiritual in Art*, New York, Dover.

**28**  Roberts, J., 2015, *Revolutionary Time and the Avant-Garde*, London, Verso, p. 55.

**29**  Roberts, *Revolutionary Time and the Avant-Garde,* p. 54.

**30**  Ibid., pp. 54–55.

**31**  Fiss, K., 2009, *Grand illusion: The Third Reich, the Paris Exposition, and the Cultural Seduction of France*, Chicago, University of Chicago Press.

**32**  Greenberg, C., [1962] 1995, 'The Identity of Art,' *Collected essays and Criticism, 4, Modernism with a Vengeance, 1957–1969*, Chicago, University of Chicago Press, p. 117.

33 Greenberg, C., [1939] 1988, *'Avant-Garde and Kitsch,' Collected essays and Criticism,1, Perceptions and Judgments, 1939–1944*, Chicago, University of Chicago Press, p. 6 [my italics].

34 Greenberg, 'Avant-Garde and Kitsch,' p. 8.

35 Ibid., p. 9.

36 Macdonald, D., 1939, quoted, Greenberg, 'Avant-Garde and Kitsch,' p. 14, no original source given.

37 Greenberg, 'Avant-Garde and Kitsch,' p. 15.

38 Ibid., p. 8.

39 Ibid., p. 22.

40 Adorno, [1981] 1991,'The Schema of Mass Culture,' *The Culture Industry*, London, Routledge, p. 80.

41 Leslie, E., 2000, *Walter Benjamin: Overpowering Conformism*, London, Pluto, p. 150.

42 Marx, K., [1845] 1968, *Theses on Feuerbach, Marx and Engels Selected Works*, London, Lawrence and Wishart, p. 29.

43 Heller, A., 2011, *Aesthetics and Modernity*, ed. Rundell, J., Plymouth, Lexington Books, p. 49.

44 Fuller, P., 1980, 'Where Was the Art of the Seventies?' *Beyond the Crisis in Art*, London, Writers and Readers Cooperative, pp. 16–43.

45 Miles, M., 2015, *Limits to Culture*, London, Pluto, pp. 98–101.

46 Wood, O., 1999, 'Conclusion: For and against the Avant-Gzarde,' *The Challenge of the Avant-Garde*, New Haven (CT), Yale, p. 265.

47 Clark, *Farewell to an Idea*, p. 407.

48 Williams, 'The Politics of the Avant-Garde,' p. 51.

49 www.dissentathome.org/missjulieinutopia [accessed 3 July 2020].

50 https://lssuu.com/twoaddthree/docs/miss_julie_in_utopia_perfprmance_text [accessed 3 July 2020] future quotes from the new Preface are from the same source.

51 As note 50.

52 Ibid.

# Chapter 3

1 Kandinsky, W., [1911] 1977, *Concerning the Spiritual in Art*, New York, Dover, p. 50.

2 The original German title of the text is *Uber das Geistige in der Kunst*, usually translated as concerning the spiritual in art; but *Geistige* also means intellectual or mental, thus referring to states of psyche.

3 Long, R-C. W., 1975, 'Kandinsky's Abstract Style: The Veiling of Apocalyptic Folk Imagery,' *Art Journal*, XXXIV, Spring, p. 227.

4 Marcuse, H., 1978, *The Aesthetic Dimension*, Boston, Beacon Press, p. 41.

5 Ibid.

**6** Adorno, T. W., [1969] 1999, *Aesthetic Theory*, trans. Hullor-Kentor, R., London, Athlone, p. 82.

**7** Marcuse, H., [1922] 2007, 'Introduction: The German Artist Novel,' Marcuse, H., *Art and Liberation*, ed. Kellner, D., Collected Papers IV, London, Routledge, p. 71.

**8** Marcuse, H., [1922; 1979] 2007, *Der deutsche Künstlerroman*, Schriften, I, Frankfurt, Suhrkamp, p. 16, quoted, Kellner, 'Introduction,' *Art and Liberation*, p. 8.

**9** Marcuse, *Der deutsche Künstlerroman*, p. 75, quoted, Kellner, 'Introduction,' *Art and Liberation*, p. 9.

**10** Ibid.

**11** Marcuse, 'Introduction: The German Artist Novel,' p. 75.

**12** Marcuse, H. [1978] 2007, interview with Larry Hartwick, *Art and Liberation*, p. 235.

**13** Marcuse, 'Introduction: The German Artist Novel,' p. 72.

**14** Ibid.

**15** Ibid., p. 79.

**16** Marcuse, H., [1937] 1968, *'The Affirmative Character of Culture,'* *Negations*, Harmondsworth, Penguin, p. 86.

**17** Ibid.

**18** Ibid.

**19** Ibid.

**20** Ibid., p. 89.

**21** Ibid., p. 90.

**22** Ibid., p. 103.

**23** Ibid., p. 101.

**24** Marcuse, H., [1956] 1987, *Eros and Civilisation: A Philosophic Inquiry into Freud*, London, Ark, p. 274.

**25** Marcuse, H., [1967] 1968, 'Liberation from the Affluent Society,' *The Dialectics of Liberation*, ed. Cooper, D., Harmondsworth, Penguin, p. 181.

**26** Buck-Morss, S., 2002, 'A Global Public Sphere?' *Radical Philosophy*, 111, January–February, p. 6.

**27** Nairn, T. and Singh-Sandhu, J., 1969, 'Chaos in the Art Colleges,' *Student Power: Problems, Diagnosis, Action*, ed. Cockburn, A. and Blackburn, R., Harmondsworth, Penguin, p. 115.

**28** Davis, A., 1974, *An Autobiography*, New York, Random House, p. 134, quoted, Katz, B., 1982, *Herbert Marcuse and the Art of Liberation*, London, Verso, p. 163.

**29** Gorz, A., [1980] 1982, *Farewell to the Working Class*, London, Pluto.

**30** Marcuse, 'Liberation from the Affluent Society,' p. 185.

**31** Ibid., p. 175.

**32** Ibid., p. 176.

**33** Ibid., p. 177.

**34** Ibid., p. 178.

35 Marcuse, H., [1967] 1970, 'The End of Utopia,' *Five Lectures*, Harmondsworth, Penguin, p. 80.

36 Marcuse, 'Liberation from the Affluent Society,' p. 182.

37 Ibid., p. 184.

38 Ibid.

39 Marcuse, H., [1967] 2007, 'Society as a Work of Art,' *Art and Liberation*, p. 124.

40 Marcuse, 'Society as a Work of Art,' p. 125.

41 Rilke, R. M., [1913] 1963, *Duino Elegies*, I, trans. Leishman, J. B. and Spender, S., London, Hogarth Press, p. 25 [parallel German-English text].

42 Marcuse, 'Society as a Work of Art,' p. 126.

43 Ibid., p. 128.

44 Ibid., p. 129.

45 Marcuse, *Essay on Liberation*, pp. 34–35.

46 Ibid., p. 27.

47 Marcuse, *The Aesthetic Dimension*, p. 54.

48 Ibid., p. 5.

49 Ibid., p. 6 [italics original].

50 Ibid., p. 8.

51 Ibid., p. 30, citing Goldmann, L., 1975, *Towards a Sociology of the Novel*, London, Tavistock, p. 10f.

52 Marcuse, *The Aesthetic Dimension*, p. 31 [no citation for Adorno is given but the following is included in the bibliography: Adorno, T. W., 1958, *Noten sur Literatur*, Frankfurt, Suhrkamp].

53 Marcuse, *The Aesthetic Dimension*, pp. 32–33.

54 Ibid., p. 38.

55 Ibid., pp. 55–56.

56 Ibid., p. 71.

57 Marcuse, H. [1945–c.1970] 1998, 'Some Remarks on Aragon: Art and Politics in the Totalitarian Era,' *Technology, War and Fascism*, ed. Kellner, D., Collected Papers, I, London, Routledge, pp. 199–214.

58 Marcuse, 'Some Remarks on Aragon,' p. 203.

59 Ibid., p. 204.

60 Ibid., p. 205.

61 Miles, M., 2011, Herbert Marcuse: *An Aesthetics of Liberation*, London, Pluto, pp. 65–85.

62 Eluars, P., [1942] 1987, *Selected Poems*, London, John Calder, pp. 72–77.

63 Marcuse, 'Some Remarks on Aragon,' p. 206.

64 Ibid., p. 207.

65 Ibid., p. 213.

66 Ibid., p. 214.

67 Kellner, 'Introduction,' *Art and Liberation*, p. 29.

68 Kristeva, J., 2002, *Revolt She Said*, Los Angeles, Semiotext(e), p. 18.

69 Kristeva, *Revolt She Said*, p. 18.

70 Ibid.

71 Ibid., p. 23.

72 Ibid., p. 114.

73 Marcuse, H., 1958, *Soviet Marxism: A Critical Analysis*, New York, Columbia University Press.

74 Ross, K., 2002, *May '68 and Its Afterlives*, Chicago, University of Chicago Press, p. 191; 193.

75 Sjöholm, C., 2005, *Kristeva and the Political*, London, Routledge, p. 8.

76 Kristeva, *Revolt She Said*, p. 39.

77 Goldman, L., cited in Roudinesco, E., 1993, *Jacques Lacan*, Paris, Fayard, p. 444, quoted in *Ross, May '68 and Its Afterlives*, p. 191.

78 Kristeva, *Revolt She Said*, p. 85.

79 Kristeva, J., [1999] 2001, *Hannah Arendt*, New York, Columbia University Press.

80 Kristeva, *Revolt She Said*, p. 85.

81 Ibid., p. 100.

82 Ibid., p. 86.

83 Ibid., p. 100.

84 Marcuse, *Eros and Civilisation*, pp. 157–158.

85 Kristeva, J., [1974] 1984, *Revolution in Poetic Language,* New York, Columbia University Press, p. 209.

86 Kristeva, *Revolution in Poetic Language,* p. 56 [italics original].

87 Ibid., p. 210.

88 Ibid., p. 205.

89 Sjöholm, *Kristeva and the Political*, p. 67.

90 Marcuse, 'Introduction: The German Artist Novel,' p. 75.

91 Marcuse, H. [1978] 2007, interview with Larry Hartwick, *Art and Liberation*, p. 235.

# Chapter 4

1 Leslie, E., 2000, *Walter Benjamin: Overpowering Conformism*, London, Pluto; Buck-Morss, S., 1991, *The Dialectics of Seeing: Walter Benjamin and the Arcades Project*, Cambridge (MA), MIT; Buci-Glucksmann, C., [1984] 1994, *Baroque Reason: The Aesthetics of Modernity*, London, Sage.

2 In the text I use the translation 'On the Concept of History' from Löwy, M., [2005] 2016, *Fire Alarm: Reading Walter Benjamin's 'On the Conception of History,'* London, Verso; in references I use 'Theses on the Philosophy of History' from the English translation, Benjamin, W., 1973, *Illuminations*, ed. Arendt, H., London, Fontana, pp. 255–266.

3 Benjamin, 'Theses on the Philosophy of History,' XIII, p. 263.

4 Benjamin, 'Theses on the Philosophy of History,' B, p. 266.

5   Löwy, *Fire Alarm*, p. 4.

6   Lorey, I., 2015, *State of Insecurity: Government of the Precarious*, London, Verso, p. 1.

7   Butler, J., 2015, 'Foreword,' Lorey, *State of Insecurity*, p. xi.

8   Benjamin, 'Theses on the Philosophy of History,' VIII, p. 259.

9   Bloch, E., [1959] 1968, *The Principle of Hope*, Cambridge (MA), MIT, p. 813.

10  Personal memory, undocumented, probably between 1975 and 1980.

11  Bakhtin, M., [1981] 2007, *Problems of Dostoevsky's Poetics*, Manchester, Manchester University Press, p. 165, quoted, Beasley-Murray, T., 2007, *Mikhail Bakhtin and Walter Benjamin: Experience and Form*, Basingstoke, Palgrave, p. 12.

12  Bakhtin, M., [1996] 2007, *The Dialogic Imagination*, Austin (TX), University of Texas Press, p. 307, quoted in Beasley-Murray, *Mikhail Bakhtin and Walter Benjamin*, pp. 131–132.

13  Ibid., p. 13.

14  Ibid., p. 6.

15  Ibid., p. 144.

16  Buck-Morss, *Dialectics of Seeing*, p. 29, citing Benjamin, W., [1927], 1987, *Moscow Diary*, trans. Smith, G., Cambridge (MA), Harvard, pp. 367–368.

17  Buck-Morss, *Dialectics of Seeing*, p. 30.

18  Benjamin, W. [1935] 2002, 'The Arcades of Paris,' *The Arcades Project*, trans. Eiland, H. and McLaughlin, K., Cambridge (MA), Harvard, p. 879.

19  Benjamin, 'Theses on the Philosophy of History,' XV, p. 264.

20  Benjamin, W., [1934] 2003, 'The Author as Producer,' *Understanding Brecht*, London, Verso, pp. 85–104.

21  Benjamin, 'The Author as Producer,' p. 89.

22  Benjamin, W., [1940] 2016, letter to Adorno, quoted, Löwy, *Fire Alarm*, pp. 120–121 n. 1.

23  Benjamin, *The Arcades Project*, p. 361.

24  Ibid., p. 462.

25  Ibid., p. 473.

26  Benjamin, 'Theses on the Philosophy of History,' VIII, p. 259.

27  Leslie, *Walter Benjamin: Overpowering Conformism*, p. 201.

28  Ibid.

29  Benjamin, *Theses on the Philosophy of History*, IX, pp.259–260.

30  Löwy, *Fire Alarm*, p. 62.

31  Baudelaire, C. [1861] 1975, 'Correspondances,' *Selected Poems*, trans. Richardson, J., Harmondsworth, Penguin, pp. 42–43 [parallel French-English text].

32  Löwy, *Fire Alarm*, p. 63.

33  Abensour, M., 1986, *Walter Benjamin et Paris*, Paris, Cerf, quoted [in English trans.], Löwy, M., 2017, *Redemption and Utopia: Jewish Libertarian Thought in Central Europe*, London, Verso, p. 112.

34  Löwy, *Fire Alarm*, p. 20.

35 Leslie, *Walter Benjamin*, p. 201, quoting Benjamin, 'These on the Philosophy of History,' *Illuminations*, p. 257.
36 Wolin, R., 1994, *Walter Benjamin: An Aesthetic of Redemption*, Berkeley (CA), University of California Press, p. 263.
37 Wolin, *Walter Benjamin*, p. 264 [italics original].
38 Buci-Glucksmann, *Baroque Reason*, p. 88 [italics original].
39 Ibid., pp. 88–89.
40 Ibid., p. 68.
41 Benjamin, W. [1925] 1985, *The Origin of German Tragic Drama*, trans. Osborne, J., London, Verso, p. 65 [my italics].
42 Benjamin, *Origin of German Tragic Drama*.
43 Ibid., p. 69.
44 Ibid., p. 70.
45 Ibid., p. 71.
46 Ibid., p. 73.
47 Ibid., p. 74.
48 Schmitt, C., [1922] 2005, *Political Theology*, Chicago, University of Chicago Press, p. 5.
49 Agamben, G., 2005, *State of Exception*, Chicago, Chicago University Press, p. 2.
50 Schwab, G., 2005, 'Introduction,' Schmitt, *Political Theology*, p. xliv.
51 Ibid., p. 6.
52 Ibid., pp. 6–7.
53 Benjamin, 'Theses on the Philosophy of History' IX, p. 259.
54 Schmitt, *Political Theology*, p. 13.
55 Ibid., p. 14.
56 Ibid., p. 36.
57 Agamben, *State of Exception*, p. 28.
58 Ibid., p. 29.
59 Ibid., p. 30.
60 Ibid., p. 36.
61 Ibid., p. 71.
62 Ibid., p. 73.
63 Bloch, E., [1933] 1991, 'Inventory of Revolutionary Appearance,' *Heritage of Our Times*, Cambridge, Polity, pp. 64–69.
64 Benjamin, W., [1921] 1996, 'Critique of Violence,' *Selected Writings, I, 1913–1926*, ed., Bullock, M. and Jennings, M. W., Cambridge (MA), Harvard, p. 236.
65 Benjamin, 'Critique of Violence,' p. 237.
66 Ibid., p. 238.
67 Ibid., p. 241.
68 Ibid., p. 244.
69 Ibid., p. 247.
70 Ibid., p. 252.

**71** Adorno, T.W., [1969] 1997, *Aesthetic Theory*, trans. and ed. Hullor-Kentor, R., London, Athlone, p. 31.

**72** Löwy, *Fire Alarm*, p. 97.

**73** Ibid., p. 98.

**74** Ibid., p. 96 [Löwy's translation; the passage is omitted in the English translation in *Illuminations*].

**75** Lorey, *State of Insecurity*, p. 1.

**76** Ibid., p. 14.

**77** Ibid., p. 51, quoting Castel, R., 2003, *L'insécurité sociale* Paris, Seuil, p. 29.

**78** Lorey, *State of Insecurity*, p. 57.

**79** Holloway, J., [2002] 2019, *Change the World without Taking Power: The Meaning of Revolution Today*, London, Pluto, p. 22.

**80** Benjamin, 'Theses on the Philosophy of History,' VIII, p. 259.

# Chapter 5

**1** Butler, J., 2004, *Precarious Life: The Powers of Mourning and Violence*, London, Verso, p. 35.

**2** Adorno, T. W., [1949] 1983, 'Cultural Criticism and Society,' *Prisms*, Cambridge (MA), MIT, p. 34.

**3** Adorno, 'Cultural Criticism and Society'.

**4** Ibid.

**5** Ibid., p. 19.

**6** Ibid., p. 20.

**7** Ibid., p. 22.

**8** Ibid., p. 27.

**9** Adorno, T.W., [1966] 1973, *Negative Dialectics*, trans. Ashton, E. B., London, Routledge, p. 361.

**10** Schweppenhauser, G., 2009, *Theodor W. Adorno: An Introduction*, Durham (NC), Duke University Press, p. 67.

**11** Rabinbach, A., 2000, *In the Shadow of Catastrophe: German Intellectuals between Apocalypse and Enlightenment*, Berkeley (CA), University of California Press, p. 9.

**12** Goebbels, J., 1941, from Götz, A., 1999, *Final Solution: Nazi Population Policy and the Murder of the European Jews*, London, Arnold, p. 245. quoted, Sloterdijk, P., 2009, *Terror from the Air*, Los Angeles (CA), Semiotext(e), p. 46.

**13** Sloterdijk, *Terror from the Air*, p. 44.

**14** Bauman, Z., 1989, *Modernity and the Holocaust*, Cambridge, Polity, p. 87.

**15** Bauman, *Modernity and the Holocaust*, p. 88 [italics original].

**16** Lindqvist, S., [1990] 1996, *Exterminate All the Brutes*, London, Granta, pp. 142–143.

17 Tille, A., 1893, *Volkdienst*, Berlin, Weiner'sche Verlag, p. 21, quoted, Lindqvist, *Exterminate All the Brutes*, p. 143.

18 Ibid., p. 148, quoting *Alldeutsche Blatter* 1894 from Lange, K., 'Der Terminus Lebensraum,' in Hitler, A., *Mein Kampf* [no details given].

19 Graf Schweinitz, K., 1906, *Der Krieg in Deutsche Südwestafrika*, quoted in Lindqvist, *Exterminate All the Brutes*, p. 149 [no pagination stated].

20 Lindqvist, S., [2001] 2012, *A History of Bombing*, London, Granta, para. 101 [unpaginated].

21 Lindqvist, *A History of Bombing*, illus. above para. 134.

22 Coombes, A., 1994, *Reinventing Africa: Museums, Material Culture and Popular Imagination*, New Haven (CT), Yale.

23 Bohm-Duchen, M., 1995, 'Fifty Years On,' *After Auschwitz* [exhibition catalogue], London, Lund Humphries, p. 103, quoting Adorno, 'Cultural Criticism and Society,' p. 34.

24 Bohm-Duchen, 'Fifty Years On,' p. 103.

25 Rabinach, *In the Shadow of Catastrophe,* p. 9.

26 Goldfarb, A., 1998, 'Select Bibliography of Holocaust Plays 1933–1997,' *Staging the Holocaust: The Shoah in Drama and Performance*, ed. Schumacher, E., Cambridge, Cambridge University Press, pp. 298–334.

27 Greenspan, P., 1998, 'The Power and Limits of the Metaphor of Survivors' Testimony,' Schumacher, *Staging the Holocaust*, p. 32.

28 Young, J. E., 2000, *At Memory's Edge: After-images of the Holocaust in Contemporary Art and Architecture*, New Haven (CT), Yale, p. 9.

29 Young, *At Memory's Edge*, p. 105.

30 Gerz, J. and Gerz, E. S., 186, inscription, *Harburg Monument against Fascism*, quoted in Young, *At Memory's Edge*, p. 130.

31 Ibid., p. 131.

32 Quoted in Gibson, M., 1987, 'Hamburg: Sinking Feelings,' *Art News*, (Summer), p. 107, requoted, Young, *At Memory's Edge*, p. 139 [no original source given].

33 quoted in Albertini, R., 1999, 'Biron – the Living Monument: White Memory on Red Glaze,' *Res Publica: The Public Works 1968–1999*, ed. Gerz, J., Bolzano, Hatje Cantz, p. 32.

34 Resident of Biron, quoted, Albertini, 'Biron – the Living Monument,' p. 30.

35 Ibid.

36 Cited and illus. Young, J. E., 1996, 'Memory and Counter-Memory: Towards a Social Aesthetic of Holocaust Memorials,' *After Auschwitz*, p. 92.

37 Young, 'Memory and Counter-Memory,' p. 80.

38 Hornstein, S. and Jacobowitz, F., 2003, *Image and Remembrance: Representation and the Holocaust*, Bloomington (IA), Indiana University Press, p. 266.

39 Amishai-Maisels, Z., 'Art Confronts the Holocaust,' *After Auschwitz* [catalogue], p. 49.

40 Neuman, E., 2014, *Shoah Presence: Architectural Representations of the Holocaust*, Farnham, Ashgate, p. 170.

41 Eisenman, P., 2008, interview, Grobman, Y. and Neuman, E., *Performalism: Form and Performance in Digital Architecture*, [DVD] quoted in Neuman, *Shoah Presence*, p. 149.

42 Krauss, R., 1985, *The Originality of the Avant-Garde and Other Modernist Myths*, Cambridge (MA), Yale, pp. 11–12, quoted, Neuman, *Shoah Presence*, p. 171.

43 Ibid., p. 175.

44 Ibid., p. 177.

45 Young, *Memory's Edge*, p. 110.

46 Kelly, N. A., 2018, *Imagining the Great Irish Famine: Representing Dispossession in Visual Culture*, London, I.B. Tauris, p. 4.

47 Kelly, *Imagining the Great Irish Famine*, p. 6.

48 Quoted, Kelly, *Imagining the Great Irish Famine*, p. 211, original text c. 1870.

49 Nossack, H. E., [1948] 2004, *The End: Hamburg 1943*, Chicago, University of Chicago Press, pp. 12–13.

50 Nossack, *The End*, p. 43.

51 Sebald, W. G., 2003, *On the Natural History of Destruction*, London, Penguin, p. 42.

52 Adorno, T. W., [1981] 1991, 'The Schema of Mass Culture,' *The Culture Industry: Selected Essays on Mass Culture*, ed. Bernstein, J. M., London, Routledge, p. 58.

53 Adorno, 'The Schema of Mass Culture,' p. 67.

54 Witkin, R. W., 2003, *Adorno on Popular Culture*, London, Routledge, p. 172.

55 Beckett, S., [1954] 2018, *The End*, London, Penguin, p. 9.

56 Beckett, S., [1983] 1996, *Worstward Ho*, New York, Grove Press, p. 87.

57 Adorno, T. W., [1969] 1999, *Aesthetic Theory*, ed. and trans. Hullot-Kentor, R., London, Athlone, p. 81.

58 Adorno, *Aesthetic Theory*, p. 82.

59 Ibid., p. 250.

60 Anderton, J., 2016, *Beckett's Creatures: Art of Failure after the Holocaust*, London, Bloomsbury, p. 43.

61 Anderton, *Beckett's Creatures*, p. 49.

62 Casanova, P., [1997] 2020, *Samuel Beckett: Anatomy of a Literary Revolution*, London, Verso, p. 11.

63 Casanova, *Samuel Beckett*, p. 16.

64 Lloyd, D., 2018, *Beckett's Thing: Painting and Theatre*, Edinburgh, Edinburfh University Press, p. 156.

65 Beckett, S., 1967, 'For Avigdor Arikha,' quoted, Lloyd, *Beckett's Thing*, p. 154.

66 Ibid., p. 172.

67 Casanova, *Samuel Beckett,* p. 106.

68 Ibid., p. 17.

69 Ibid.

70  Ibid., p. 26.

71  Ibid., p. 89.

72  Ibid.

73  Celan, P., [1963] 2001, 'Mandorla,' from the collection *No-Man's Rose*, trans. Felstiner, J., *Selected Poems of Paul Celan*, New York, Norton, pp. 172–173 [parallel German-English text].

74  Celan, P., [1958] 2001, 'Speech on the Occasion of Receiving the Literature Prize of the Free Hanseatic City of Bremen,' *Collected Poems and Prose*, New York, Norton, pp. 395–396.

75  Felstoner, J., 1995, *Paul Celan: Poet, Survivor, Jew*, New Haven (CT), Yale, p. 287.

76  Adorno, 'Cultural Criticism and Society,' p. 19.

77  Ibid., p. 21.

78  Eagleton, T., 1990, *The Ideology of the Aesthetic*, Oxford, Blackwell, p. 341.

79  Eagleton, *The Ideology of the Aesthetic*.

80  Butler, *Precarious Life*, p. xii.

81  Ibid., p. 10.

82  Ibid., p. 11.

83  Ibid., p. 20 [italics original].

84  Ibid., p. 21.

85  Ibid., p. 28.

86  Ibid., p. 33.

87  Ibid., p. 142.

88  Ibid., p. 143.

89  Ibid., p. 150.

90  Shown to undergraduates on a course co-taught with John Goto, Oxford Brookes University, c. 1996.

91  Personal memory after spending a day with Ukeles, New York, c. 2002 [unrecorded].

# Chapter 6

1  www.bristolmuseums.org.uk/m-shed/whats-on/the-colston-statue-what-next [accessed 19 October 2021].

2  www.bbc.co.uk/news/uk-england-bristol-52962356, 8 June 2020 [accessed 11 May 2021].

3  Ibid.

4  Douglas, D., Chrisafis, A. and Mohdin, A., 'One Year On – George Floyd's Murder Shook the World, but What Has Changed?' *The Guardian*, 22 May 2021, p. 38.

5  Ibid.

6  Reid, J., 2020, quoted, www.marcquinn.com/studio/news/a-joint-statement-from-marc-quinn -and-jen-reid [accessed 19 May 2021].

7　Ibid.

8　Beckford, R., quoted, Douglas, Chrisafis and Mohdin, 'One Year On,' p. 39.

9　Nevil, A., 2019, *New Model Island*, London, Repeater, p. 38

10　Nevil, *New Model Island,* p. 42

11　Salecl, R., 1999, 'The State as a Work of Art,' *Architecture and Revolution*, ed. Leach, N., London, Routledge, p. 99.

12　Salecl, 'The State as a Work of Art.'

13　Ibid.

14　www.bbc.co.uk/news/uk-england-south-yorkshire-33107090 [accessed 31 January 2022].

15　Poole, R., 2019, *Peterloo: The English Uprising*, Oxford, Oxford University Press, p. 389.

16　www.tolpuddlemartyrs.org.uk [accessed 19 October 2021].

17　Benjamin, W., [1940] 1977, 'Theses on the Philosophy of History,' *Illuminations*, London, Fontana, p. 259.

18　Miles, M., 2019, *Cities and Literature*, London, Routledge, pp. 100–104.

19　Sadler, S., 1999, *The Situationist City*, Cambridge (MA), MIT, p. 100.

20　Holloway, J., [2002] 2019, *Change the World without Taking Power: The Meaning of Revolution Today*, London, Pluto, p. 225.

21　Holloway, *Change the World without Taking Power*, p. 22.

22　Ibid., p. 223.

23　Sommer, D., 2014, *The Work of Art in the World: Civic Agency and Public Humanities*, Durham (NC), Duke University Press, p. 155.

# Chapter 7

1　Flood, C. and Grindon, G., 2014, 'Introduction,' *Disobedient Objects*, [exhibition catalogue], London, Victoria & Albert Museum, p. 23.

2　Traugott, M., 2014, 'Barricades as Material and Social Constructions,' *Disobedient Objects*, pp. 27–31.

3　Traugott, 'Barricades as Material and Social Constructions,' p. 32.

4　Feigenbaum, A., 2014.'The Disobedient Objects of Protest Camps,' *Disobedient Objects*, p. 35.

5　*Disobedient Objects*, illus. p. 67, top left.

6　Feigenbaum, 'The Disobedient Objects of Protest Camps,' p. 37.

7　www.kriyaarts.co.uk/rebel-clown-army [accessed 8 November 2021].

8　*Disobedient Objects*, illus. p. 76.

9　Longoni, A., 2014, 'Disobedient Bodies: Art Activism in Argentina,' *Disobedient Objects*, p. 103.

10　Holmes, B., 2003, 'Liars's Poker: Representation of Politics / Politics of Representation,' *Springeren*, 1, [no page reference] quoted, Longoni, 'Disobedient Objects: Art Activisim in Argentina,' pp. 107–108.

11  Platform, 1996, *Ignite*, London, Platform, p. 1.

12  Platform, 1997, *Ignite* (2), London, Platform, p. 2.

13  Reclaim the Streets, 1997, *Evading Standards*, London, Reclaim the Streets, p. 1.

14  Reclaim the Streets, *Evading Standards*, pp. 3, 6, 7, 8.

15  Author's conversations with Platform, c. 1999 [from memory].

16  Flood and Grindon, 'Introduction,' *Disobedient Objects*, pp. 8–9.

17  Bishop, C. 2013, *Radical Museology, or What's Contemporary in Museums of Contemporary Art*, London, Koenig Books, p. 6.

18  Bishop, *Radical Museology*, pp. 49–50.

19  Bishop, C., 2012, *Artificial Hells: Participatory Art and the Politics of Spectatorship*, London, Verso, p. 275.

20  Carnevale, G., [1967] 2004, in Katzenstein, I., ed., *Listen, Here, Now! Argentine Art of the 1960: Writings of the Avant-Garde*, New York, Museum of Modern Art, p. 299, quoted, Bishop, *Artificial Hells*, p.120.

21  Bishop, *Artificial Hells*, p. 120.

22  Bishop, *Artificial Hells*, pp. 126–127.

23  Bishop, *Artificial Hells*, p. 235.

24  Leslie, E., 2001, 'Tate Modern: A Year of Sweet Success,' *Radical Philosophy*, 109 (Sep–Oct), p. 3.

25  Leslie, 'Tate Modern,' p. 5.

26  Evans, H., 2013, 'Fracking Futures: A Taste of What's to Come,' *New Internationalist*, 6 November, p. 117.

27  HeHe, 2016, *Man Made Clouds*, Orléans, Editions Hyx, p. 303.

28  *The Echo*, [on-line, n.d.] reproduced in HeHe, *Man Made Clouds*, p. 308.

29  Ibid.

30  www.forensic-architecture.org/programme/exhibitions/cloud-studies [accessed 29 November 2021].

31  www.mif.co.uk/whats-on/cloud-studies [accessed 30 November 2021].

32  Sloterdijk, P. [2002] 2009, *Terror from the Air*, Los Angeles (CA), Semiotext(e), p. 28.

33  www.forensic-architecture.org/programme/exhibitions/cloud-studies [accessed 29 November 2021].

34  www.forensic-architecture.org/programme/news/forensic-architecture-stands-with-palestine-whitworth-exhibition-statement [accessed 16 November 2021].

35  Bryant, M., 2022, 'Artists Shun Exhibition amid Whitworth Row over Palestine Statement,' *The Guardian*, 28 February [accessed on-line 18 March 2022].

36  Fuller, M. and Weisman, E., 2021, *Investigative Aesthetics: Conflicts and Commons in the Politics of Truth*, London, Verso, p. 35.

37  Fuller and Weisman, *Investigative Aesthetics*, p. 36.

38  Lesdema, E., 2021, 'The Practitioner in Alter Space,' *Fortunes of War*, Bristol, Intellect, p. 61.

**39** Ibid.

**40** Lesdema, 'The Practitioner in Alter Space,' p. 62.

**41** Camerotti, A., 2021, 'The Immateriality of Culture, Lesdema, *Fortunes of War*, p. 8.

**42** Cripps, F. H. and Stimson, A., 1961, *Distribution of Uranium 235 and Plutonium 239 around the United States Air Force base at Greenham Common*, Aldermaston, Atomic Weapons Research Establishment, en.wikipedia.orhg/RAF_Greenham_Common [accessed 11 November 2021].

**43** Philopoulos-Mihalopoulos, A., 2021, 'What's in a Day?' Lesdema, *Fortunes of War*, p. 9.

**44** Ibid.

**45** Philopoulos-Mihalopoulos, 'What's in a Day?' p. 10.

**46** Barsdorf-Liebchen, N., 'A Reading, in Retrospection,' Lesdema, *Fortunes of War*, p. 30.

**47** Hewitt, A. and Jordan, M., 2004, *I Fail to Agree*, Sheffield, Site Gallery, p. 22.

**48** Hewitt and Jordan,*I Fail to Agree*, p. 21.

**49** Hewitt, A. and Jordan, M., eds., 2004, *Futurology: Issues, Contexts and Conditions for Contemporary Art Practice*, Walsall, New Art Gallery, p. 13.

**50** Adorno, T.W., [1981] 1991, 'The Schema of Mass Culture,' *The Culture Industry: Selected Essays on Mass Culture*, ed., Bernstein, J., London, Routledge, p. 79.

**51** Miles, M., 2015, *Limits to Culture*, London, Pluto, pp.161–163.

**52** Freee Art Collective, 2007, [from photocopied leaflet, author's collection].

**53** Freee Art Collective, 2018, *The Carracci Institute Yearbook*, Northampton, NN Contemporary Art, p. 16.

**54** Freee Art Collective, *The Carracci Institute*, p. 16.

**55** Freee Art Collective, *The Carracci Institute*, p. 51.

**56** Ibid.

**57** Freee Art Collective, *The Carracci Institute*, p. 55.

**58** Rancière, J., 2010, *Dissensus*, London, Continuum, p. 37.

**59** Rancière, *Dissensus*, p. 133.

**60** Freee Art Collective, *The Carracci Institute*, p. 61.

**61** Adorno, 'The Schema of Mass Culture,' p. 67.

**62** Grosz, E., 2004, *The Nick of Time: Politics, Evolution and the Untimely*, Durham (NC), Duke University Press, p. 29.

**63** Grosz, *The Nick of Time*, p. 90.


# Chapter 8


**1** E mail, Mel Jordan to author, 20 December 2021.

**2** Zoom conversation between Jordan, Hewitt and author, 12 November 2021.

**3** Marcuse, H., 1968, 'Liberation from the Affluent Society,' *The Dialectics of Liberation*, ed. Cooper, D., Harmondsworth, Penguin, p. 175.

**4** Miles, M., 2015, *Limits to Culture*, London, Pluto, pp. 157–163.

**5** Charnley, K., 2021, *Sociopolitical Aesthetics: Art, Criticism and Neoliberalism*, London, Bloomsbury, p. 153.

**6** Charnley, *Sociopolitical Aesthetics*, p. 154.

**7** Ibid.

**8** Freee Art Collective, 2009, *Revolution Is Sublime*, London, Camberwell Art Space, p. 3.

**9** Freee Art Collective, *Revolution Is Sublime*, p. 4.

**10** Ibid.

**11** Ibid., p. 5.

**12** Ibid., p. 9.

**13** Ibid., p. 10.

**14** Beech, D., 2019, *Art and Postcapitalism: Aesthetic Labour, Automation and Value Production*, London, Pluto, p. 51, quoting Gorz, A., 1985, *Paths to Paradise: On the Liberation from Work*, London, Pluto, p. 34.

**15** Beech, *Art and Postcapitalism*, p. 53, quoting Weeks, K., 2011, *The Problem with Work: Feminism, Marxism, Antiwork Politics, and Postwar Imaginaries*, Durham (NC), Duke University Press, p. 103.

**16** Berardi, F., 2009, *The Soul at Work: From Alienation to Autonomy*, Los Angeles, Semiotext(e), p. 24, quoted in Beech, *Art and Postcapitalism,* p. 52.

**17** Ibid., p. 52.

**18** Clark, T. J., 1999, *Farewell to an Idea: Episodes from a History of Modernism*, New Haven (CT), Yale, p. 242.

**19** Clark, *Farwell to an Idea*, p. 291.

**20** Ibid.

**21** Marcuse, 'Liberation from the Affluent Society,' p. 184.

**22** Marcuse, H., 1969, *An Essay on Liberation*, Harmondsworth, Penguin, p. 37.

**23** Marcuse, 'Liberation from the Affluent Society,' p. 185.

**24** Frank, J., 2014, 'Delightful Horror: Edmund Burke and the Aesthetics of Democratic Revolution,' *The Aesthetic Turn in Political Thought*, ed. Kompridis, N., London, Bloomsbury, p. 5.

**25** Burke, E., [1756] 1998, *A Philosophical Enquiry into the Origins of the Sublime and the Beautiful: And Other Pre-Revolutionary Writings*, New York, Penguin, p. 142, quoted in Frank, 'Delightful Horror,' p. 8.

**26** Burke, *Enquiry*, p. 24, quoted, Frank, 'Delightful Horror,' p. 9.

**27** Ibid., p. 9.

**28** Woodward, C., 2002, *In Ruins*, London, Vintage, p. 121.

**29** Pugh, S., 1988, *Garden, Nature, Language*, Manchester, Manchester University Press, pp. 21–22.

**30** Burke, E., [1790] 1987, *Reflections on the Revolution in France*, Indianapolis (IN), Hacket, p. 30, quoted, Frank, 'Delightful Horror,' p. 13.

**31** Burke, E., [1789] 1984, letter to Lord Charlemond, 9 August, *Selected Letters,* Chicago, University of Chicago Press [no page stated], quoted in Frank, 'Delightful Horror,' p. 15.

**32** Ibid., p. 21.

**33** Ibid., p. 25.

**34** Schiller, F., [1794] 1982, *On the Aesthetic Education of Man in a Series of Letters*, Oxford, Oxford University Press, p. 7.

**35** Schiller, F., letter 8 February 1793, 2005, quoted, Wilkinson, M. E. and Willoughby, L. A., 'Introduction,' Schiller, *Aesthetic Education*, p. xvii.

**36** Ibid., p. 25.

**37** Ibid., p. 7.

**38** Ibid., 'Introduction,' p. xii.

**39** Schiller, *Aesthetic Education*, p. 11.

**40** Ibid., p. 17.

**41** Ibid., p. 55.

**42** Ibid., pp. 55; 57.

**43** Ibid., p. 57.

**44** Marcuse, H., [1974] 1978, *The Aesthetic Dimension*, Boston, Beacon Press, p. 54.

**45** Schiller, *Aesthetic Education*, p. 215.

**46** Beech, *Art and Postcapitalism,* p. 33.

**47** Ibid., p. 103.

**48** Harding, A., 2018, *Artists in the City: SPACE in '68 and beyond*, London, Space.

**49** Marcuse, *The Aesthetic Dimension*, p. 1.

**50** Ibid.

**51** Schiller, *Aesthetic Education*, p. 195.

**52** Ibid., p. 197.

**53** Ibid., p. 209.

**54** Ibid.

**55** Ibid., p. 213.

**56** Ibid., Glossary, p. 307.

**57** Schiller, *Aesthetic Education*, p. 187.

**58** Freee Art Collective, *Revolution Is Sublime*, p. 3.

**59** Edelstyn, D., 2020, 'Revelations: Debt and Money,' *Bank Job*, Powell, H. and Edelstyn, D., London, Chelsea Gteen, p. 48.

**60** Edelstyn, 'Revelations: Debt and Money'.

**61** Clarke, C., 2021, 'Bank Job Review: A Classic Print Money to Cancel Debt Caper,' *The Guardian*, 26 [accessed 5 January 2022].

**62** Edelstyn and Powell, *Bank Job*, p. 77.

**63** Ibid., p. 82.

**64** Ibid., p. 110.

**65** Ibid., p. 113.

**66** Ibid., p. 173.

67  Powell, H., 2018, interview with Hopkins, R., *Transition Network*, 12 April, www.transitionnetwork.org [accessed 5 January 2022].
68  Edelstyn and Powell, *Bank Job*, p. 173.
69  Ibid., p. 107.
70  Skeltys, N., 2019, in petition, quoted Powell and Edelstyn, *Bank Job*, p. 108.
71  Ibid., p. 108, citing the title of Hopkins, R., 2019, *From What Is to What if: Unleashing the Power of Imagination to Create the Future We Want*, White River Junction (CT), Chelsea reen.
72  Bloch, *The Principle of Hope*, pp. 509–515.

# Chapter 9

1  Sommer, D., 2014, *The Work of Art in the World, Civic Agency and Public Humanities*, Durham (NC), Duke University Press, p. 89.
2  Blazwick, I., quoted, Evans, M., 2015, *Artwash: Big Oil and the Arts*, London, Pluto, p. 144 [no source given].
3  Images: www.amyscaife.co.uk/2011/liberate-tate-at-tate-britain [accessed 24 February 2021].
4  Evans, *Artwash*, p. 145.
5  Stallabrass, J., 2011, 'Art Pollutes Oil,' *Culture beyond Oil*, ed. Clarke, J., Evans, M., Newman, H., Smith, K. and Tarman, G., London, Art Not Oil, Liberate Tate and Platform, p. 70.
6  Marriott, J., 2011, Clarke et al, *Culture beyond Oil*, p. 12.
7  Liberate Tate, 2011, 'About Us,' Clarke et al, *Culture beyond Oil*, p. 86.
8  Evans, *Artwash*, p. 147.
9  Athanasiou, A., 2017, *Agonistic Mourning: Political Dissidence and the Women in Black*, Edinburgh, Edinburgh University Press, p. 59.
10  Women in Black, 1993, quoted in Athanasiou, *Agonistic Mourning*, p. 60.
11  Athanasiou, *Agonistic Mourning*, pp. 61–62.
12  www.womeninblack.org.uk/about-us [accessed 1 January 2022].
13  www.womeninblack.org.uk [accessed 1 January 2022].
14  www.womeninblack.org.uk [accessed 1 January 2022].
15  Marcuse, H., [1972] 2005, 'Ecology and Revolution,' *The New Left and the 1960s*, ed. Kellner, D., Collected Papers III, London, Routledge, pp. 173–174.
16  Butler, J., and Athanasiou, A., 2013, *Dispossession: The Performative in the Political*, Cambridge, Polity, p. 67.
17  Arendt, H., 1958, *The Human Condition*, Chicago, University of Chicago Press.
18  Butler, *Dispossession*, p. 122.
19  Butler, J., *The Force of NonViolence: An Ethico-Political Bond*, London, Verso, p. 69.

20 Butler and Athanasiou, *Dispossession*, p. xi.
21 Holst-Warhaft, G., 1992, *Dangerous Voices: Women;' Lament and Greek Literature*, London, Routledge, pp. 129–130.
22 Athanasiou, *Agonistic Mourning*, p. 73.
23 Marcuse, H., 1969, *An Essay on Liberation*, Harmondsworth, Penguin, p. 30.
24 www.redrebelbrigade.com [accessed 3 January 2022].
25 Ibid.
26 Ibid.
27 Ibid.
28 www.redrebelbrigade.com/cistume-robes [accessed 3 January 2021].
29 Holst-Warhaft, *Dangerous Voices*, p. 163.
30 Ibid., p. 165.
31 Haque, M., 2019, 'Feeding the Rebellion,' Extinction Rebellion, *This Is Not a Drill: An Extinction Rebellion Handbook*, ed. Farrell, C., Green, A., Knights, S. and Skeaping, W., London, Penguin, p. 112.
32 Lucas, C., 2019, 'A Political View,' Extinction Rebellion, *This Is Not a Drill*, p. 144.
33 James and Ruby, 2019, 'Cultural Roadblocks,' *This Is Not a Drill*, p. 119.
34 Gayle, D. and Carrington, D., 2021, 'Extinction Rebellion eyes shift in tactics as police crack down on protests,' *The Guardian*, 3 September [accessed 3 January 2022].
35 Ibid.
36 McKay, G. ed., 1998, 'Notes towards an Introduction,' *DiY Culture: Party and Protest in Nineties Britain*, London, Verso, p. 18 [italics original].
37 Jordan, J., 1998, 'Anti-Road Protest and Reclaim the Streets,' McKay, *DiY Culture*, p. 133.
38 www.goodchance.org/thejungle [accessed 7 January 2022].
39 www.walkwithamal.org/the-journey [accessed 7 January 2022].
40 https://issuu.com/storymuseum/docs/issu_amal_meets_alice [accessed 7 January 2022].
41 Adorno, T. W. and Horkheimer, M., [1944] 1997, *Dialectic of Enlightenment*, London, Verso, p. 4.

# Bibliography

Adorno, T. W., [1969] 1999, *Aesthetic Theory*, trans. Hullor-Kentor, R., London, Athlone.

Adorno, T. W., 1991, *The Culture Industry: Selected Essays on Mass Culture*, ed. Bernstein, J., London, Routledge.

Agamben, G., 2005, *State of Exception*, trans. Attell, K., Chicago, Chicago University Press.

Anderton, J., 2016, *Beckett's Creatures: Art of Failure after the Holocaust*, London, Bloomsbury.

Arendt, H., 1958, *The Human Condition*, Chicago, University of Chicago Press.

Argüelles, J., 1972, *Charles Henry and the Formation of a Psychophysical Aesthetic*, Chicago, University of Chicago Press.

Athanasious, A., 2017, *Agonistic Mourning: Political Dissidence and the Women in Black*, Edinburgh, Edinburgh University Press.

Bakhtin, M., [1996] 2007, *The Dialogic Imagination*, Austin (TX), University of Texas Press.

Bakhtin, M., [1981] 2007, *Problems of Dostoevsky's Poetics*, Manchester, Manchester University Press.

Bauman, Z., 1989, *Modernity and the Holocaust*, Cambridge, Polity, p. 87.

Beasley-Murray, T., 2007, *Mikhail Bakhtin and Walter Benjamin: Experience and Form*, Basingstoke, Palgrave.

Beckett, S., [1954] 2018, *The End*, London, Penguin.

Beckett, S., [1983] 1996, *Worstward Ho*, New York, Grove Press.

Beech, D., 2019, *Art and Postcapitalism: Aesthetic Labour, Automation and Value Production*, London, Pluto.

Benjamin, W., [1939] 2003, 'What Is Epic Theatre?' [second version], *Understanding Brecht*, London, Verso, p. 18.

Benjamin, W., [1939] 1999, *The Arcades Project*, trans. Eiland, H. and McLaughlin, K., Cambridge (MA), Harvard.

Benjamin, W., [1935] 1997, *Charles Baudelaire*, London, Verso.

Benjamin, W., [1925] 1985, *The Origins of German Tragic Drama*, London, Verso.

Benjamin, W., 1973, *Illuminations*, London, Fontana.

Berardi, F., 2009, *The Soul at Work: From Alienation to Autonomy*, Los Angeles, Semiotext(e).

Bishop, C., 2013, *Radical Museology, or What's Contemporary in Museums of Contemporary Art*, London, Koenig Books.

Bloch, E., [1933] 1991, 'Inventory of Revolutionary Appearance,' *Heritage of Our Times*, Cambridge, Polity, pp. 64–69.

Bloch, E., [1959] 1986, *The Principle of Hope*, Cambridge, MIT.

Bohm-Duchen, M., 1995, 'Fifty Years On,' *After Auschwitz* [exhibition catalogue], London, Lund Humphries.

Buci-Glucksmann, C., [1984] 1994, *Baroque Reason: The Aesthetics of Modernity*, London, Sage, p. 88 [italics original].

Buck-Morss, 1991, *Dialectics of Seeing: Walter Benjamin and the Arcades Project*, Cambridge (MA), MIT.

Burke, E., [1790] 1987, *Reflections on the Revolution in France*, Indianapolis (IN), Hacket.

Butler, J., 2020, *The Force of NonViolence: An Ethico-Political Bond*, London, Verso.

Butler, J., 2004, *Precarious Life: The Powers of Mourning and Violence*, London, Verso.

Butler, J., 1990, *Gender Trouble*, London, Routledge.

Butler, J., and Athanasiou, A., 2013, *Dispossession: The Performative in the Political*, Cambridge, Polity.

Casanova, P., [1997] 2020, *Samuel Beckett: Anatomy of a Literary Revolution*, London, Verso.

Celan, P., 2001, *Selected Poems of Paul Celan*, trans. Felstiner, J., New York, Norton.

Charle, C., [1990] 2015, *Birth of the Intellectual 1880–1900*, Cambridge, Polity.

Charnley, K., 2021, *Sociopolitical Aesthetics: Art, Crisis and Neoliberalism*, London, Bloomsbury.

Clark, T. J., 1999, *Farewell to an Idea: Episodes from a History of Modernism*, New Haven (CT), Yale.

Clark, T. J., 1973, *Image of the People: Gustave Courbet and the 1848 Revolution*, London, Thames and Hudson.

Clarke, J., Evans, M., Newman, H., Smith, K. and Tarman, G., eds., 2011, *Culture Beyond Oil*, London, Art Not Oil, Liberate Tate and Platform.

Collini, S., 2019, *The Nostalgic Imagination: History in English Criticism*, Oxford, Oxford University Press.

Coombes, A., 1994, *Reinventing Africa: Museums, Material Culture and Popular Imagination*, New Haven (CT), Yale.

Cooper, D., ed., 1968, *The Dialectics of Liberation*, Harmondsworth, Penguin.

Cottington, D., 1998, *Cubism in the Shadow of War: The Avant-Garde and Politics in Paris 1905–1914*, New Haven (CT), Yale.

Crimethinc, 2018, *There's No Such Thing as Revolutionary Government*, Croatia, In the Spirit of Emma Publications.

Eagleton, T., 1990, *The Ideology of the Aesthetic*, Oxford, Blackwell.

Evans, M., 2015, *Artwash: Big Oil and the Arts*, London, Pluto.

Extinction Rebellion, 2019, *This Is Not a Drill: An Extinction Rebellion Handbook*, London, Penguin.

Felstoner, J., 1995, *Paul Celan: Poet, Survivor, Jew*, New Haven (CT), Yale.

Figes, O., 2019, *The Europeans: Three Lives and the Making of a Cosmopolitan Culture*, London, Penguin, p. 194.

Fiss, K., 2009, *Grand Illusion: The Third Reich, the Paris Exposition, and the Cultural Seduction of France*, Chicago, University of Chicago Press.

Flood, C. and Grindon, G., eds., 2014, 'Introduction,' *Disobedient Objects*, [exhibition catalogue], London, Victoria & Albert Museum.

Foucault, M., [1975] 1991, *Discipline and Punish: The Birth of the Prison*, London, Penguin.

Fuller, P., 1980, *Beyond the Crisis in Art*, London, Writers and Readers Cooperative.

Freee Art Collective, 2018, *The Carracci Institute Yearbook*, Northampton, NN Contemporary Art.

Freee Art Collective, 2009, *Revolution Is Sublime*, London, Camberwell Art Space.

Frisby, D. and Featherstone, M., eds., 1997, *Simmel on Culture*, London, Sage.

Fuller, M. and Weisman, E., 2021, *Investigative Aesthetics: Conflicts and Commons in the Politics of Truth*, London, Verso.

Gerz, J., 1999, *Res Publica: The Public Works 1968–1999*, Bolzano, Hatje Cantz.

Gorz, A., 1985, *Paths to Paradise: On the Liberation from Work*, London, Pluto.

Greenberg, C., 1995, *Collected Essays and Criticism, 4, Modernism with a Vengeance, 1957–1969*, Chicago, University of Chicago Press.

Harding, A., 2018, *Artists in the City: SPACE in '68 and beyond*, London, Space.

Harvey, D., 1989, *The Urban Experience*, Baltimore (MD), Johns Hopkins University Press.

Hazan, E., [2013] 2015, *A History of the Barricade*, London, Veso.

Hess, T. B. and Ashbery, J., eds., 1968, *Avant-Garde Art*, New York, Collier.

Hewitt, A. and Jordan, M., 2004, *I Fail to Agree*, Sheffield, Site Gallery.

Hill, C., 1975, *The World Turned Upside Down: Radical Ideas during the English Revolution*, Harmondsworth, Penguin.

Holloway, J., [2002] 2019, *Change the World without Taking Power: The Meaning of Revolution Today*, London, Pluto.

Holst-Warhaft, G., 1992, *Dangerous Voices: Women;' Lament and Greek Literature*, London, Routledge.

Hornstein, S. and Jacobowitz, F., 2003, *Image and Remembrance: Representation and the Holocaust*, Bloomington (IA), Indiana University Press.

House, J., 2004, *Impressionism: Paint and Politics*, New Haven (CT), Yale.

Jaurès, J., [1901] 2015, *A Socialist History of the French Revolution*, London, Pluto.

Jordan, T. and Lent, A., eds., 1999, *Storming the Millennium: The New Politics of Change*, London, Lawrence and Wishart.

Kandinsky, W., [1912] 1977, *Concerning the Spiritual in Art*, trans. Sadler, M. T. H., New York, Dover.

Kelly, N. A., 2018, *Imagining the Great Irish Famine: Representing Dispossession in Visual Culture*, London, I.B. Tauris.

Kompridis, N., ed., 2014, *The Aesthetic Turn in Political Thought*, London, Bloomsbury.

Krauss, R., [1986] 1993, *The Originality of the Avant-Garde and Other Modernist Myths*, Cambridge (MA), MIT.

Kristeva, J., 2002, *Revolt She Said*, Los Angeles, Semiotext(e).

Kristeva, J., [1999] 2001, *Hannah Arendt*, New York, Columbia University Press.

Leach, N., ed., 1997, *Architecture and Revolution*, London, Routledge.

Lefebvre, H., [1974] 1991, *The Production of Space*, Oxford, Blackwell.

Leighton, J. and Thomson, R., 1997, *Seurat and the Bathers*, London, National Gallery.

Lesdema, E., ed., 2021, 'The Practitioner in Alter Space,' *Fortunes of War*, Bristol, Intellect, pp. 61–72.

Leslie, E., 2000, *Walter Benjamin: Overpowering Conformism*, London, Pluto.

Lloyd, D., 2018, *Beckett's Thing: Painting and Theatre*, Edinburgh, Edinburgh University Press.

Lindqvist, S., [1990] 1996, *Exterminate All the Brutes*, London, Granta.

Lingwood, J., ed., 1995, *House*, London, Phaidon.

Lorey, I., 2015, *State of Insecurity: Government of the Precarious*, London, Verso.

Lowy, M., [2001] 2016, *Fire Alarm: Reading Walter Benjamin's 'On the Concept of History,'* London, Verso.

McKay, G., 1996, *Senseless Acts of Beauty: Cultures of Resistance since the Sixties*, London, Verso.

McKay, 1998, 'DiY Culture: Notes towards an Introduction,' *DiY Culture: Party and Protest in Nineties Britain*, London, Verso, pp. 1–53.

Marcuse, H., 2007, *Art and Liberation*, ed. Kellner, D., Collected Papers IV, London, Routledge.

Marcuse, H., 2005, *The New Left and the 1960s*, ed. Kellner, D., Collected Papers III, London, Routledge.

Marcuse, H., [1974] 1978, *The Aesthetic Dimension*, Boston, Beacon Press.

Marcuse, H., 1969, *An Essay on Liberation*, Harmondsworth, Penguin.

Marx, K. and Engels, F., 1968, *Collected Works*, London, Lawrence and Wishart, p. 42.

Miles, M., 2021, *Paradoxical Urbanism: Anti-Urban Currents in Modern Urbanism*, Singapore, Palgrave.

Miles, M., 2019, *Cities and Literature*, London, Routledge.

Miles, M., 2015, *Limits to Culture*, London, Pluto.

Neuman, E., 2014, *Shoah Presence: Architectural Representations of the Holocaust*, Farnham, Ashgate, p. 170.

Nevil, A., 2019, *New Model Island*, London, Repeater.

Powell, H. and Edelstyn, D., 2020, *Bank Job*, London, Chelsea Green.

Proudhon, P. J., 1970, *Selected Writing*, ed. Edwards, S., London, Macmillan.

Pugh, S., 1988, *Garden, Nature, Language*, Manchester, Manchester University Press.

Rabinbach, A., 2000, *In the Shadow of Catastrophe: German Intellectuals between Apocalypse and Enlightenment*, Berkeley (CA), University of California Press.

Rancière, J., [1988] 2011, *Staging the People*, London, Verso.

Rancière, J., 2010, *Dissensus*, London, Continuum.

Rancière, J., [2000] 2004, *The Politics of Aesthetics*, London, Continuum.

Reed, J., [1919] 1977, *Ten Days That Shook the World*, London, Penguin.

Rilke, R. M., [1913] 1963, *Duino Elegies*, I, trans. Leishman, J. B. and Spender, S., London, Hogarth Press, p. 25 [parallel German-English text].

Roberts, J., 2015, *Revolutionary Time and the Avant-Garde*, London, Verso.

Ross, K., 2015, *Communal Luxury: The Political Imaginary of the Paris Commune*, London, Verso.

Ross, K., [1988] 2008, *The Emergence of Social Space: Rimbaud and the Paris Commune*, London, Verso.

Ross, K., 2002, *May '68 and Its Afterlives*, Chicago, University of Chicago Press.

Sadler, S., 1999, *The Situationist City*, Cambridge (MA), MIT.

Saint-Simon, H. de, [1825] 1975, 'The Artist, the Scientist and the Industrial: Dialogue,' *Opinions littéraires, philosophiques et industriels*, trans. Taylor, K., *Selected Writings on Science, Industry and Social Organisation*, London, Croom Helm, pp. 279–288.

Schiller, F., [1794] 1982, *On the Aesthetic Education of Man in a Series of Letters*, Oxford, Oxford University Press.

Schweppenhauser, G., 2009, *Theodor W. Adorno: An Introduction*, Durham (NC), Duke University Press.

Schumacher, E., ed., 1998, *Staging the Holocaust: The Shoah in Drama and Performance*, Cambridge, Cambridge University Press.

Sebald, W. G., 2003, *On the Natural History of Destruction*, London, Penguin.

Shattuck, R., 1969, *The Banquet Years: The Origins of the Avant-Garde in France 1885 to World War I*, London, Cape.

Sjöholm, C., 2005, *Kristeva and the Political*, London, Routledge.

Sloterdijk, P., 2009, *Terror from the Air*, Los Angeles (CA), Semiotext(e).

Smith, P., 1997, *Seurat and the Avant-Garde*, New Haven (CT), Yale.

Sommer, D., 2014, *The Work of Art in the World: Civic Agencies and Public Humanities*, Durham (NC), Duke University Press.

Spate, V., 1979, *Orphism: The Evolution of Non-figurative Painting in Paris 1910–1914*, Oxford, Oxfoprd University Press.

Tisdall, C. and Bozzola, A., 1977, *Futurism*, London, Thames and Hudson.

Williams, R., [1988] 1999, 'The Politics of the Avant-Garde,' *The Politics of Modernism*, London, Verso, pp. 49–64.

Witkin, R. W., 2003, *Adorno on Popular Culture*, London, Routledge.

Wolin, R., 1994, *Walter Benjamin: An Aesthetic of Redemption*, Berkeley (CA), University of California Press.

Wood, P., ed., 1999, *The Challenge of the Avant-Garde*, New Haven (CT), Yale.

Woodward, C., 2002, *In Ruins*, London, Vintage.

Young, J. E., 2000, *At Memory's Edge: After-images of the Holocaust in Contemporary Art and Architecture*, New Haven (CT), Yale.